*Ethical Decisions for Social Work Practice*

**Fifth Edition**

# Ethical Decisions for Social Work Practice

## Frank M. Loewenberg
*Professor Emeritus, Bar-Ilan University*

## Ralph Dolgoff
*University of Maryland at Baltimore*

F. E. PEACOCK PUBLISHERS, INC.   •   Itasca, Illinois

Copyright © 1996 by F. E. Peacock Publishers, Inc.
All rights reserved
Library of Congress Catalog Card No. 95-71666
ISBN 0-87581-399-2
Printed in the United States of America
Printing 10 9 8 7 6 5 4 3
Year 00 99 98

**What is the ethical way for a social worker to respond when:**

- Your client tells you that he intends to commit a serious crime.
- A twenty-six-year-old married woman wants a tubal ligation because she does not want to have any more children. She asks you to help her find a physician who will perform this procedure.
- A social worker in a residential detoxification center believes that one of the residents is potentially violent and may become a danger to other residents.
- A client who is HIV-positive tells you that he has unprotected sex with his wife because he does not want her to know of his condition.
- A social worker learns that another social worker knows about a child abuse situation but has failed to report the case to the Child Abuse Center.
- A board member has helped to obtain a substantial grant which has made it possible for your agency to serve adult alcoholics and members of their families. Now this board member wants you to report that more clients have been served by this program than actually did participate so that the agency can receive a larger grant next year.
- Physicians and a nurse in a pediatric hospital believe strongly that a child should have a tracheostomy. The child's parents are resistant because the child's lungs can fail, the procedure looks very painful, and death is possible. The chief physician asks you to convince the parents to agree *no matter what.*

# Contents

# Figures, Tables, and Exemplars

# Preface

Change seems to have accelerated in the years since the appearance of the fourth edition of *Ethical Decisions for Social Work Practice*. The breakup of the Soviet Union and Eastern bloc has meant the end of the Cold War regimes. East and West Germany have united. Wars, famines, and changing governments as well as new technologies and internationally interdependent economies have produced dramatic changes around the world. The Pacific Rim nations have become a third major economic bloc; the Caribbean and South and Central America also impact on the world scene. The United States too has experienced rapid change in which many complex issues confront the nation. Questions of ethics continue to remain high on the public agenda of all countries as many groups press often conflicting moral claims.

Ethical problems arise whenever and wherever people deal with human lives, human survival, and human welfare. These are activities in which social workers are involved daily. For this reason we believe that concern for ethical conduct should be included in every curriculum for professional education. But those who teach in this area must keep in mind Thomas Aquinas's caution that when it comes to ethics "we cannot discuss what we ought to do unless we know what we can do" (Commentary on *De Anima*, I.1.2). In other words, teaching the theory of ethical action is not worth much unless we also teach the skill of making ethical decisions. In this book, therefore, we will follow this dual focus. Some have said that virtue cannot be taught in a college classroom and that ethical dilemmas cannot be resolved by textbooks. But we believe that the principles and techniques of ethical assessment and ethical decision making do have a place in a professional curriculum.

However, we agree with those who have suggested that the concern of instructors should be less focused on presenting solutions to dilemmas than with efforts to encourage students to be alert in discovering and perceiving ethical issues, in considering competing arguments, in examining both the strengths and limitations of their own positions, and in reaching for thoughtfully reasoned conclusions. Our approach to ethical decision making is designed to assist social workers in reasoning carefully about ethical issues, to help them clarify their moral aspirations at the level demanded by the profession, and to achieve a more ethical stance in practice.

The exercises at the end of each chapter have been prepared to heighten students' sensitivity to the ethical aspects of social work practice, to aid them in developing a personal approach to such issues, and to help them consider the essential elements in ethical decision making in professional practice. Suggestions for additional readings also appear at the end of each chapter.

In our continuing effort to make this book more useful, we have added new material, dropped some dated material that appeared in earlier editions, and rewritten many chapters. At the suggestion of colleagues and students who have used earlier editions of this book, we have included new sections on the recently adopted standards regarding dual relationships, practitioner impairment, and advertisements and solicitation as well as new material on the ethical implications of technology, macro practice, racism, the aging, managed care, group practice, health and mental health, and the NASW policy on assisted suicide.

We have retained the two ethical decision screens first presented in the fourth edition, revising one. We have received numerous comments that the screens have proved helpful in the rank ordering of ethical principles and ethical obligations, thus helping social work practitioners identify priorities among competing ethical obligations. We have tried to suggest some principles and guidelines which can really help social workers making ethical practice decisions. While ethical and moral perfection remains an unattainable goal, social workers, like all others, must continue to strive toward that goal.

The exemplars in this book are taken from the real world, but none of them occurred in exactly the way described or to the people identified in each situation. Neither names nor other identifying information came from social agency records nor from social workers who worked with these people. Many new exemplars have been added to reflect newer areas of practice. Needless to say, the exemplars do not always typify good or desirable practice. They were chosen simply to illustrate ethical practice problems occurring in the real world of practice.

We want to thank our colleagues and students for helping us think through many of the issues involved in social work ethics. Thanks are due to the anonymous reviewers of earlier editions; they drew our attention to several areas that should be added. To Jura Avizienis, our editor, special thanks for encouraging us to prepare this fifth edition. We also want to express our appreciation to Bernetta Hux for her assistance and to Beverly Bowles, librarian of the Learning Resource Center of the School of Social Work, as well as the Health Sciences Library at the University of Maryland at Baltimore and to the Milton S. Eisenhower Library of the Johns Hopkins University. Harris Chaiklin gave useful suggestions.

The appearance of this edition marks a quarter century of association with Ted and Sarah Peacock, our publishers. We wish to express our gratitude to them.

Finally, we thank our wives, Chaya and Sylvia, who have continued their everlasting patience with our not so minor personal foibles.

Frank M. Loewenberg
Ralph L. Dolgoff

# PART ONE

# Introduction to
## Ethical Decision Making

# 1. Ethical Choices in the Helping Professions

Every day most social workers are confronted with the necessity to make ethical decisions. Sometimes they have an opportunity to think about the choices, perhaps to talk things over with a colleague or to consult with an expert. However, more often social workers, even student social workers, are alone when they must make difficult ethical decisions; they cannot wait because of the immediacy of the problem that faces them. At best, they have a few hours or a few days to consider what should be done.

➤ **1.1 The Dilemma of Huntington's Disease**

Roberta Jackson is eager to have a baby and has just asked you as her social worker not to tell her husband or family members that she has a genetic marker which identifies her as a carrier of Huntington's disease, a disease for which there is no cure but which will not show up until twenty to thirty years from now. This is an inherited condition which potentially affects all family members and inflicts premature senility on those affected. She is afraid that her husband will not be willing to have a child if he knows about her genetic condition.

What ethical issues does this request pose? Where will the social worker find help with the ethical aspects of this practice problem? How will the social worker decide what course of action to follow?

Ms. Jackson's request poses a number of ethical dilemmas for herself and for her social worker. The personal dilemmas are outside the scope of this book, but her social worker is confronted by a number of professional dilemmas whose solutions should be congruent with ethical professional practice. We will briefly analyze three of these.

*Competing values.*    Client self-determination and protection of human life are two values to which all social workers are deeply committed. But as is so often the case, in this instance the social worker cannot honor both. Not revealing the facts to Ms. Jackson's husband deprives him of the knowledge he needs for making a thoughtful decision about having children, including the risk of having a child who will carry this disease. Informing Mr. Jackson of the presence of the genetic marker provides him with decision-making opportunities, but interferes with Ms. Jackson's right to determine her own fate. It also may prevent the possibility of the birth of a defective or severely disabled child. Yet not informing him may result in a child whose life expectations may be limited. There may be good reasons for giving priority to one, rather than the other, of these values. Nevertheless, this is a problem in professional ethics which the social worker must resolve either knowingly or unconsciously.

*Multiple client system.*    Ordinarily a social worker gives priority to her client, just as ordinarily she would respect the confidentiality rule. Both of these principles are relevant to Ms. Jackson's request "Don't tell my husband or kinfolk." However, the social worker also has responsibilities toward others, including Ms. Jackson's husband. This practitioner must decide to whom she[*] owes first obligations.

*Value dilemma.*    Ms. Jackson's request for confidentiality places the social worker before additional value dilemmas. While she is committed to provide service to her client, she is not at all sure which professional values are relevant in this situation. She believes that both professional and personal situations are always better served by telling the truth; yet she does not want to impose her own values on a client nor does she

---

[*] Some social workers are men, many more are women. In recent years many writers have used such terminology as *his* or *her* or *she* and *he*. Or they have used the plural, such as "social workers believe." However, these usages are clumsy and often tend to interfere with the clarity of the message. Since most social workers are women, we will refer to the social worker as *she* (except in exemplars where the worker has been identified as a man, as in Exemplar 3.2) and to the recipient of the service as *he* (except where the recipient is a woman, as in Exemplar 1.2). We hope that male social workers and female recipients will bear with our usage.

think it right to remain quiet when her silence leaves Mr. Jackson without important information. Will the least harm be accomplished by not informing him, thus enabling the birth of an infant whose quality and length of life are threatened?

There are many ways to prepare for this practice reality. First, it is important to recognize that every decision in social work practice includes ethical aspects. Next, social workers need knowledge and skill to clarify these aspects of practice in order to engage in effective ethical decision making. Knowledge and skill in this area (as in all other aspects of social work practice) must be developed and refined throughout a social worker's professional career.

This book has been written to help social workers, students as well as practitioners, prepare for informed and skillful reasoning in ethical decision making. Part of this preparation consists of considering such questions as: Who is my client? What obligations do I owe to my clients? Do I have professional obligations to people other than my clients? What about my family? My agency? My profession? What are my own personal values? Are these compatible with the profession's values? With societal values? What are my ethical priorities when these value sets are not identical? What is the ethical way to respond when I have conflicting professional responsibilities to different people?

In this chapter we will introduce this complex and important topic and define what we mean by *ethical decision making*. There are those who charge that some social workers have not yet developed a strong enough sense of morality, and that therefore they find it hard to cope with the ethical implications of their practice. Others think that social workers are aware of ethical issues that occur in practice, but that they make decisions on the basis of incomplete knowledge, value judgments and biases, and insufficient conscious use of self. Social work students and practitioners have repeatedly asked for guides to help them grapple with ethical practice issues. Until recently these requests were answered only by the adoption of codes of ethics which were helpful in some ways, but left too many questions unanswered. The requests for help continue because most social workers know instinctively that ethics are supremely important. Even those who have never heard of Gewirth tend to agree with him that ethical requirements "take precedence over all other modes of guiding action" (1978, p. 1).

The very subject of professional ethics was once almost completely ignored in the social work curriculum. But there has been a change. In the past two generations scientists have cracked the genetic code, split the atom, put a man on the moon, replaced hearts and other vital organs, and have successfully transferred an embryo from the test tube to the womb. From a technological point of view it is nowadays possible to do almost anything we want to do. The key question now is how to decide what ought to be done. In line with this, more and more social workers have come to recognize that they too face questions that go beyond the "technology" of social work. This recognition has made the subject of professional ethics more visible in the professional social work curriculum. Beginning in 1982 and again in 1992, the Council on Social Work Education (CSWE) *Curriculum Policy Statement* (1992) required the inclusion throughout the curriculum of values and ethics that guide professional social workers in their practice.

What does the term *ethics* mean? The word comes from the Greek root *ethos* which originally meant custom, usage, or habit. In contemporary use it deals with the question of what actions are morally right and with how things ought to be. General ethics clarify the obligations that are owed by one person to another person. But some obligations are based on the specific relations between two people (such as a mother and her son), or they are based on a particular role voluntarily accepted by one of the parties. The latter are special obligations which apply only to those who have consented to accept that role position (Fishkin, 1982, pp. 25–27). Professional ethics are a codification of the special obligations that arise out of a person's voluntary choice to become a professional, such as a social worker. Professional ethics clarify the ethical aspects of professional practice. Professional social work ethics are intended to help social work practitioners recognize the morally correct way of practice and to learn how to decide and act correctly with regard to the ethical aspects of any given professional situation.

## CONTEMPORARY INTEREST IN PROFESSIONAL ETHICS

Jane Addams talked many years ago about the importance of ethical practice, but until recently most professional social workers were less than clear about the ethical aspects of practice. Even though it is difficult to avoid ethical problems in everyday practice, a powerful tradition has attempted to deemphasize questions of morals, values, and ethics from the practitioner's purview. Social workers accepted this "scientific" stance and preferred objective explanations over moralistic ones. But this approach has not helped them in making ethical decisions when difficult problems arise, especially in such controversial practice areas as abortion, genetic technology, allocation of scarce resources, and similar situations.

One of the paradoxes of modern times is the fact that the interest in professional ethics is high even though the level of morality of our society is rather low. In this century more people have been killed by

violence than ever before. Genocide was perfected in our own lifetime. The Nuremberg trials after World War II, the Civil Rights movement in the late 1950s and 1960s, the killings in Cambodia in the 1970s,
as well as the many rapid advances in medical and computer technology, have resulted in a greater awareness of human rights, including the
rights of clients. The renewed interest in social work ethics is, in part,
related to this emphasis on human rights and, in part, it is an expression of the maturation of the social work profession. Another explanation for the growing interest in social work ethics lies in the
increasing concern of practitioners with the proclivity of clients to re-
sort to litigation in order to resolve claims of ethical malfeasance and
malpractice. Though the number of complaints and lawsuits that involve social workers is still small, there has been an upswing of these
in recent years.

Unethical conduct, corruption, and scandals in government as well as
in industry have become commonplace. Newspapers report almost daily
unethical practices by some scientific researchers, physicians, lawyers,
accountants, and other professionals. No wonder that ethics generally,
and ethics for professional practitioners in particular, have attracted so
much interest that one writer spoke of an "ethics explosion" (Brennan,
1983) and another noted "a widespread cultural ado about morality"
(Frankena, 1980, p. 5). Courses in ethics are spreading rapidly and are offered today not only by universities but also by businesses, industries,
professional groups, and even by the military.

Social work practitioners are searching for guides that will direct
their practice behavior along ethical lines. For many, neither science nor
religion has provided satisfactory answers to the ethical problems that
they face. The renewed emphasis on professional ethics is due to a "desire to retrieve human values and moral concerns from the high-tech influence of science, professionalization and rapid technical innovation"
that is so characteristic of all areas of contemporary life, including professional social work (Walrond-Skinner & Watson, 1987, p. 5).

## ETHICAL PROBLEMS IN SOCIAL WORK PRACTICE

Some suggest that ethics are a problem that occurs only on very special
occasions. In most situations a practitioner requires only a high level of
professional skill and insight since such situations do not involve any
ethical questions. This approach to professional practice, established by
Sigmund Freud himself, has been accepted by generations of practitioners in all of the helping professions. The assumptions underlying this approach are supported by some philosophers who argue that most actions

do not involve any moral question but are the result of a free choice among the various available alternatives. These alternatives are located in the area that Fishkin (1982) has identified as the "zone of moral indifference." But other philosophers insist that there are ethical implications or ethical aspects to almost every professional decision. We follow the latter approach because we believe that professional social workers are not merely technical problem solvers but are also moral agents.

An examination of social work practice will reveal that almost all practice principles involve (or are based on) ethical principles. One of the sources for ethical problems in social work practice may be located in the multiplicity and contradiction of values which characterize contemporary society. While we often speak of ethical problems, it would be more correct to speak of the ethical dimensions or ethical aspects of social work practice problems. In the past it was assumed that ethical issues arose out of, and were limited to, the dyadic relation between social worker and client. Current ethical concerns also include those that arise out of the newer practice models that include many participants in addition to client and worker. The breakdown of consensus concerning societal goals, the increasing scarcity of resources that are available for social welfare, and the utilization of new technologies not only have intensified traditional ethical dilemmas but have also given rise to what may well be a new generation of ethical issues in social work practice.

In this book we will examine *ethical problems* and *ethical dilemmas*. Ethical problems raise the question: What is the *right* thing to do in a given practice situation? How can a social worker avoid unethical behaviors in that situation? Ethical dilemmas occur in situations where the social worker must choose between two or more relevant, but contradictory, ethical directives, or when every alternative results in an undesirable outcome for one or more persons. The seedbed for ethical problems in social work practice is graphically portrayed in Figure 1.1.

Any disagreement that different participants of the action system (Block B) have with regard to alternate decision options (Block A) or alternative assumptions (Block C) will intensify the difficulties that social workers will encounter in ethical decision making. Examples of such difficulties occur when

- A client wants a service that may affect another member of the family who does not want to receive that service: an adult son may want to place his aged father in a nursing home, but the father wants to remain in his own home.
- Conflicting values impinge on the decision facing the social worker: a young woman asks whether her fiancé (who is your client) is HIV-positive, while the client wants to keep this information secret.

**Figure 1.1   Ethical Problems in Social Work Practice**

| | | |
|---|---|---|
| Ethical problems arise when there is a conflict in | **A** | problem definition<br>goal setting<br>priority setting<br>decision on means<br>decision on strategy<br>desired outcomes |
| proposed by | **B** | client<br>practitioner<br>agency<br>community<br>profession<br>society |
| because each relates to different assumptions about | **C** | human nature<br>values<br>issues<br>system levels |

- The community and the profession have different priorities: everyone agrees that something must be done about homeless families, but community leaders believe that better police protection is more important than building another shelter.
- The social agency prescribes a treatment modality based on one social work theory, while the practitioner knows that another approach is indicated for a particular client: the agency is committed to insight therapy, while research evidence indicates that in this situation behavior modification may be more effective.

Some social workers try to ignore the ethical problems and dilemmas that arise in these and similar situations either because they are too uncomfortable in making ethical decisions or because they think that they already have the answer. Other social workers are aware of the ethical aspects of these problem situations, but are uneasy because they think that they do not yet have the skill to deal with ethical problems of this nature.

Two root causes for ethical problems are (1) competing values and (2) competing loyalties. Social workers may benefit from paying special attention to these root causes.

*Competing values.*   An ethical dilemma may arise when a practitioner is faced by two or more competing values, such as justice and equality, or confidentiality and protecting life. Similarly, in a period of rapidly shrinking budgets no practitioner can ignore considerations of efficiency and efficacy, even though these constraints may do violence to what is thought to be best for a particular client. A worker may feel equally committed to two values, even when both cannot be actualized in a specific situation.

*Competing loyalties.*   When competing or conflicting groups make claims for the social worker's loyalties, she may face an ethical dilemma. A classic example of this dilemma is the social worker who represents both the agency and the client, with each making conflicting demands. There is little need to point to the more blatant examples of this cause of ethical problems. But even less blatant incidents, such as a request for giving preferential treatment to relatives and friends, can be problematic from an ethical point of view. Multiple loyalties are also a source for ethical quandaries when a social worker serves a multiple-client system, as is so common today. In these circumstances, identifying the person or unit that should receive priority attention becomes a key ethical issue.

Several exemplars from social work practice will now be examined. Consider how ethical issues arise in each exemplar.

The ethical problems faced by the social worker who has been assigned to work with Blanca Gabelli are similar to, yet different from, those faced by the worker of Roberta Jackson (in Exemplar 1.1).

➤   **1.2 Blanca Gabelli Costs Too Much**
Blanca Gabelli, an eighty-four-year-old retired physician, participates in a day treatment program and resides in an assisted living residence. Recently she has become slightly more forgetful, falls more frequently, and has been somewhat less able to care for herself. She has also become increasingly irascible, and several staff members have complained about her demanding behavior. As the social worker who serves the residents, your supervisor has asked you to arrange a transfer to a nursing home because Ms. Gabelli is a "pain" and she is costing the residential program too much. Although you believe that Ms. Gabelli is not yet in need of nursing home care, you contacted the one possible nursing home to arrange for a transfer. You just received a call from Ellen Brito, the nursing home administrator, who is asking about Ms. Gabelli's health, behavior, and attitudes. How should you respond?

Let us consider some of the ethical choices this social worker might make.

## Goal Setting

Who should set the goals in this situation? If you comply with your supervisor's demand, you and your supervisor determine Ms. Gabelli's future while also undermining her sense of autonomy. Do you and your supervisor have an ethical right to do so? What part should Ms. Gabelli play in deciding her own living arrangements?

### Role Conflict

A social worker is an agency employee. What are the implications if you do not comply with your supervisor's demand? Does the social worker's role require that you always comply with the suggestions of your supervisor or that you always serve as Ms. Gabelli's protector? Whose interests should receive priority consideration? Your supervisor's? The agency's? Yours? Ms. Gabelli's? What role should you play in relation to the non-social work colleague who works for the nursing home? Should you share with the nursing home staff some or all of the facts about Ms. Gabelli's behavior?

### Value Dilemma

This social worker's supervisor is demanding the worker comply with the agency's decision rather than with her client's choice. In addition, her supervisor is asking her to lie and manipulate the situation so that the agency can transfer Ms. Gabelli. But this social worker personally places a high value on honesty. In what ways do her professional and personal values clash? Should the social worker tell Ms. Gabelli what her supervisor said? How honest should this social worker be and with whom?

Another set of ethical problems faces Sharon Gillette, the social worker in the following exemplar.

➤ **1.3 A Tornado Hits Warrensville**

It was 7:35 a.m. in Warrensville when the phone in the Gillette home rang. Sharon Gillette rushed to answer the phone because her husband had left for work over an hour ago. About half an hour after he left the radio and TV aired warnings of tornados in the vicinity. Mrs. Carlyle who baby-sits for Sharon's children just called to say she could not get there this morning. Just a few minutes ago fire sirens had sounded indicating a very dangerous weather condition would hit the town momentarily. All Warrensville families knew they should take cover in their prepared sheltered spaces. Now the phone rang for Sharon. The Civil Emergency Center asked her to report immediately for duty at her assigned Emergency Center because there were already homes destroyed and people in shock.

*Competing values.*    Is it right for Sharon to leave her family? What mother can leave her children frightened and confused by tornados? On the other hand, what are her obligations as a social worker to the homeless families being served at the Emergency Center? This social worker cannot simultaneously be in her shelter with her children and at the Emergency Center.

*Ambiguity.*    Sharon would have been far less troubled by her decision if she knew there would be no damage to her house and children or if she knew for certain that her presence at the Emergency Center would make a critical difference in the lives of the homeless victims of the tornados.

What other ethical issues does this case pose? Where in the *Code of Ethics* will this social worker find help with the ethical aspects of this practice problem encountered in emergency situations such as floods, hurricanes, outbreaks of violence, and war? How will the social worker decide what course of action to follow? The ethical aspects of the situation are relatively straightforward. As a social worker, Sharon is charged with professional responsibilities, perhaps especially in an emergency situation, but she also has responsibilities to her family, which in this case includes very young, frightened, and potentially at-risk children. Which of these two obligations has priority?


## CAN PROFESSIONAL ETHICS BE TAUGHT?

Teaching professional ethics is based on the assumption that knowledge about ethics will lead to the acquisition of attitudes and values, and that these, in turn, will produce the desired ethical behavior. But is there any reason to think that studying ethics will motivate ethical behavior any more than studying biochemistry will inspire a person to become a physician? In fact, some have suggested that learning about ethics may not be the best way to promote ethical behavior. Social work students and practitioners who spend too much time reflecting about professional ethics may find themselves in the same situation as the centipede who became incapable of moving about when it tried to understand how its legs worked. Further empirical research is needed to discover whether and to what extent learning about ethics is helpful. Educators still do not know much more about value-and-ethics education than Socrates did more than two thousand years ago when he told Meno that he did not know how values were acquired and whether they could be taught at all. These questions still require answers.

The widely accepted view is that attitudes determine behavior, but some leading attitude theorists have proposed that behavior determines attitudes. Generally it is held that our behavior is a direct consequence of our attitudes about the world, but the revisionist theorists suggest that a person tends to select beliefs and attitudes that are in consonance with or support his or her behavior (Bem, 1970; Festinger, 1957). Following the traditional theory, it is widely believed that a social worker's values influence the selection of treatment methods. The Council on Social Work Education (CSWE) requirement for curriculum content on values and ethics is also based on the assumption that a student who learns to value professional ethics will, as a practitioner, choose to behave in ethical ways.

It may be that both approaches are correct. Acock and Fuller (1984) have indicated that both the attitude → behavior and the behavior → attitude models are far too simplistic and not fully in accord with reality. Instead they suggest a reciprocal model in which, at the same time, attitudes influence behaviors and behaviors influence attitudes.

In earlier times professional ethics were transmitted by watching a master practitioner. This apprentice model was satisfactory for training professionals as long as the new practitioner faced the same type of problems as did the master teacher. Social work's traditional emphasis on concurrent field instruction and educational supervision suggests a partial continuation of the apprentice model. But in today's world of rapid changes, this model may no longer be optimally effective; alternate teaching methods must be developed to supplement this traditional curriculum approach.

The impact of college and university curricula on changes in values and ethics is not entirely clear. Feldman and Newcomb, on the basis of an examination of more than 1,500 empirical studies, conducted over four decades in many different parts of the United States, reported some positive findings, though these differed for various types of colleges and curricula. Most interesting was their conclusion that with few exceptions faculty members exerted an impact only "where the influence of student peers and of faculty complemented and reinforced one another" (1970, p. 330). Feldman and Newcomb surveyed primarily undergraduate colleges and focused on general value systems. There are only a few empirical studies of value changes in professional social work education. These raise some questions about the efficacy of teaching values. A number of studies report either negative outcomes or no significant changes (Varley, 1963; Varley, 1968; Hayes & Varley, 1965; Brown, 1970; Cyrns, 1977; Judah, 1979). Three other studies (Sharwell, 1974; Moran, 1989; Wodarski et al., 1988) report some positive findings. However, all of these studies attempted to measure value changes as reflected by answers to a questionnaire and did not assess ethical behaviors in practice settings.

More than thirty years ago Pumphrey (1959) noted that social work students viewed the teaching of values as something quite apart from (or even irrelevant to) practice. Changes have occurred since Pumphrey undertook her study, but a recent observer noted that too many students still think that the major objective of ethics education is to pass an exam at the end of the semester. It is no wonder that social work students, like medical students, are often unable to recognize ethical problems in practice situations (Reiser et al., 1987).

It is doubtful whether an academic course limited to thinking and talking about professional ethics will suffice to make students more ethical practitioners. Thinking and talking must be supplemented by doing. Skill in utilizing the decision-making tools that we will present in this book, as well as the discussions and exercises, should help to improve the ability of students and practitioners to reason more effectively about ethical issues, improve the quality of ethical decision making, and result in more ethical professional behaviors in day-by-day practice. At the same time we try to avoid giving pat answers. Instead, we hope to convey the need for tolerance of ambiguity when it comes to professional ethics. In professional practice there is rarely, if ever, only one correct ethical way. Our approach is to focus on ethical applications in practice situations rather than merely on the philosophical foundations of professional ethics. We agree with Hokenstad (1987) that instruction that is limited to ethics and values and does not at the same time concern itself with knowledge and practice will not facilitate the development of ethical social work practice. The purpose of teaching professional ethics is not to develop philosophers or ethicists, but more effective and more ethical practitioners.

Social work educational programs are expected to provide specific knowledge about social work values and their implications, to help students to develop an awareness of their personal values and to clarify conflicting values and ethical dilemmas. One goal of social work education is to educate social workers who are responsible for their own ethical professional conduct (CSWE, 1992).

The following are reasonable objectives for a course in professional ethics:

1. Become more aware of and more sensitive to ethical issues in professional practice;
2. Identify and grapple with competing arguments by examining their limitations and strengths;
3. Learn to recognize the ethical principles involved in their practice situations;
4. Develop a greater understanding of the complexities of ethical decision making;
5. Be able to reach thoughtfully reasoned conclusions and apply ethical principles to their professional activities;

6. Be able to clarify their moral aspirations and standards and evaluate the ethical decisions they have made within the context of the profession.

## ABOUT THIS BOOK

In this book we try to help students to acquire skill in analyzing ethical quandaries, to learn techniques in making better ethical decisions, and to become aware of the ethical aspects of practice. We will not present detailed prescriptions for solving specific ethical problems, nor will we offer a cookbook approach that indicates what to do in every given practice situation. Instead, we will offer various models to help social work students and practitioners gain skill in analyzing and assessing the ethical dimensions of practice problems so that they can develop an ethically appropriate professional behavior. We will suggest several analytic schemes which may help social workers resolve the ethical dilemmas that they face in practice.

It is important to recognize that ethical practice is an individual, an organizational, and a social phenomenon. Though ethical conduct is intentional and willed behavior for which each individual bears responsibility, the peer group and the agency setting can and must encourage professional behavior that is ethical. Joseph (1983) noted that "ethical concerns are generated by the structural and interactional arrangements of organizations, as well as from their goals and objectives." For too long ethics have been the exclusive concern of the individual. Ethics must become the concern of the social group—in this instance, the concern of each social agency as well as of the total profession.

In Chapter 2 we will review the relation between values, general ethics, and professional ethics. Widespread concern about the relation between law and ethics has led us to include a section on the relationship of ethical and legal behavior. We will also examine the manifest and latent functions of professional ethics as well as present a brief history of the evolution of professional ethics in the field of social work.

In Chapter 3 we will develop our decision-making framework. After briefly presenting several basic ethical theories and various approaches to ethical decision making in the helping professions, we will develop two decision-making screens, specifically designed to help in assessing the ethical alternatives that social workers face in their day-by-day practice.

Part II of the book will be devoted to the presentation of a number of ethical problems and ethical dilemmas in professional practice. The nine chapters in this section cover a variety of practice problems. Each ethical problem and dilemma is important in its own right, but no claim is made that any one is more important than any other. For each dilemma we have presented some relevant background information in order to help the reader examine the ethical dilemmas that arise out of the exemplars presented. The decision screens developed in Chapter 3 should be applied in analyzing each of these ethical dilemmas.

In the thirteenth and final chapter we again discuss the question of who is responsible for professional ethics. From what we have written in this chapter and from the development of our argument throughout the book, it will not come as a surprise that we place the responsibility for professional ethics not only on each individual social worker but also on the employing organization and on the organized professional group.

Exercises and suggestions for additional readings will appear at the end of every chapter. The codes of ethics of several social work professional groups, as well as additional exemplars, will be found in the appendixes.

Ethical issues will continue to cause discomfort even after reading this book. This is so because every decision which a social worker makes entails ethical risks. Perhaps the most agonizing of these risks is the danger of making a choice that may hurt or damage a client. Every effort must be made to avoid such dangers; yet these hazards are unavoidable and must not lead to inaction. We hope that the tools for ethical decision making that we will present, as well as the discussions and questions that will be raised, will alert social workers to their ethical responsibilities and help them become more skilled and more ethical practitioners.

## EXERCISES

1. Read Exemplar A.9 (see Appendix A). Try to answer the following questions:
   a. What ethical issues are involved in this exemplar?
   b. What provisions of the NASW *Code of Ethics* address themselves to the ethical issues you have identified?
   c. What ethical problems and ethical dilemmas that occur in this exemplar are not covered by the NASW *Code of Ethics?*
   d. What do you think is the ethical thing to do? Do you think there is more than one solution?
2. Compare and contrast the ethical principles that relate to *confidentiality* in the five codes of professional ethics presented in Appendix B.
   a. Which code do you consider most helpful when a practitioner must make ethical decisions involving this principle? Why?

      b. Are there any additional points you would want to add when the *Code* is revised?

      c. Put yourself in the Roberta Jackson situation (Exemplar 1.1). What options are open to you? Analyze these in terms of the four questions raised in Exercise 1 (above).

3. Study your local TV and newspapers for one week. Identify the ethical issues that have implications for social workers.

## SUGGESTIONS FOR ADDITIONAL READINGS

A short list of readings that we have found particularly helpful is found at the end of each chapter. Emphasis is given to the more recent literature rather than to the classics. The readings may amplify points that have been made, present other points of view, or raise additional questions. Reference to an article does not necessarily mean that we agree with it. But in each instance we have found that the author has made a thoughtful contribution to one or more of the subjects discussed in the chapter. The articles are mentioned only by author and year; the full citation can be found in the bibliography at the end of the book.

    Goldstein (1987) presents a critical analysis of the moral aspects of social work practice. From a somewhat different perspective Conrad (1988) examines the ethical considerations of clinical practice. Dean and Rhodes (1992) argue that good clinical practice is not necessarily good ethical practice and recommend ethical deliberation be a more explicit focus of practice and of practitioners' self-examination. Brieland and Korr (1987) present their ideas for a code of ethics for student social workers.

# 2. Values and
   Professional Ethics

Values are a very important element in social work practice. According to Brown (1968), "no other profession, with the exception perhaps of philosophy, concerns itself as deeply with the matter of values as does the profession of social work," Goldstein (1973) described social workers as "value laden individuals." For Vigilante (1974) social work values are "the fulcrum of practice." Imre added that "moral theory for social work must begin with an understanding of the essentially moral nature of social work practice" (1989). Frankl (1968) also emphasized the centrality of values, not only for professional practitioners but for everyone. Life without values has no meaning, but only creates an "existential vacuum." For Frankl the "will to meaning" is considerably more important than the "will to pleasure."

## Values

Social workers, like so many others, often fail to distinguish between such terms as *values*, *ethics*, and *morality*. They use them rather loosely. But values are not the same as virtues, though the two terms are often used interchangeably. Neither are values the same as ethics. One popular dictionary offers seventeen definitions of *value*. Timms (1983) reviewed reports and publications from a number of social science fields and found no less than 180 different definitions for the term *value*. A survey of the social work literature suggests that social work writers have used most of these definitions.

Maslow (1962) once observed that values are like a big container that holds all sorts of miscellaneous and vague things. Many philosophers have used the term *value* as if it meant the same as *interest*, but John Dewey used the term in a more precise way by noting that it must include some element of appraisal or preference. Most social scientists have followed Dewey's definition, indicating that values are meant to serve as guides or criteria for selecting good and desirable behaviors. Williams defines values as "those conceptions of desirable states of affairs that are utilized in selective conduct as criteria for preference or choice or as justifications for proposed or actual behavior" (1967, p. 23). Kluckhohn adds that "a value is not just a preference but it is a preference which is felt and/or considered to be justified..." (1951, p. 306). Most writers draw attention to the differences between societal values, group values, and individual values. Usually values at these different levels are complementary or reciprocal, though at times they may be in conflict. Within any one society, most people, most of the time, agree about societal values.

## Professional Values

Social work practitioners take their basic professional values from societal values, that is, from the values held by the larger society in which they practice. These professional values are most often compatible with societal values, but there may be important differences in emphasis, priorities, or interpretation. It stands to reason, just as there is wide agreement about societal values, so is there a wide consensus about basic professional values.

The central role that values play in social work has been recognized by many, as was noted in the beginning of this chapter. According to Gordon, values constitute "the major substance of social work" (1965b, p. 20). The revised *Curriculum Policy Statement* of the Council on Social Work Education (1992) summarized the core values of the social work profession, as follows:

1. Social workers' professional relationships are built on regard for individual worth and dignity and are furthered by mutual participation, acceptance, confidentiality, honesty, and responsible handling of conflict.
2. Social workers respect people's right to make independent decisions and to participate actively in the helping process.
3. Social workers are committed to assisting client systems to obtain needed resources.

4. Social workers strive to make social institutions more humane and responsive to human needs.
5. Social workers demonstrate respect for and acceptance of the unique characteristics of diverse populations.
6. Social workers are responsible for their own ethical conduct and the quality of their practice; they should seek to attain continuous growth in the knowledge and skills of their profession.

There is a general consensus about social work values. For example, most professional social workers agree that client participation, self-determination, and confidentiality are among basic social work values. However, disagreements are likely to occur when it comes to implementing these generalized professional values. Social workers may differ about priorities, specific objectives, and the means necessary to put these generalized values into practice. Thus the value "enhancing the dignity of life" may be used by one social worker to support a client's request for an abortion, while her social work colleague may call on the same generalized value to support her professional decision to try to persuade the client to go through a full-term pregnancy. This situation led Perlman to conclude that "a value has small worth, except as it is moved, or is moveable, from believing into doing, from verbal affirmation into action" (1976, p. 381).

Vigilante asks whether values can "be transmuted into instruments of professional practice, or do they serve only to guide practice and morally justify the profession" (1983, p. 59)? Bloom suggests that philosophic definitions of values do not really assist practitioners in the helping professions; according to him the focus should be on "what values look like as expressed in action" (1975, p. 138). Professional values that do not provide guidance and direction are only of limited use. Nevertheless, they are important because ethical principles and ethical rules can be derived from these values. When framed as a professional code of ethics, such rules and principles may provide social workers with the ethical criteria necessary for making difficult practice decisions. Note should be taken that ethical principles are always derived from values. A rule or principle that is not derived from values but from another source is not an ethical rule. Such a rule may be a bureaucratic rule, a principle derived from practice wisdom, or something else, but it is not an ethical rule.

## Ethics

How to move from values to behavior is a problem that is not limited to professional practitioners. It is a more general problem that has become the focus of attention of ethicists. Ethics are generally defined as that branch of philosophy that concerns itself with human conduct and moral decision making. It seeks to discover the principles that guide people in deciding what is right and wrong. Another definition points to a key function of ethics. "Ethics is not primarily concerned with getting people to do what they believe to be right, but rather with helping them to decide what is right" (Jones et al., 1977, p. 8).

Though the terms *value* and *ethics* are often used interchangeably, they are not identical. Ethics are deduced from values and must be in consonance with them. The difference between them is that values are concerned with what is *good* and *desirable*, while ethics deal with what is *right* and *correct*. A person's right to privacy, for example, is a first-order value of American society. One of the social work ethical rules deduced from this value states, "The social worker should obtain informed consent of clients before taping, recording, or permitting third party observation of their activities" (NASW, 1993, Section II-H-5).* In the same manner *privacy* is a desirable value, while *informed consent* is the ethical rule and the correct way of practice that is derived from this value.

Even though values are meant to serve as guides for selecting desirable behavior, they do not always lead to these results since a person's behavior is not always consistent with his or her professed values. Social workers, like other professionals, at times practice in ways that are inconsistent with professional values or in ways that do not reflect societal values. For example, client participation in decision making is highly valued by social workers, yet some practitioners do not always make sufficient effort to involve their clients fully. One reason for the lack of congruence between values and behaviors may be that values are usually stated at a very high level of generality, while behaviors are very specific. Another reason for this incongruence may be the gap between professed (or public) and real (or personal) values of the person.

There is broad agreement about the most generalized values, such as cooperation and success, but these are not sufficiently specific to help identify appropriate behavior patterns. The more specific a value, the more useful will it be as a behavioral guide. On the other hand, the more specific a value, the smaller the chance that it will gain wide acceptance. For example, everyone agrees that *family life* is a highly desired value— that is, everyone agrees as long as that value is not defined in more specific operational terms. But this generalized value does not help an adult son who has to make difficult decisions about how to care for his paralyzed, senile father without increasing the tensions that already exist

---

* Note: This reference is to the NASW *Code of Ethics* (1993). All such citations encountered subsequently in this work refer to the same source.

between his present wife and his children from a previous marriage. Nor will the son's social worker find any specific ethical referents which may provide her with guidance in this situation

## Morality

George Bernard Shaw (1932) once wrote, "I don't believe in morality." His reference may have been to traditional values and rules of behavior promulgated by some external authority. Yet it is hard to conceive of life in a society that is essentially amoral.

Morality consists of principles or rules of conduct which define standards for right behavior. One might hope that morality consists of a set of general rules that apply to everyone in a society. These rules are neither enacted nor revoked by a legislature, but are accepted and changed by general consensus. They define the relationship between the members of a society. As Goldstein observed, "a moral sense...involves not only individual thoughts and actions but relationships with others" (1987, p. 181). While in the United States there is a broad consensus about some issues, we are witnessing nowadays a growing diversity and multimoralities. There are deep divisions in American society about such issues as euthanasia and the right to commit suicide, abortion, the responsibilities of individuals, families, and governments, and on another level clashing values among immigrant, racial, generational, religious, and ethnic and cultural groups. Social workers are increasingly confronted by a diversity of values and moralities; they practice in a society where there is less and less consensus about what is *the* proper moral stance.

The *Curriculum Policy Statement* of the Council on Social Work Education (1992) expects every social work education program to provide specific knowledge about social work values and their ethical implications, including assisting students to develop an awareness of their own values and ethical dilemmas. The *Statement* also sets forth a series of social work professional values such as respect for and acceptance of the unique characteristics of diverse populations and striving to make social institutions more humane and responsive to human needs.

Curriculum content must be offered so that students can understand and appreciate human diversity. Content must be included about population groups relevant to each program's mission, such as race, ethnicity, culture, class, gender, sexual orientation, religion, physical or mental disability, age, and national origin. Such a diversity of groups represents a diversity of values and perspectives which, for many social workers, raises value dilemmas, both for themselves and for their clients. Such a diversity also complicates their ethical decision making in practice.

**Figure 2.1    The Ethics of Interpersonal Relations**

|  |  |
|---|---|
| GENERAL ETHICS: | All persons shall be respected as equals. |
| PROFESSIONAL ETHICS: | All persons shall be respected as equals, but priority shall be given to the interests of the client. |

## Professional Ethics

Professional ethics provide the guide that enables a social worker to transform professional values into practice activities. Ethical principles do not describe professional practice, but provide screens in terms of which practice options can be assessed. Codes of professional ethics identify and describe the ethical behavior expected of professional practitioners.

Professional ethics are closely related to, but not identical with, general societal ethics. Just as social work values are derived from the values held by society but are not necessarily identical with those values, so professional ethics come from the same sources as societal ethics but may differ from them in important details. There may be differences in priorities, emphases, intensities, or applications. Illustrative of these crucial differences are the ethical principles governing the relationships among people. Both societal and professional ethics stress the *principle of equality*, but professional ethics give priority to the client's interests ahead of the interests of all others. Figure 2.1 spells out these differences in concise form.

For social workers this professional ethics principle is expressed in at least three rules of the NASW *Code of Ethics* (Paragraphs F-1, P-2, and P-3). The implications of these professional ethical principles for social workers and their practice are manifold because every social worker is almost continually forced to choose (knowingly or not) between general ethics and professional ethics. It is, of course, often easier to deduce and formulate an ethical principle in theory than it is to apply it in practice. The framers of the CSWE *Curriculum Policy Statement* recognized the importance of professional ethics for social work practice. They therefore mandated that there should be infused throughout the curriculum the values and ethics that guide professional social workers in their practice (Council on Social Work Education, 1992).

Some social workers can discuss professional ethics at length at staff meetings but fail to see how these principles affect their own practice. In the following exemplar the situation faced by one social worker will be analyzed; pay particular attention to the questions of professional ethics that this worker faces.

### ➤ 2.1 Diana Can't Go Out

Ms. Macedonia is a single parent, the mother of three children ranging in age from seven to sixteen. Her oldest daughter, Diana, is a sixteen-year-old high school student. Until the beginning of this school year she received good grades, but at midterm she was failing all courses. She seems to have lost all interest in school. For the past three weeks she has not been in school at all.

Ms. Macedonia is a clerical worker in the town's only industry. She goes to work early in the morning before her children leave for school, and returns home late in the afternoon, hours after the children finish school. Ms. Macedonia is a good home manager. However, she has no friends and is always at home by herself.

Recently Ms. Macedonia turned to the local family service agency to ask for help. She told the social worker that she felt depressed since she did not know what to do with Diana. By talking with both Ms. Macedonia and Diana the social worker learned that Diana has to stay home every evening and every weekend because her mother does not want to be alone. Even though Diana wants to go out with her friends, her mother never allows her to do so.

Ms. Macedonia's social worker faced a number of practical and ethical questions, including the following: Who is "the client" to whose interest the social worker should give priority? Is it Diana? Or her mother who made the initial request for help? Or both? Is it ethical for the social worker to intervene with Diana even though she has not asked for help and who (on being contacted by the worker) claims to have no need for help? What other ethical considerations are evident in this case?

No profession can establish for itself ethical rules which grossly violate the general ethical standards of the community. If a profession fails to take into consideration general societal ethics, it risks severe sanctions, including the possible revocation of part or all of its professional authority. Yet society recognizes that practice requirements make it impossible for professional practitioners to follow the identical ethical rules that people generally are expected to follow. Social workers, for example, may ask the kind of questions which in general conversation might be considered inappropriate or even an invasion of a person's privacy. However, before asking such questions a social worker must be certain that this information is necessary and that she can keep it confidential.

Society often sets limits to what a social worker may do. These limits can add to the ethical problems that social workers face. In a number of foreign countries, particularly in some of the developing countries, social workers have been jailed because they chose to follow a practice modality and professional ethics contrary to their government's expectations. Their fate highlights the fact that ethical problems in professional practice are real and at times can result in dire consequences. In a number of countries, including our own, some social workers have lost their jobs, have not received promotions, or have been shunned because they practiced in accord with professional ethical principles and in this way ran afoul of societal values.

## LAW AND ETHICS: THE PROBLEM OF UNETHICAL BUT LEGAL BEHAVIOR

Within the last two decades Congress and all state legislatures have passed a large number of laws that have affected and will continue to affect social work practice. At the same time the various state and federal courts, including the U.S. Supreme Court, have handed down a number of decisions that are of critical importance for social workers. "Good intentions" and "ignorance of the law" are no longer acceptable excuses for social workers who run afoul of the law. Lack of knowledge not only exposes practitioners to possible litigation for malpractice but may also contribute to unprofessional and unethical practices.

The purpose of this section is to help social work students and practitioners understand the interdependence of law and practice. We will also explore a number of key legal principles that are of vital importance for social workers. Little attention will be paid to specific legal questions because (1) in many instances the "law" differs in each of the fifty states, (2) law is constantly evolving so that if we were to discuss a specific law, there is a real possibility that it would be out-of-date even before this book got into the hand of the reader, and (3) we do not intend to make lawyers out of social workers.

### Characteristics of Law

*Law* has been variously defined by different authorities. According to Albert (1986), laws are concerned with protecting people against excessive or unfair power—government as well as private power. Black (1972) emphasizes the social control aspect of law; for him, law defines the normative relations between a state and its citizens. Selznick (1961) considers justice to be at the very center of any adequate definition of law. Others note that law tells people what they can and cannot do. The law informs them what is likely to happen if they are caught doing something that is prohibited (Van Hoose & Kottler, 1985). A crucial characteristic of law is that it is enacted by legislatures, interpreted by courts, and enforced by the threat of punishment. Its observance is held to be obligatory.

Law changes continually. At any given time it tries to reflect current knowledge and mores. The adaptation and change of law to reflect contemporary culture is exemplified by the evolution of the laws on abortions. When the California Supreme Court, in the *Belous* case (1969), reversed the lower court conviction of an obstetrician who had been found guilty of procuring an abortion, it discussed at length the history of the statute that classified procuring an abortion as a crime. It noted that when the statute was enacted in 1850, almost every abortion resulted in the woman's death because of the complete lack of modern antiseptic surgical techniques. The legislature in the mid-nineteenth century therefore limited abortions to those rare cases where the danger to the woman's life from continuing the pregnancy was greater than the danger of her dying from the abortion. The Court noted that nowadays abortions during the first trimester are relatively safe, in fact, statistically safer than going through with the pregnancy. For this and other constitutional reasons the Court reversed the conviction under what it considered the antiquated abortion statute and thus, in effect, revised the law in line with contemporary knowledge and technology.

In societies where the broad moral consensus has eroded, laws may be more effective than "moral persuaders" because they are enforced by the police power of the state. For example, in 1970 the U.S. Supreme Court held in *Goldberg* v. *Kelly* that the due-process clause of the Fourteenth Amendment of the Constitution also applied to social welfare programs. This new legal protection for the poor resulted almost immediately in a steep increase in appeals against administrative decisions made by welfare bureaucrats and public assistance caseworkers. In the decade following this decision, Aid to Families with Dependent Children (AFDC) alone witnessed an eightfold increase in administrative appeal hearings.

No matter how defined, law is of direct and immediate concern to social workers. There are many different ways in which law impacts on social work practice. Laws authorize payment for specified services; laws direct that certain social services be provided for all who need them; laws authorize professional social workers to engage in some activities that other people are not allowed to perform, but they also limit social workers from other activities which can be performed only by practitioners of another profession. Laws require social workers to report certain information to designated government agencies. Since laws differ from state to state, we avoid mentioning specific laws. Our purpose is merely to indicate the importance of laws for all social workers, no matter whether they are agency-employed or in private practice. Yet many social workers remain ignorant of the law. They practice as if the law were of little or no concern to them. Though *all* states now require that cases of suspected child abuse and neglect be reported to a designated public child protective agency, no matter whether the social worker is employed by a public or voluntary agency or is in private practice, some social workers still are not familiar with this requirement. They are also not aware that most state laws include a criminal penalty for those failing to report (Butz, 1985).

A national study of the reporting patterns of professionals involved with child abuse and neglect (physicians, nurses, dentists, mental health professionals, social workers, teachers and other school officials, child care workers, and law enforcement personnel) found that a large proportion of serious abuse known to professionals is not reported. Professionals fail to report almost 40 percent of the sexually abused children they have seen; nearly 30 percent of fatal or serious physical abuse cases (life-threatening or requiring professional treatment to prevent long-term impairment); almost 50 percent of moderate physical abuse cases; and about three-fourths of physical neglect cases (Finkelhor, 1990; Besharov, 1990).

Researchers are still not certain how to explain this failure to report child abuse and neglect. At one time it was thought that professionals feared that reporting might result in a lawsuit, but nowadays all jurisdictions give immunity from civil and criminal liability to professionals who report child abuse and neglect cases (Daro, 1988).

## Differences between Law and Ethics

What are the similarities and differences between law and ethics? Law has an ethical dimension. Thus Albert insists that "it is altogether misleading to say...that legal duties have nothing to do with moral duties" (1986, p. 9). But there are differences. While law observance is obligatory and enforced by threat of punishment, compliance with ethical principles is voluntary and reinforced only by a moral respect for values. Professional ethics, however, may also be enforced by professional sanctions; such sanctions may range from a simple censure to cancellation of permission to practice. A professional who is guilty of unethical or unprofessional behavior may be punished by a court of law and also may be disciplined for the same offense by his professional association.

While ethics are often characterized by a sense of ambiguity and indeterminacy, law is said to be definitive. Yet the outcome of legal disputes is far from certain or predictable. Legal rules are pliable; whether a particular legal rule will apply often depends on the arguments presented by one or the other side.

Law is enacted by legislatures and can be changed by a subsequent enactment or by legal interpretations. Ethical rules, though they do change over time, are generally immune from deliberate changes. Yet there is a close relationship between law and ethics since laws are often based on ethical principles. Thus, the legal principle of *privileged communication* is based on the ethical principles of *confidentiality* and *privacy*. (See Chapter 4 for a discussion of these principles.)

## CONFLICT BETWEEN LAW AND PROFESSIONAL ETHICS

Treating people wrongly does not become ethically right even when this is required or sanctioned by law. At times a practitioner may follow the law and still be guilty of unethical professional behavior. In the past a number of state legislatures enacted laws that mandated the involuntary sterilization of certain groups of felons and developmentally disabled persons. Can we say that a social worker who participated in these "lawful" programs practiced in an ethical manner? Many social workers claim that compliance with the law requiring the deportation of political refugees who have entered this country illegally is contrary to professional ethics. Other social workers state that the application of the death penalty, even when authorized by law, is always unethical. Some suggest that there is a moral right, even a moral duty, to violate unjust laws (Pemberton, 1965).

Yet there is a general assumption that human service professionals have an ethical duty to obey the law. From the time of John Locke to our own day there have only been a few who have openly challenged this assumption. Yet "in some circumstances, competing ethical principles may be so fundamental that they justify disobedience of the law" (Melton, 1988, p. 944). This dilemma is highlighted by the *Tarasoff* decision. The wider implications of this decision will be discussed in greater detail in Chapter 4. Here we will only note that in *Tarasoff* the California Supreme Court held that in some situations the welfare of the community may be more important than the confidentiality principle. Some social workers view this legal requirement to break confidentiality as forcing them to choose between professional ethics and law. Some social workers hold that a law cannot override professional ethical duties. But most have accepted the principles of the *Tarasoff* decision and do not think that they have to choose between professional ethics and law.

Social work with HIV-positive persons may make the dilemma of the *Tarasoff* decision even more critical for many social workers. What are the ethical and the legal requirements when such a client admits to his social worker that he continues to share needles or engage in unprotected sexual relations without notifying his or her partner of his condition? Should this social worker break confidentiality and warn the endangered partner? This ethical dilemma will be discussed in greater detail in Chapter 11.

Another example of the law/ethics dilemma may arise in connection with the legal requirement to report cases of suspected child abuse. Should a social worker disobey the law requiring that such cases be reported to the child protective agency when she knows (on the basis of past experiences) that the staff of that agency is not competent to deal with this problem? The *Code of Ethics* of the National Federation of Societies of Clinical Social Work (1988) addresses the possible conflict between professional ethics and law in Section VIb:

> Clinical social workers practice their profession in compliance with legal standards. They do not participate in arrangements undermining the law. However, when they believe laws affecting clients or their practice are in conflict with the principles and standards of the profession, clinical social workers make known the conflict and work toward change that will benefit the public interest.

## Malpractice and Unethical Behavior

A social worker's activities may be unprofessional, unethical, or both. An activity is *unprofessional* when it departs from the usual practice that a "prudent professional" would have rendered in the same situation. It is *unethical* when it violates the professional principles established by the profession's *Code of Ethics*. Thus Levy writes, "Failure to apply accepted principles of social work practice because of incompetence or negligence would subject social workers to the charge of malpractice. Failure to apply accepted principles of professional ethics in dealing with clients and others would subject social workers to the charge of unethical conduct" (1988, p. 477).

Failure to provide proper professional service (that is, rendering unprofessional service) can make a social worker liable to civil suits and/or criminal charges. Failure to provide ethical service can make a social worker liable to professional sanctions. In some situations a social worker faces all three risks. For example, a social worker who has sexual relations with a client may face criminal charges, a civil damage suit, and professional sanctions for unethical behavior. (See Chapter 8 for a more extensive discussion of the ethical issues involved in client/social worker relations.) Having sexual relations with a *former* client may also be unethical and illegal, but after a lapse of a period of time there may no longer be a case for civil liability. Thus, in Minnesota and California, civil liability is limited to a two-year period. But no state law specifies when (after the end of treatment) it is legal to have a sexual relationship with a former client. The question, both legally and ethically, is not the elapsed time, but rather whether such relations still constitute an exploitation of the therapeutic relationship (Conte et al., 1989, pp. 40–41).

Civil suits to recover damages resulting from unprofessional actions are known as *malpractice suits.* The relatively low premium rates for malpractice insurance that social workers pay (in contrast to the premiums paid by physicians and other high-risk occupations) suggest that successful malpractice suits against social workers are still rare, but their number is increasing every year. In the early 1970s there were almost no lawsuits against social workers, but by 1985 these had increased to over two thousand annually. It must be remembered that all professions experienced a growth in lawsuits in recent decades; this is characteristic of our "increasingly litigious society" (Besharov & Besharov, 1987, p. 518). In the past there were relatively few malpractice suits against social workers because most clients believed in their social workers' selfless dedication to client welfare. But this assessment may change as more social workers go into private practice (where service is provided for payment of a fee); as a result, all social workers may expect to become more vulnerable to malpractice suits (Jones & Alcabes, 1989).

Social workers who want to protect themselves properly should know what is involved in malpractice. By learning how liability develops, they can take precautions that will reduce the hazards they may face. One need not be a lawyer to understand the principles involved. However, in specific situations legal consultation is desirable. Nevertheless, it is important to keep one's perspective about malpractice and not panic. Yet social workers should not underrate the potential risk they face.

A client must prove these four conditions in order to win a malpractice suit:

1. The defendant (that is, the social worker) must have a legal duty to provide a professional service to the plaintiff (client). Ordinarily, a social worker has such a legal duty once a person becomes a "client" (whether in an agency or in private practice).
2. The social worker's performance must have been negligent or below generally accepted professional standards of competence. What would other social workers have done under the same circumstances? "Good intentions" or "ignorance" are rarely an effective defense.
3. The plaintiff (client) must have suffered an injury or loss.
4. The social worker's actions must have "caused" the alleged injury or loss.

There appears to be no limit to the reasons for which malpractice suits can be started, as the following list, based on Besharov & Besharov (1987, pp. 519–20), shows:

1. Treatment without consent
2. Improper and incorrect diagnosis
3. Inappropriate treatment
4. Failure to consult with a specialist
5. Failure to refer to a specialist
6. Failure to prevent a client's suicide
7. Causing a client's suicide
8. Failure to protect a third party against damage
9. Inappropriate release of client from hospital
10. False imprisonment
11. Failure to provide adequate care for a client in residential care
12. Assault and battery
13. Sexual involvement with a client
14. Breach of confidentiality
15. Defamation
16. Violation of a client's civil rights
17. Failure to be available when needed
18. Abrupt or inappropriate termination
19. Inappropriate bill collection methods
20. Inadequately protecting a child
21. Violating parental rights
22. Inadequate foster care
23. Failure to report suspected child abuse
24. Failure to report suspected child neglect
25. Failure to cure or failure to achieve satisfactory results

Many social workers are not familiar with the general principles of malpractice litigation. In one research study, 105 New Jersey social workers were asked whether a malpractice suit would be successful in the case of a therapist who had asked the police to pick up an emotionally disturbed client. This client had threatened to assault his therapist because he imagined that the therapist had revealed confidential information about him. Only twenty-nine respondents (27.6 percent) gave the correct answer to this vignette. However, just over half of the social workers (55 percent) gave the correct answer to another illustrative case example. The second such example involved a case where a depressed client threatened to commit suicide and also kill her two children. Social workers were asked whether there was a basis for a successful malpractice litigation against the worker if she failed to inform the client's husband of the threat and the client succeeded in the murder-suicide she had threatened. The publicity given to the *Tarasoff* decision in professional journals may explain the higher percentage of correct responses in this instance. Nevertheless, even in this case 45 percent of the social workers did not seem to know what is involved in malpractice litigation (Gerhart & Brooks, 1985).

The question remains, How can a social worker defend herself against the possibility of a malpractice suit? Knowledge and information are important, but "good practice is the best defense to possible liability" (Besharov & Besharov, 1987, p. 520).

## WHO NEEDS PROFESSIONAL ETHICS?

Do professional practitioners require special norms and ethical principles to guide their well-intentioned activities? Are not general ethical principles sufficient?

Whenever two ethical principles or two ethical rules provide contradictory directions, social workers need guidelines to help them decide which takes precedence. Professional ethics seek to provide such guidelines. Yet there are those who see no need for professional ethics. They argue that "common sense" or "practice wisdom" is all that a social worker needs in order to make the right decision. While no one should underrate the importance of sound judgment and practice wisdom, many recall the occasions when these simply were not sufficient to arrive at an ethically correct and effective practice decision.

Those who argue that professional ethics are not necessary for social workers cite one or more of the following arguments:

1. *Competence is enough.* Correct practice is based on competence and skill, not on the mastery of ethical principles. Many so-called ethical problems merely reflect poor practice. For example, good contracting will avoid many situations which are presented as ethical problems. Social workers will make more appropriate ethical decisions by becoming more competent.

2. *Uniqueness of each case.* Every case is different and every client presents unique problems. No code of ethical principles can provide adequate guidance for every unique situation that a social worker faces.

3. *Scientific social work is value-free.* Scientific social work must pay more attention to knowledge and technology than to religion and morality. An exaggerated interest in ethics will deflect the practitioners from developing further skill and knowledge, two

areas which are most important for strengthening professional practice.

4. *No time.* Social work practitioners have no time for lengthy ethical reflections because practice demands that they act quickly. They do what they think is best for their clients. A code of abstract ethical principles will not help. If social workers were to analyze each ethical problem, they would never get anything done.

5. *Philosophers' ambiguity.* At least since Aristotle's days philosophers have been unable to agree whether anyone can determine the truth of an ethical principle. Under these circumstances it is not possible to know the correctness of any ethical proposition. It is best not to fool ourselves into believing that professional ethics can help us know what is "right."

6. *Relativity.* What is thought to be "right" varies from country to country and even within a country at different times and for different population groups. In one society it is rude to come late for appointments, in another it is rude to come on time. Which is correct? In one culture a social worker is encouraged to recommend abortions when appropriate, while in another culture this option is taboo. Which is right? Within American society, different ethnic and cultural groups provide conflicting guidelines to what is "correct." In the social welfare field the emphasis has shifted pendulumlike between individual well-being and societal welfare. Which emphasis reflects professional social work ethics? Those citing this reason conclude that there are no fixed ethical principles which hold over time or space. Everything is relative and there is no way of indicating which choice or option is correct.

7. *Instinct and "gut" feeling.* Practitioners usually know what is right in any given practice situation without having to turn to an authoritative ethical guide prescribed by some superior body. It is far better to trust a worker's intuition than to depend on the enforcement of bureaucratic rules.

8. *Coercion.* The adoption of a code of professional ethics will result in latent, if not overt, coercion on practitioners to act only in accordance with that document. Such coercion contradicts the basic social work and societal value of self-determination. A code also tends to stifle professional creativity because it places every social worker in the same mold and expects the same routine standard behavior from every practitioner. Personal ethics and regard for client welfare are far more important for ethical behavior than any fear of sanctions imposed by a professional organization.

9. *Wastage.* There are so few valid complaints about unethical behavior that a code of ethics and an enforcement machinery really are wasted efforts. The number of complaints concerning ethics violations increased during the 1980s, peaking during the latter years of the decade. An NASW study indicates that in a ten-year period between 1982 and 1992, on the average, only thirty-three ethics violations occurred each year for the entire country (NASW, 1995).

These arguments against a code of professional ethics are not entirely persuasive. Some are fallacious, others distort reality. Here a brief response to some of the arguments must suffice. The philosophical and clinical bases for these arguments will be dealt with in greater detail in the next chapter.

Anyone who practices social work knows that social workers seldom take time for drawn-out theoretical debates. Large caseloads and constant client demands for service do not leave time for calm contemplation and leisurely thinking. But ethical decisions need not take a long time. Social workers need help in making correct choices, precisely because they have so little time.

Every social worker knows that each case is unique and different; yet there are commonalties. Ethical codes address these common elements. Principles and rules in a code of ethics are stated on a generalized level in order to permit adjustment to the unique features of each situation.

The voluntary acceptance of professional discipline, including a code of ethics, can hardly be viewed as a violation of the self-determination principle. A person becomes a professional social worker as a result of a voluntary decision. In Kohlberg's theory of moral development, this occupational choice could be identified as Level 5 moral behavior, which is a very high level of moral development, characteristic of "postconventional morality" (1976).

Even though a code of professional ethics does not supply all of the answers that contemporary social workers need, there is a real demand for such a code. In time, improvements will make such a code even more useful. But no code will ever provide "all" the answers—that is not and should not be a code's function.

## CODES OF PROFESSIONAL ETHICS

Every occupation which strives to achieve professional status attempts to develop a code of professional ethics. Such a code usually contains a compilation of the ethical principles relevant to the practice of that profession, principles to which the members of that profession are expected to adhere. Many codes of professional ethics also describe the sanctions that will be invoked against those who are unable or unwilling to meet these expectations.

The code of almost every contemporary profession has been written with the following functions in mind:

1. Provide practitioners with guidance when faced by practice dilemmas that include ethical issues.
2. Protect the public from charlatans and incompetent practitioners.
3. Protect the profession from governmental control; self-regulation is preferable to state regulation.
4. Enable professional colleagues to live in harmony with each other by preventing the self-destruction that results from internal bickering.
5. Protect professionals from litigation; practitioners who follow the code are offered some protection if sued for malpractice.

Since a code of professional ethics tries to provide guidance for every conceivable situation, it is written in terms of general principles, not specific rules. Yet when we compare codes written two or three decades ago with those written in more recent years, we note that the contemporary ones tend to be more specific and try to cover a greater variety of specific situations. Thus, the NASW *Code of Ethics* of 1967 had many fewer paragraphs and was written in much more general terms than the one adopted in 1979 and reconfirmed in 1984 and 1993. On the other hand, the American Medical Association's code of ethics, adopted in 1980, is much briefer than its previous code. One reason for the lack of detail in this new code was the desire to prevent lengthy litigation that resulted from the detailed provisions of the previous code (*New York Times*, July 23, 1980).

One of the possible consequences of greater specificity is the possibility of internal inconsistencies between various paragraphs of the same code. The NASW task force which prepared the *Code of Ethics* was aware that ethical principles often conflict with one another, even though each may be valid. By avoiding any formulation of ethical principles in a hierarchical order, the task force provided the ingredients for many of the ethical dilemmas which we will examine in the following chapter (Cohen, 1980a). Yet it should be remembered that codes of ethics "are not intended as a blueprint that would remove all need for the use of judgment or ethical reasoning" (Conte et al., 1989, p. 5). Marcuse (1976), on the other hand, suggested that codes of professional ethics fail to provide answers to many ethical dilemmas because their orientation is more likely to be system-maintenance than system-challenging.

Codes of ethics generally provide guidance only for good/bad decisions. They are far less effective in helping practitioners make decisions of the good/good and bad/bad variety. But it is precisely these types of decisions that trouble many social workers. Good/bad decisions are those where one of the two options under consideration is thought to be correct or right, while the alternative is assumed to be incorrect or wrong. In most instances, social workers have no trouble making ethical decisions of the good/bad variety. Common sense and sound ethical judgment are usually sufficient to guide the practitioner's choice. Good/good decisions, on the other hand, are those where all of the options are beneficial, while bad/bad decisions are those for which all options result in undesirable consequences (Keith-Lucas, 1977). In many of these latter situations social workers need help to sort out the ethical aspects in order to make a correct decision.

The following exemplar illustrates a practice situation that includes an ethical dilemma that is not of the good/bad variety.

➤ **2.2 John Miller's Return to State Hospital**

John Miller is mentally ill and has been so diagnosed by several psychiatrists. For the past three years this twenty-one-year-old young adult has been living at home with his elderly parents. He can take care of his own minimal needs, but he has no interest whatsoever in any personal contact. Most of every day he sits in the living room, either staring into empty space or at TV. His parents dare not leave him home alone. They have approached you, John's social worker, requesting that you make arrangements to have him returned to the state hospital since they feel that they can no longer give him the care he needs. You appreciate their situation, but you also know that returning John to a state hospital may harm him.

You know that it is unethical to deprive anyone, even a mentally ill person, of his freedom except under certain clearly specified circumstances. What are the circumstances which would warrant a social worker to consider involuntary hospitalization? Is the parents' request sufficient? How would this social worker's dilemma differ if the psychiatric diagnosis indicated that sooner or later John would inflict serious harm on others or to himself, even though he has been entirely harmless until now?

## A BRIEF HISTORY OF CODES OF PROFESSIONAL ETHICS

All modern professions have developed codes of professional ethics. These became common only in the past century, but their long and checkered history goes back to antiquity. More than two thousand years ago,

Hippocrates (c. 460–c. 377 B.C.) demanded that all Greek physicians pledge themselves to a high level of professional and ethical conduct. There is no record of similar codes for theologians and lawyers, the only other professions in the ancient world. But the Hippocratic oath became a guide, informing medical doctors in many parts of the ancient and medieval world of the correct way of professional behavior.

Just as medicine was the first profession in the ancient world to develop a code of ethics, so did it lead the way in modern times. Dr. Thomas Percival of England is credited with writing the first of the modern professional codes of ethics in 1803. The first American code was promulgated by the American Medical Association in 1847 and was modeled on Percival's code. Pharmacists followed a few years later with their own code. Contemporary accounts suggest that pharmacists wrote this code because they wanted the public to know that their professional conduct differed from that of physicians, who in those days did not enjoy a very high repute.

For most American occupational groups the development of a code of ethics coincided, more or less, with the decision to formalize the transformation of the occupation into a profession. Social workers, for example, were aware that a code of ethics was one of the prerequisites for professional recognition long before the appearance of Greenwood's important article on the attributes of a profession (1957). They tried to draft codes of professional ethics soon after Flexner (1915) told them that social work was not yet a profession. An experimental draft code of ethics for social case workers, printed in 1920, has been attributed to Mary Richmond (Pumphrey, 1959, p. 11).

The prestigious *Annals of the American Society for Political and Social Sciences* devoted its entire May 1922 issue to ethical codes in the professions and in business. Contemporary observers viewed the appearance of this journal issue as crucial to the emerging interest in such codes. In the *Annals* article on social work ethics, Mary Van Kleeck and Graham R. Taylor, two veteran social workers, wrote that social work did not have a written code of professional ethics, but that social work practice was ethical because practitioners were guided by the ideal of service and not by any thought of financial gain. Several local and national groups developed draft codes during the twenties. The American Association for Organizing Family Social Work prepared, but did not adopt, a detailed draft code in 1923. Many of the thirty-eight paragraphs of that draft still sound relevant today.

The American Association of Social Workers (AASW), the largest organization of professional social workers of that day, endorsed the need for a code of professional ethics. An editorial in the April 1924 issue of *The Compass*, the official journal of the AASW, came out in favor of a code of professional ethics and asked, "Hasn't the public a right to know how the ordinary social worker is likely to act under ordinary circumstances?" The Research Committee of the AASW tried to identify common problems of ethical practice. The AASW Executive Committee appointed a National Committee on Professional Ethics even before this study was completed. This action spurred many local chapters to discuss the need for a code. Several chapters tried to produce draft documents. The Toledo (Ohio) chapter reportedly was the first local AASW chapter to publicize a draft code. Though that draft was limited to a few general ethical principles, it inspired other chapters to try their hand at preparing their own draft code of professional ethics. However, despite much interest the adoption of a nationwide professional code had to await further organizational developments. It was only in 1951 that the AASW Delegate Assembly adopted a code of ethics.

When the historic merger of all professional social work organizations took place in the mid-1950s, work on drafting a new code of professional ethics was started almost immediately, but the NASW Delegate Assembly adopted a code of ethics only in 1960. Seven years later this code was amended to include a nondiscrimination paragraph. The absence of such a provision from earlier codes tells much about the change in the moral climate of the country and of the profession.

Before long many social workers called for a complete revision of the code in order to produce a document that would provide clearer guidance for practitioners and that would be more in tune with the realities of contemporary practice. A completely new code was adopted by the 1979 NASW Delegate Assembly. But soon it became evident that this code did not yet provide sufficient guidance for social work practitioners who sought help when facing difficult ethical issues. In an early discussion of the draft code, one prominent social worker noted that its usefulness was limited because of "its high level of abstraction and lack of practice utility" (McCann, 1977, p. 18).

The revised NASW *Code of Ethics* placed a much greater emphasis on the welfare of individuals than did the earlier 1967 document. This change is problematic because it tends to shift the focus away from the common welfare. One analysis of different codes of professional ethics found that all other helping professions (with the exception of medicine) placed a greater emphasis on the common welfare than did social work (Howe, 1980). Social workers affiliated with the National Association of Black Social Workers have prepared a code of ethics that gives expression to their belief that individual welfare can be served best by promoting the common welfare of all African-American people. Social workers in clinical practice have adopted a code of ethics that reflects their specific concerns. The Code of Ethics of Canadian social workers preflects some of the special concerns of Canadian society.

A Feminist Code of Ethics for feminist therapy is based upon feminist philosophy, psychological theory and practice, as well as political theory. In 1993 the NASW *Code of Ethics* was revised partially when new standards were approved related to practitioner impairment and dual/multiple relationships. A more comprehensive revision is planned for 1996. All of the professional codes mentioned above can be found in Appendix B.

## EXERCISES

1. Ethical principles and rules are derived from societal values. Identify the relevant social work ethical rules for the following societal values:

    cultural diversity
    equality
    freedom
    integrity
    knowledge building
    privacy
    social justice

    Note the differences in the ethical rules offered in the different Codes of Ethics that appear in Appendix B.

2. Discuss in small groups whether it is possible and desirable for a social worker to remain neutral and keep her own values from influencing clients.

3. As a social worker if you had to choose between a child's right to confidentiality and a parent's right to know things which affect the child, how would you go about making this decision?

4. Study the Feminist therapy Code of Ethics in Appendix B. When you compare that code or guidelines with the NASW *Code*, can you identify themes which are not emphasized in the NASW *Code* but are found in the Feminist Code? Are there any standards which conflict?

5. Discuss in small groups whether it is preferable that social workers work only with clients whose values are similar to their own.

## SUGGESTIONS FOR ADDITIONAL READINGS

An excellent introduction to the place of moral philosophy in social work practice can be found in Siporin (1982), Goldstein (1987), and Imre (1989). Conrad (1988), Walden, Wolock, and Demone (1990), Kugelman (1992), and Proctor, Morrow-Howell, and Lott (1993) report on research on the ethical aspects of social work practice in various settings. Besharov and Besharov (1987) include a discussion of steps a social worker should take to prevent the possibility of litigation. Gothard (1989) discusses what a social worker needs to know when she is called to be an expert witness in a court. Lytle-Vieira (1987) reviews a social worker's role in a child custody litigation. Barker (1988b) raises a question that faces social workers who are members of several professional associations: Which code of ethics should they follow?

# 3. Guidelines for Ethical Decision Making

Social workers must make ethical choices every day. A client tells her social worker that she is planning to commit suicide. A group member who has been unemployed for the past nine months asks his social worker not to tell a prospective employer about his criminal past so that he can get the job which he needs so desperately. Another client has been telling his worker that he has been embezzling funds from his employer in order to pay for his son's open-heart surgery. A young man threatens to harm a fellow worker who he believes has raped his fiancée. Each of these situations confronts the social worker with one or more ethical dilemmas because they involve conflicting obligations. What are a social worker's obligations toward her clients? Toward others who may be harmed or benefited by what the client did or will do? Toward society? Toward her own values?

A better understanding of the philosophical and practical components of ethical decision making is desirable in order to encourage ethical behavior among social work practitioners. An analysis of a practice situation, the case of Debbie Roberts, will illustrate this approach.

➤ **3.1 Debbie Roberts Is Pregnant**

Debbie Roberts, a twelve-year-old sixth grader, is ten weeks pregnant. She has been a good student. Her teacher reported that she never had any trouble with her. Debbie was not known by the school social worker. She was referred to the social worker only because she refused to talk to the school nurse about her condition.

At first Debbie also refused to speak to the social worker, but later she told her that she did not want to have an abortion. She asked the social worker to make arrangements so that she could carry to full term. She emphasized repeatedly that she did not want her parents to know that she was pregnant.

The facts seem fairly clear, as are several of the ethical dilemmas which face this worker. There are many questions that arise out of the social worker's professional knowledge and experience; among these are the following:

1. Debbie's request is not realistic. A twelve-year-old pregnant girl cannot carry to full term without her parents knowing about her pregnancy. Good professional practice would suggest that the worker help Debbie understand this and help her discuss her situation with her parents. But there may not be sufficient time to follow this strategy since time is of the essence if there is to be an abortion. Under these circumstances, is the social worker ethically justified to talk with Debbie's parents even if Debbie does not agree to this and even if she specifically requested that the worker not do so?

2. Childbirth may cause emotional and physical damage to a twelve-year-old girl, as well as place serious barriers to her achieving social, educational, and life goals. Given these negative consequences, is the social worker ethically justified to ignore Debbie's wishes and make plans for her abortion?

3. Is a twelve-year-old girl competent to decide whether to have a child? Is she competent to decide whether to have an abortion? What ethical implications do the answers to these questions have for this social worker?

4. Can or should this worker impose a decision? Would the worker be ethically justified in persuading Debbie to have an abortion?

Ethical decision making does not involve the automatic application of arbitrary rules. MacIver wrote that "ethics cannot be summed up in a series of inviolate rules or commandments which can be applied everywhere and always without regard to circumstances, thought of consequences, or comprehension of the ends to be attained" (1922, p. 7). If the situation were otherwise, social workers would find it easier to deal with the ethical problems they encounter. Generally social workers do not face a simple choice between one good option and one bad option. Instead, there are a number of choices, each one of which contains both positive and negative features, as in the above exemplar.

In such a situation, the skilled worker must assess and weigh all options and outcomes and then select the one that appears to be the most ethical. But how does a social worker know which option is "the most ethical"?

## FOUNDATIONS FOR ETHICAL DECISION MAKING

Decisions about ethical questions are rarely idiosyncratic. Since such decisions involve questions of right and wrong, they are deeply rooted in that value system which is most important to the decision maker. Though philosophy has had a major impact on the development of ethics, there have also been other influences. Frankena (1980) made reference to traditional, political, religious, racial, and gender influences on the development of contemporary ethics.

Aristotle and other Greek philosophers sought to discover the most *rational* way to live. Consequently they did not pay much attention to *moral* choices, nor were they greatly concerned with interpersonal relations. Many contemporary philosophers, on the other hand, emphasize moral choices in their search for the best way to live together with fellow humans. While Greek ethics were guided by a sense of egoism, altruism has become the moral principle that guides many modern ethicists.

Contemporary philosophers have identified two major theories that encompass most approaches to ethical decision making. We will call these two theories (*a*) ethical relativism and (*b*) ethical absolutism. These two theories have also been known by a variety of other names and have been subdivided into many subtheories.

### Ethical Relativism

Ethical relativists reject fixed moral rules. They justify ethical decisions on the basis of the context in which they are made or on the basis of the consequences which they create. An option is chosen because it will lead to desired results, or it is rejected because it will lead to results that are not wanted. The amount of good that is produced or the balance of good over evil—not any absolute standard—serves as the major criterion for reaching an ethical decision.

Among ethical relativists there are differences with respect to identifying the target or the intended beneficiary of the planned decision. Ethical egoists believe that one should always maximize what is good for oneself, no matter what the consequences for others. Ethical utilitarians, on the other hand, argue that the most important thing is to seek the greatest good for the largest number of persons. Philosophers who base their ethical reasoning on the consequences of the activity are known as *teleologists*. Ethical relativism was already known in ancient Greece, where among its followers were the Sophists and Herodotus. In more recent times John Stuart Mill, Jeremy Bentham, and Sigmund Freud were among those who followed this approach. For them and for other teleologists, ethical decisions are made on the basis of maximizing pleasure and avoiding pain.

Ethical relativists say that the only thing that matters is the result. But is this position always defensible? Is there really no difference between an armed robber who kills a bystander during a bank holdup, a soldier who kills an enemy in combat, and a social worker who, by following the provisions of the welfare code, contributes to the death of a child by not removing him from his abusive parents? Different motivations and differing activities seem to lead to the "same" results, but are they really the same? Some are even more critical of ethical relativism, suggesting that it is essentially asocial and perhaps even amoral because it assumes that individual satisfaction is *the* primary value.

## Ethical Absolutism

Ethical absolutists, on the other hand, stress the overriding importance of fixed moral rules. They hold that an action is inherently right or wrong, apart from any consequences that might result from it. "The morality of an action is inherent in action itself," according to MacMurray, "and does not supervene in cases where a particular action has consequences which impinge in a critical fashion on the lives of other people" (1961, p. 116). Ethical absolutists maintain that ethical rules can be formulated and that these should hold under all circumstances. For example, they will argue that the rule, "A social worker shall tell the truth to her client," is always correct and applies in every situation, no matter how much damage may be caused by telling the truth in any particular situation. Philosophers who follow this theory are known as *deontologists*.

Immanuel Kant (1724–1804) was the first of modern philosophers to adopt deontological concepts. He insisted that categorical imperatives are morally necessary and obligatory under *all* circumstances. Ethical systems in which humans determine moral rules are known as *autonomous ethics*. Ethical systems which derive moral rules from nonhuman sources are known as *heteronomous ethics*. When religious philosophers teach that moral rules are of divine origin, they exemplify a heteronomous ethical system. Kant's philosophy, on the other hand, is an example of an autonomous ethical system.

Ethical absolutism and ethical relativism represent two approaches to ethics. Each has its followers. Some contemporary moral philosophers, such as Henry Sidgwick and William Frankena, have tried to synthesize ethical absolutism and ethical relativism.

Teleologists may argue for situational ethics, but there are times when they also will follow fixed rules. Jeremy Bentham (1748–1832), one of the earliest exponents of English utilitarianism, accepted "the greatest good for the greatest number" as a binding principle that applies in every situation. Some present-day philosophers who are committed to situation ethics argue that "love" is the principle which should guide all human behavior (Fletcher, 1966). On the other hand, many ethical absolutists, even those who teach a heteronomous ethics, allow for situations where the fixed rules do not apply. Many theologians have accepted the argument, first proposed by the Dutch jurist, Hugo Grotius (1583–1645), that one must always tell the truth and never lie, but that it is permissible to speak falsely to thieves because no one owes them the truth. However, there is an important difference between not applying a rule in an exceptional situation and deciding each situation as if there were no rules (Diggs, 1970).

Practitioners may not be aware of these efforts by professional philosophers. Neither do they always know which of the two ethical theories they follow in making ethical decisions. As a matter of fact, the differences between the major theories frequently are not as clear in practice as they are on the printed page. The two theoretical approaches often seem to merge in practice, but it does make a difference in ethical decision making whether a social worker follows one or the other theory, as the following analysis will illustrate.

### Different Approaches of Two Social Workers

We will examine how two social workers—Ruth, an ethical relativist, and Anne, an ethical absolutist—might approach the ethical aspects of Debbie's problem (Exemplar 3.1). Our focus will be on learning how these differences might lead to different worker activities. Debbie requested that the worker not inform her parents about her pregnancy. Social worker Anne believes that every person has an absolute right to make decisions about himself or herself, even if the consequences of these decisions might harm that person. She also believes that confidentiality is a first-order professional value which social workers must follow at all times. Anne therefore has no hesitation about respecting Debbie's request that her parents not be informed about her pregnancy. She might also argue that, from a practical point of view, it is important to honor Debbie's request because violating the confidential relationship will destroy the trust that a client must have in her worker. But this "practical" consideration is not the crucial ethical criterion for Anne's decision. No doubt Anne would give high priority to helping Debbie see the advantage of confiding in her parents. However, as far as social worker Anne is concerned, the principles of confidentiality and client autonomy are absolute, no matter who the client or what the situation.

Social worker Ruth views the ethical aspects of Debbie's problems in another light. Being an ethical relativist, she assesses the consequences of respecting Debbie's request for confidentiality against the consequences of delaying the involvement of her parents. She concludes that any delay might have very serious immediate and long-term consequences for Debbie's physical and emotional health. Therefore, she tells Debbie that either Debbie herself or the worker must without delay inform her parents of the pregnancy. If Debbie is unwilling or unable to do so, social worker Ruth will tell Debbie's parents, waving aside any considerations of client autonomy and confidentiality in order to prevent any harmful consequences.

Another ethical aspect of this problem situation involves the question of terminating Debbie's pregnancy. Social worker Ruth, after assessing the consequences of various options, decides to persuade Debbie to have an abortion since it has been established that childbirth for a twelve-year-old girl often results in serious medical problems. Social worker Anne, on the other hand, will approach this issue from a different vantage point. Unless there is an immediate and direct danger to Debbie's life, the statistical risk of possible medical complications will be less crucial a consideration than determining the ethical and moral rules that apply in this situation.

Not all deontologists follow identical ethical rules with respect to any given problem. Identification of the relevant rules is therefore of the greatest importance. For example, some ethical systems consider abortion to be the same as murder and prohibit it altogether, no matter what the circumstances; others take a more moderate position and permit abortions under specified conditions, such as danger to the mother's life. Still other ethical systems are mute on this issue, leaving any decision to the individual involved. But social worker Anne may face yet another ethical dilemma after she has identified the relevant moral rules. This dilemma arises out of a conflict between two categorical imperatives—the professional rule that calls for client self-determination and her own values that may prohibit abortion. Here is a situation where the social worker cannot honor both categorical imperatives, but must make a choice about which one to follow. How to make this choice will be discussed later in this chapter.

The above discussion illustrates some of the differences that arise when a social worker follows one or the other ethical approach. These are not the only differences. You are urged to attempt to identify others.

## CONTEMPORARY APPROACHES TO ETHICAL DECISION MAKING

Philosophers have identified ethical absolutism and ethical relativism as two major ethical theories. We discussed their implications for practice in the previous section. Yet these theories are usually presented at so generalized or abstract a level that practitioners do not always find them helpful when coping with the ethical issues they face in their professional practice. In the past, *conscience* was considered the key to ethical decision making; contemporary readers may want to substitute *guilt feelings* for the older concept.

But conscience or guilt feelings are too idiosyncratic to serve professionals as guides for ethical decision making. One person's conscience will not be the same as another's. Professional ethics are common to the entire professional group and should therefore be relevant to every individual member of that profession. What a social worker needs are tools of analysis that will permit a more systematic and a more rational consideration of the ethical aspects of social work intervention. Such models will of course include knowledge elements, but ethical decision making cannot be based on knowledge alone since ethics deal principally with what *ought to be* and not with what *is*. Before presenting our ethical decision-making models, we will discuss various approaches that some social workers have found useful in arriving at ethical decisions.

### Clinical Pragmatism

Many social workers indicate that they are neither philosophers nor specialists in solving ethical problems. Instead, they believe that their primary responsibility is to deliver a high level of professional service. Perhaps they agree with Jim Casey who, in John Steinbeck's *Grapes of Wrath*, said, "There ain't no sin and there ain't no virtue, there is just stuff people do." They are sure that they will not become entangled in ethical problems if they concentrate their efforts on improving practice. In addition they suggest that the type of service provided, the nature of the problems dealt with, and the modes of intervention used are determined in the first instance by society, so that a worker's personal ethical stance is far less important than societal ethics. Social workers who follow this approach focus on implementing the values of the society which sanctions their activities. For example, one of the functions of social workers in contemporary American society is to help individuals and groups who face various kinds of emotional disturbances and crises. These social workers use societal values as the only criterion to identify the types of behavior that require professional intervention. Any value conflicts that may arise in the practice context will be resolved by reference to the value priorities of the dominant social group.

While this approach seems simple, straightforward, and even supportive of scientific practice, it has a conservative tinge. Radical writers, such as Thomas Szasz and Ivan Illich, have criticized this approach as unethical because these social workers tend to act as agents of social control on behalf of dominating and exploiting societal institutions. Social workers who follow this approach rarely question society's ethics or its norms (as they understand them). Their practice supports the status quo. They rarely encourage the autonomous development of alternate life-styles nor will they be found among those who challenge society's values in other ways.

Instead, social workers have the responsibility and ethical imperative to "not practice, condone, facilitate or collaborate with any form of discrimination on the basis of race, color, sex, sexual orientation, age, religion, national origin, marital status, political belief, mental or physical handicap, or any other preference or personal characteristic, condition or status" (II, F, 3). The question for social workers is what can they do to enact this ethical imperative.

### Self-Realization

Many practitioners have found the humanistic ethical approach attractive because it combines a strong idealism with wide opportunities for individual choices. An idealistic view of human nature as essentially positive, together with an optimistic stance toward the future, provides the basis for this approach. The focus is on causal rather than on moralistic explanations of human behavior. It stresses the capacity, opportunity, and responsibility of every person to make choices that make sense to him or her. The individual client, rather than any institution or ideology, occupies the center of attention. Such an approach appears to be particularly suited to contemporary America with its emphasis on individualism and pluralism.

Self-realization has been at the center of the humanistic theories of Abraham Maslow, Erich Fromm, and other existentialists. Humanity is innately good and has the ability to behave ethically. The inner core of the human personality is intrinsically ethical. Individual freedom and responsibility form the basis of social life. Self-expression and self-actualization are postulated as the desired outcome of mature development. Personal identity is defined by each individual according to self-chosen values. These are hopefully derived from rational principles. The priority of professional intervention at the individual level will be to help people achieve self-actualization, rather than helping them to learn how to adjust to the existing social order. On the societal level, social workers following this approach will intervene to change those social institutions which inhibit the growth and self-realization of individuals.

Practitioners following this approach can be found in the forefront of many causes which promote freedom and equality. Some oppose stable social authority structures (Rogers, 1977); others emphasize hedonistic rather than traditional values (Schutz, 1967). All followers of this approach feel that they have minimized the ethical dilemmas they face. By clearly identifying value priorities, they feel that they can cope with the ethical aspects of most practice problems. More important, by emphasizing individual responsibility, the major burden for ethical decision making is shifted from the practitioner to the client.

## Situational Ethics

There is a tendency in contemporary life to deal with ethical dilemmas on a case-by-case basis. Many prefer to use "fragmentary moral rules as a substitute for universal rules" (Carlton, 1978, p. 2). The secularization of modern life has encouraged the abandonment of absolute rules and universal criteria. Instead there has emerged a plurality of ethical rules with no one able or willing to say that any one rule is correct or applicable in every situation.

Situation ethics has had many forerunners. The Danish philosopher Søren Kierkegaard (1813–1855) insisted that truth is subjective, while the French philosopher Jean Paul Sartre (1905–1980) taught that ethical decisions can be made only in the light of the prevailing situation since each case is unique and unlike every other case. Different and changing situations call for different ethical criteria and different ethical decisions. As one contemporary philosopher writes, "The good differs from culture to culture, and there is no objective way…of verifying one [culture's good] as better than another" (Shirk, 1965, p. 58). Environment, circumstance, and context shape human behavior as well as the criteria for ethical conduct. What might be considered correct or proper in one sphere will be incorrect in another. A social worker may be ethically justified to intervene in one situation, even while a similar intervention in another situation might be ethically questionable. The activity itself is neither ethical nor unethical. It is the situation in which it occurs that defines its ethical dimension.

The critical importance of the context was experimentally demonstrated in what is known as the *simulated prison experiment*. College students who volunteered to participate in this experiment were randomly assigned roles of prisoners or guards. Those who became "guards" had little notion that within less than twenty-four hours they would behave in a very authoritarian and very punitive manner. Prior to the experiment, all of these students had utilized very different ethical criteria, but the experimental context invited ethical considerations that the participants believed to be appropriate to the prison setting. In the words of the senior experimenter, "evil acts are not necessarily the deeds of evil men, but may be attributable to the operation of powerful social sources" (Haney et al., 1973, p. 90).

Social workers who follow the situation approach do not have any fixed rules to help them make decisions about the ethical aspects of practice problems. Because of this, they need support systems and guides for making such decisions.

## Religious Ethics

Religious ethics presuppose a belief in the existence of God. While secularist philosophers teach that men and women are the creators of their own values, religious philosophers maintain that humans can only try to discover divine values, not create them. Modern scientific man has denied the existence of absolute truth and absolute ethical rules, but those who follow religious ethics declare that there are eternal rules which should govern behavior at all times. Believers are convinced that religious faith and ethical morality are indivisible. They cannot conceive of the long-term effectiveness of ethical principles that come from a source other than the divine will. The ethical aspects of interpersonal relations can exist only if one accepts the authority of God. They frequently cite Ivan in Dostoyevsky's *The Brothers Karamazov* who said, "If there is no God, everything is permissible."

Jacques Maritain, a contemporary Christian philosopher, argued that in secular ethics man himself becomes the ultimate goal. Far from deifying the person, placing him or her in the center really is degrading because "the greatness of man consists in the fact that his sole end is the uncreated God" (1934, p. 269). For believers the search for meaning is meaningful, while for nonbelievers everything is futility.

One of the consequences of accepting the religious approach is that ethics and law merge into one comprehensive, interrelated system. Since ethical principles are usually stated on a very generalized and abstract level, the authorized interpreters of religious law deduce specific applications to daily problems. These deductions become precedence or law. When this occurs, law is no longer "divorced from ethics but serves as a means to implement ethical principles in the every-day life of society" (Kurzweil, 1980, p. 71). To the extent that such a conclusion is warranted, this approach provides those who follow it with a powerful tool that helps them cope with many of the ethical issues encountered in social work practice.

New Ethical Critiques and Approaches

Several additional approaches to ethical decision making have been mentioned in the recent literature. It is not clear at this time whether and in what ways these new perspectives will impact upon traditional ethical decision-making patterns. Gould (1992) discussed three relatively new critiques of traditional decision-making frameworks; these are *feminism*, *communitarianism*, and "*new*" *democratic theory.* Gould suggests that ethical relativism sacrifices individual rights to the general welfare. According to her, ethical absolutism is too formal or stringent and disregards contextual and social considerations.

The following aspects of feminist theory have importance for professional ethics:

1. The critique of domination and the concomitant articulation of the value of reciprocity;
2. The recognition of the distinctive individuality of the other;
3. The perspective of care;
4. Partiality and the rejection of abstract universality; and
5. Practical concern for the equal valuation and treatment of women's work.

Given these guidelines, the relationship between client and professional and among professionals becomes mutually consultative with each taking the other's judgments respectfully into account in codetermining the course of professional action. The professional is not just the agent of the client's will nor is the client a passive ward of the professional.

The communitarian perspective views norms as historically and socially constructed expressions which change over time. Their justification is grounded in the community's own reflection and self-understanding. There is, therefore, no ethical appeal beyond the community, though improvements and deepening of norms over time are possible. From this point of view, professional practice is a social construction, and professional norms are grounded in the self-understanding of the practitioners themselves and not in any external or suprahistorical source. Since professions are embedded in the larger society, the ultimate justification of a profession lies in its contribution to the welfare of the community in which it functions. Questions can be raised about the boundaries of the community. But, Gould suggests, communitarianism contributes a social critique which acknowledges the historical and constituted nature of the ethical norms of the profession; this means they can be changed in response to critical reflection and discussion within the profession itself. This occurs, for example, when new ethical standards are included in the NASW *Code;* this process became particularly evident when a governmental decree stimulated a change in ethical standards with regard to professional advertisements.

The third critique of traditional ethical decision making, Gould suggests, comes from what she calls new democratic theory, which emphasizes the equal right to participation in decision making by all parties involved in a common activity. Especially where a profession delivers its services in group or institutional contexts, there should be—according to new democratic theory—intraprofessional democracy among the professionals working together, a degree of joint participation in decision making (worker self-management and participative decision making). This theory, further, holds that all potential clients should have equal access to the resources necessary for their self-development or well-being, including the right of access to the services of professionals needed for meeting their basic needs. (Gould, 1992)

These new approaches challenge the traditional ethical decision-making frameworks. They present new ways of thinking about ethical decision-making patterns in professional social work practice. Just as clinical pragmatism, situational and religious ethics, among other approaches, have had their particular impact on social work ethical decision making, so these three contemporary approaches may also contribute to contemporary ethical decision making.

## PERSONAL VALUES, SOCIETAL VALUES, AND PROFESSIONAL VALUES

Values, as noted earlier, are a key element in the ethical decision-making process. No wonder that Levy (1976b) called ethics "values in action." Before clarifying the relationship between values and ethics it may be helpful to differentiate between *individual* or *personal values* (values held by one person but not necessarily by others), *societal values* (values that are recognized by an entire social system or, at least, by the leading members or spokespersons of that system), and *professional values* (values proclaimed by a professional group, such as social workers). Generally, these three value sets are complementary or reciprocal, although at times they may be in conflict. Most of the time and in most places discord between the different value sets is infrequent, though differences in interpretation, priority, and intensity are not uncommon.

### Clarifying Personal Values

Shakespeare gave sound advice when he wrote: "This above all, to thine own self be true....Thou canst not then be false to any man" (*Hamlet*, act I, scene 3, lines 78–80). This same advice may also help social workers when they consider the ethical aspects of decision making. No matter what approach social workers use in ethical decision making, it is essential that they clarify and make explicit their own personal values. Personal values are not abstract principles, but on the operational level serve to integrate and organize a person's resources and behaviors, as well as relations with others.

Frankena (1980) indicated that a person's cultural experiences and background implicitly direct the ethical decision-making process of that person. But unless these become explicit, there is danger that biases and stereotypes will impede the application of desirable professional behaviors. For example, Dunkel and Hatfield (1986) have shown how hidden and unconscious personal values and biases interfere with helping clients who are HIV-positive. Similar observations have been made when analyzing social work intervention with such client groups as cancer patients, gay persons, unmarried mothers, etc.

The difficulty that many social workers have when it comes to making ethical decisions has been noted by Siporin (1985a). He suggests that today's libertarian and relativist moral climate has made it increasingly difficult for many persons to be clear about their own values. Even when personal values have been identified, making ethical choices on the basis of these values is difficult, as Coughlin noted when he said that "in a society that is philosophically, culturally, politically, and religiously pluralistic, making value choices is no way to win friends" (1966, p. 97).

Those who agree with Siporin that "there is a moral and ethical imperative that social workers act as moral agents" (1985a, p. 20) know the importance of holding clear, unambiguous, and specific personal values. Only such values are effective in influencing and guiding behavior. In no other way can a social worker be true "to thine own self" and not act as a "hired gun" for a client, an agency, the state, or even for a "Moral Majority." It just will not do to speak in generalities. Instead, a social worker must carefully scrutinize and define her values. For example, today all reasonable persons value equality and abhor discrimination and exploitation on the basis of race, sex, or age. But how committed are you to the equality value? Does it extend to persons with different sexual orientations? To persons who prefer "unconventional" life-styles? To persons whose personal values are completely contrary to those that you hold?

It is not enough for a social worker to say that she favors (or opposes) abortions. She must be able to define her values about abortion clearly. Until when does she believe a woman has a right to have an abortion? Does she hold that abortions are permissible as late as the second trimester? If so, she needs to consider the ethical problems that may arise when a defective, but viable, baby is born prematurely at the beginning of the sixth month. Does it make an ethical difference whether such a defective body is inside or outside of the womb? These questions are raised here to emphasize that social workers must first clarify their own value stance if they want to be true to themselves and to their profession.

Some social workers question or denigrate the importance of personal values for professional practice. They suggest that a social worker must suspend or neutralize all personal values when serving clients. Charles Levy, who chaired the NASW committee that drafted most of the current *Code of Ethics*, said, "To be a professional practitioner is to give up some of one's autonomy and to relinquish some of one's right as a freely functioning being" (1976a, p. 113). However, the conflict between personal and professional values is rarely as unambiguous as Levy suggests. And the desirability, as well as the possibility, of suppressing personal values is much more problematic than Levy indicates.

Still others suggest that personal values have relatively little influence on ethical behaviors. They claim that social workers know instinctively or intuitively what is the right thing to do. Admittedly, feelings and instincts are important and do influence behavioral choices. However, having a strong feeling for something does not necessarily make for an ethical choice. A worker may feel that she wants to have sex with a client, but this instinctive feeling, strong as it may be, does not make this behavior ethical.

## Clarifying Societal Values

Societal values usually, but not always, provide guidelines for professional ethical behavior. But there may be situations when a social worker is justified, even obligated, to act in ways that are contrary to societal norms. However, in every instance the worker first has an obligation to clarify the relevant societal values. Radical changes in societal values have occurred within the lifetime of many social workers. Values that our parents or grandparents considered sacred have been swept away or have been altered so much that they are no longer recognizable. Though changes of values around life-styles and sexual mores gain headline attention, more fundamental changes have taken place with respect to inequality and equality. Not too long ago it was self-understood that all people were not equal. An unemployed person did not enjoy the same rights as a working person. Women were considered inferior to men. Whites were thought to be better than everybody else. These views were held openly, even by the "best" people in society. Public policy was designed to reflect and support these values. It does not require any lengthy discussion to point out that major changes have occurred with respect to these values. While racism, sexism, and ageism still exist in our society, these are no longer accorded the general respect and public recognition that they once enjoyed.

The equality value is not the only value that has changed dramatically in our lifetime. Similar changes can be observed with respect to many other values. To the extent that ethical behavior in general reflects what society values, a social worker must have accurate knowledge of the current societal value stance. *Knowing* does not mean that a social worker must follow these values blindly, but she must take them into consideration when assessing a problem situation and when making her decisions. The application of societal norms may become problematic when a society accepts values which previously were disvalued, especially when the adoption of the new value occurs unevenly among different groups within society. For example, today the value to choose one's life-style freely, whether it be heterosexual, bisexual, or homosexual, is accepted by many but not all Americans. Gay rights, derived from this value, are an issue that still divides Americans because the acceptance of this new value has not been uniform across American society.

## Clarifying Professional Values

The social work profession takes its basic values from those held by the larger society, but there may be differences in emphasis, interpretation, and priorities. These differences can, at times, result in ethical problems. By selecting and emphasizing certain values, while attaching lesser importance to others, social workers may place themselves at risk of engaging in unpopular behaviors and of being charged with unethical behaviors.

Social work professional ethics are based on "the fundamental values of the social work profession that include the worth, dignity, and uniqueness of all persons as well as their rights and opportunities. It [also]...fosters conditions that promote these values" (NASW, 1993, Preamble). Essentially, the social work value system reflects a democratic ethos which provides for individual and group fulfillment. It calls for respect of individuals and their differences, while at the same time recognizing the need for mutual aid and societal supports so that all persons can attain their maximum potential.

Finding the correct balance between the rights of the group or community and the rights of the individual is often not an easy matter and is a challenge not unique to social work. Such choices present serious dilemmas for which there are few guidelines. But within this balance, ethical decisions clearly follow a democratic ethos.

Social work practice always involves ethical decision making. Assumptions about morals and values are basic to social workers' theories, policies, and practice decisions. Also dilemmas arise because the values and allegiances of social workers, personally and professionally, sometimes conflict. In addition, clients introduce their own moral conflicts to which social workers must respond. The "absence" of conflict for the social worker may indicate either that the social worker is unconscious of the moral nature of the choices she faces or that the social worker is so clear about her values and societal priorities that the choice is *prima facie* correct (child abuse, suicide threats) or so routine because of habit and repeated justification that making the decision is not problematic (Fleck-Henderson, 1991).

## THE DECISION-MAKING PROCESS

Ethical decision making is far too complex to permit the development of a simple "how to" problem-solving model. Yet some model is necessary if we are to understand what decision making is all about. Making decisions is seldom a split-second act. Typically it is a process or series of thoughts and activities that occur over time and that result in a person or group acting (or not acting) in a particular manner. Every decision is approached step-by-step so that one moves gradually through a series of stages until, at the end of the process, one makes *the* decision. It is erroneous to assume that only one person, the decision maker, participates in this process. Many different persons present information, react to assessments, introduce additional options, or make changes in the environment; these in turn change the nature of the decision or the nature of the data on which the decision is based.

In real life it is almost impossible to point to any one discrete decision. Observing decision making is like watching the ocean waves approach the shoreline. Choices are always influenced by previous decisions that in turn lead to new directions. A simpler model of decision making may help social workers understand what is involved in ethical decision making. Such a model, like all models in science, will simplify reality by focusing on only one decision. A model is a permissible didactic device as long as it is understood that in real life every decision is preceded and followed by other decisions, many of which have a direct bearing on the matter under consideration. In Figure 3.1, we present one such general model for decision making.

The decision-making model presented in Figure 3.1 is a general model applicable to many different situations and is not limited to ethical decisions. This model is based on the assumption that social workers can plan rationally what is needed for intervention in human situations and that they want to minimize the irrational, the impulsive, and the unplanned

---

**Figure 3.1   A General Decision-Making Model**

Step  1   Identify the problem and the factors that contribute to its maintenance.

Step  2   Identify the persons and institutions involved in this problem, such as clients, victims, support systems, other professionals, and others.

Step  3   Identify the values relevant to this problem held by the several participants identified in step 2, including societal values, professional values, and client's and worker's personal values.

Step  4   Identify the goals and objectives whose attainment may resolve (or at least reduce) the problem.

Step  5   Identify alternate intervention strategies and targets.

Step  6   Assess the effectiveness and efficiency of each alternative in terms of the identified goals.

Step  7   Determine who should be involved in decision making.

Step  8   Select the most appropriate strategy.

Step  9   Implement the strategy selected.

Step 10   Monitor the implementation, paying particular attention to unanticipated consequences.

Step 11   Evaluate the results and identify additional problems.

---

consequences of purposeful actions. In Figure 3.2 we present an ethical assessment screen designed to help social workers further clarify and integrate the ethical aspects of decision making in social work practice.

## ETHICAL ASSESSMENT SCREEN

The social worker who is alert to the ethical aspects of practice will examine and assess the available options and alternatives somewhat differently than her colleague who is not as concerned with the ethical aspects of practice. This becomes clear when we consider various assessment criteria.

### Protection of Clients' Rights and Welfare

The definition of rights and privileges changes over time. What is thought to be a right at one time may not be so defined in another era. These changes may create ethical problems. Journalists, for example, were once expected to get the news, no matter what the obstacles. Nowadays, when there is a greater concern for the privacy rights of individuals and families, journalists often face an ethical dilemma—whether to pursue the news even if this means disregarding a person's privacy.

The changing definitions of what constitutes rights may also create ethical problems for social workers. Consider the ethical problems faced by social workers in the adoption field as the right of adopted persons to information about their biological parents is becoming recognized in more and more jurisdictions. At one time the biological parents as well as the adoptive parents were assured that such information would remain confidential and would never be shared with the adoptee. But when court decisions or legislative enactments in some states support the right of adopted persons to this information, social workers have little choice but to reveal it. However, is it ethical for them to continue to tell biological and adoptive parents in other jurisdictions that this information will always remain confidential?

### Protection of Society's Interest

Sometimes it is difficult to balance society's interests with a client's interests. If a client tells his social worker that he has committed a property crime, the social worker must weigh her obligations to the client against her obligations to society. Social control is one of the functions of every social worker, but so is the maintenance of a helping relationship. To which function should the practitioner give priority if she cannot pursue both at the same time? Would the same considerations apply if the client were a part-time prostitute in a town where prostitution was prohibited by law? Can lawbreaking be overlooked when a client makes progress toward attaining identified intervention goals? Does it matter whether or not the law violation harms another person? Keep these questions in mind as you assess the ethical dilemmas posed in the following exemplar.

➤ **3.2 Security or Protection?**

John Newton was a likable chap. Twenty-two years old, not steadily employed, but always willing to help. Even before Ray Dunkirk, the community worker, had arrived on the scene, Newton had organized a number of young adults into a club. This club was well known in the neighborhood for the many helpful services it provided. The community's elderly population was especially appreciative of the security services that this group gave them. Thefts, holdups, and even murder of older people had ceased ever since this club began to operate in the community.

But Dunkirk also became aware that Newton has intimidated local store owners and has obtained small payoffs from them in return for promising them "protection."

What was Ray Dunkirk to do? He considered various options, including the following:

1. He could overlook Newton's protection racket in view of the many positive things he was doing that were benefiting the community.
2. He could report Newton's protection racket to the police since illegal activities should never be condoned.
3. He could strengthen his relations with Newton with the view of helping to guide him away from the illegal activity; in the meantime he would not report the law violation to the police.

What are the ethical aspects in choosing the best option? One ethical dilemma is how to balance the best interest of the various publics involved: oldsters, storekeepers, the community, the larger society, and others. Another question concerns the ethics of doing something that might result in the return of violence against the older people of this community.

### The "Least Harm" Principle

Sometimes social workers are confronted by problems which permit only harmful options. Regardless of the option chosen by the client and/or the worker, some harm will come to one person or another, perhaps even to the client or to the social worker. What is the ethical thing to do in such situations? The "least harm" rule suggests to choose the option that will result in the least harm, the least permanent harm, or the most easily reversible harm.

Consider the options facing the social worker who has to respond to Roberta Jackson's question (Exemplar 1.1). Does the least harm principle offer guidance in choosing the most ethical alternative? How?

Some have suggested that the rigid application of the least harm principle may diminish the possibility of choosing the most effective intervention technique. There may be times when it is justified to utilize an option that has great risks but which enhances the likelihood of a successful outcome (Halleck, 1981). However, such a choice should be made only with the full consent and agreement of the client.

It has also been suggested that an intervention is ethical when the projected benefits exceed the projected risks (Diener & Crandall, 1978; Walden et al., 1990). But when the consequences of an intervention are the *only* consideration, ethics and values tend to be ignored. This is the modern version of the old maxim "The ends justify the means," a proverb that is hardly a helpful guide for ethical decision making. Such a guide does not specify whose cost or whose benefit are to determine the decision, nor does it tell the social worker how to predict future costs and benefits. This formulation also may ignore the rights of a client to control and make decisions about his own life.

## Efficiency and Effectiveness

The efficiency criterion is concerned with the relative cost (including budget, staff time, agency and community resources) of achieving a stated objective. Whenever two options will lead to the same result, the one that requires less budget, less staff, and less time is the more efficient one. The effectiveness criterion, on the other hand, relates to the degree to which the desired outcome is achieved. When the implementation of one option results in halving the number of poor people in a county, while the second option reduces the poverty population by 80 percent, the latter option is the more effective one.

Difficult choices arise when the more efficient option is the less effective one or vice versa. But ethical questions about an option may reduce the relevance of the efficiency and effectiveness criteria. The most efficient or the most effective option may be rejected because of its ethical implications. For example, deporting poor people to another country may be the most effective and the most efficient way of eliminating poverty—so long as no one is concerned with the ethical implications of the proposed plan. More often the ethical assessment of an option is not as clear as in this example so that a social worker may find it more difficult to make a decision. For example, What are the ethical implications of forcing poor people to work? Work is a desirable activity, highly valued in our society, but *force* means limiting a person's freedom, another important value in our society. The ethical assessment, in this case, demands that we assess *work* and *independence* against the loss of *freedom*. In the past, social work ideology rejected out of hand the various *workfare* programs which forced poor people to work. A change in social work ideology and values may be taking place. However, there are no widely accepted assessment procedures that can help a social worker weigh the ethical aspects of each workfare option.

Another kind of ethical quandary was raised some years ago in connection with the efforts to deinstitutionalize patients of mental hospitals. Some policymakers tried to implement these programs less out of concern for improving the lot of hospitalized patients than for the purpose of publicizing the need for additional community resources. In some instances, the option of releasing mentally ill patients from hospitals was adopted even though it was known that most communities lacked adequate resources for caring for these people. State governments were unable to help communities with this problem since at the same time they were facing major budget cuts. How ethical was it to institute a strategy that might result in some long-range improvements, but which in the short run might harm many fragile people? In this connection, see Figure 3.2.

**Figure 3.2   Ethical Assessment Screen**

1. Identify your own relevant personal values in relation to the ethical dilemma which faces you.
2. Identify any societal values relevant to the ethical decision to be made.
3. Identify the relevant professional values and ethics.
4. Identify alternative ethical options that you may take.
5. Which of the alternative ethical actions will protect to the greatest extent possible your client's rights and welfare as well as the rights and welfare of others?
6. Which alternative action will protect to the greatest extent possible society's rights and interests?
7. What can you do to minimize any conflicts among 1, 2, and 3? What can you do to minimize any conflicts between 5 and 6?
8. Which alternative action will result in your doing the "least harm" possible?
9. To what extent will alternative actions be efficient, effective, and ethical?
10. Have you considered and weighed both the short-term and long-term ethical consequences of alternative actions?

## RANK ORDERING ETHICAL PRINCIPLES

In the preceding pages we discussed a number of ethical criteria which some social workers have found helpful when assessing decision alternatives. These criteria have not been arranged in any order of priority. More specific guides are needed whenever two or more of these criteria point toward different alternatives.

The most common way of resolving such conflicts among ethical principles is a lexical ordering of these principles, that is, rank ordering them from the most important to the least important. This is necessary even though "ordering principles is not an easy task" (Christensen, 1986, p. 82). A lexical ordering of ethical principles can provide social workers with a guide, but it must be remembered that such a guide is not meant to be a magic formula that can be applied blindly. As Reamer notes, "Guidelines are guidelines, not airtight algorithms" (1982, p. 584).

In the past few years a number of authors (including Kitchner, 1984; Joseph, 1985; Lewis, 1984; Reamer, 1983; Siporin, 1983; and Zygmond & Boorhem, 1989) have prepared guides for ethical decision making, but not many social workers have found these useful in practice because these authors have not taken into sufficient consideration how social workers make decisions. Social workers rarely make direct use of theoretical knowledge or philosophical principles when making practice decisions. Instead, they have integrated knowledge and values into a set

---

**Figure 3.3    Ethical Rules Screen (ERS)**

1. Examine the *Code of Ethics* to determine if any of the Code rules are applicable. These rules take precedence over the worker's personal value system.
2. If one or more Code rules apply, follow these.
3. If the Code does not address itself to the specific problem, or if several Code rules provide conflicting guidance, use the Ethical Principles Screen (Figure 3.4).

---

of practice principles—and these are what social workers utilize at the critical points in the decision-making process.

We have used the work of the above authors, as well as additional sources and our own practice experience, to prepare two guides or screens that we believe will help social workers in making ethical decisions. We call these guides the *Ethical Rules Screen* (ERS) and the *Ethical Principles Screen* (EPS). (See Figures 3.3 and 3.4.)

The ERS should always be used first. Only when this screen does not provide any satisfactory guidance should the social worker use the EPS. To be useful, a guide for rank ordering ethical principles must clearly indicate the order of priority of such principles. Once such a priority list has been established, the operating rule is that the satisfaction of a higher-order principle takes precedence over the satisfaction of a lower-order principle. Even though there is not yet any general agreement on the rank order of professional ethical principles, we have developed the EPS on the basis of our perception of what might be the consensus among social workers. All ethical principles are important. When more than one ethical principle is relevant in the analysis of a set of practice options and these lead to different outcomes, the rank order suggested in the EPS should be utilized when making a decision. In other words, an assessment based on Ethical Principle 1 is more compelling than one using Ethical Principles 2 or 3. Thus, if both *confidentiality* (Principle 6) and *full-disclosure* (Principle 7) apply, the ethical principle of confidentiality should receive priority. Since the EPS is the key ethical assessment tool for resolving ethical practice dilemmas, we will comment in some detail on several of these principles.

*Ethical Principle 1.* The protection of human life applies to all persons, that is, both to the life of a client and to the lives of others. This principle takes precedence over every other obligation. "The right to life," according to Kuhse and Singer, "is the most basic of all rights, for if one's right to life is violated one cannot enjoy any other rights" (1985, p. 509).

**Figure 3.4   Ethical Principles Screen (EPS)**

ETHICAL PRINCIPLE 1   Principle of the protection of life
ETHICAL PRINCIPLE 2   Principle of equality and inequality
ETHICAL PRINCIPLE 3   Principle of autonomy and freedom
ETHICAL PRINCIPLE 4   Principle of least harm
ETHICAL PRINCIPLE 5   Principle of quality of life
ETHICAL PRINCIPLE 6   Principle of privacy and confidentiality
ETHICAL PRINCIPLE 7   Principle of truthfulness and full disclosure

Most physicians follow this principle of saving and prolonging human life, irrespective of the quality of life and the economic costs involved. The best-known application of this biophysical version of the life-sustaining principle was the case of Karen Ann Quinlan whose physicians refused to withdraw life-support systems, even though this patient had been unconscious for many years and there was no further hope for any positive change. More than ten thousand other Americans are also kept "alive" by high-tech life-sustaining instruments. Most social workers, on the other hand, tend to limit the application of this life-sustaining principle to acute situations when the question of life or death is actual and immediate. At other times they tend to place more emphasis on improving the quality of life for individuals, groups, and communities. Most of the time social workers are not aware of any conflict between the biophysical principle of sustaining life and the psychosocial principle of improving life. But Roberts (1989) discusses the case of a middle-aged man with marked hypertension. The medication which brought down his life-threatening blood pressure also caused sexual impotence. Is it ethical for a social worker to support this client's decision to stop taking the medication so that he can once again enjoy sexual relations? Such a decision may improve the quality of his life (Ethical Principle 5), but may also shorten his life (Ethical Principle 1).

*Ethical Principle 2.* The Principle of Equality and Inequality suggests that equal persons have the right to be treated equally and non-equal persons have the right to be treated differently if the inequality is relevant to the issue in question. This principle, as formulated by Kitchner (1984), is based on the seminal work of Rawls (1971). One situation where this principle applies is that of child abuse. Since the abused child is not in an "equal" position, the principles of confidentiality and autonomy with respect to the abusing adult are of a lower rank order than the obligation to protect the child even when it is not a question of life and death.

*Ethical Principle 3.* A social worker should make practice decisions that foster a person's autonomy, independence, and freedom. Freedom, though highly important, does not override the right to life or survival of the person himself or of others. A person does not have the right to decide to harm himself or herself or anyone else on the grounds that the right to make such a decision is her or his autonomous right. When a person is about to make such a decision, the social worker is obligated to intervene since Ethical Principle 1 takes precedence.

The risk/benefit ratio may also help determine when the autonomy principle applies and when it is ethical to ignore a client's "decision." If the condition facing a client is life threatening and if the risk of intervention is minimal (while the potential benefit of the intervention is great), the social worker may consider proceeding even without a client's consent. In this situation, the client's refusal can be considered an indication of his lack of competency. On the other hand, if the risk is great and the potential benefit minimal, the client's refusal is logical and should be accepted.

*Ethical Principle 4.* A social worker should always choose the option that will cause the least harm, the least permanent harm, and/or the most easily reversible harm.

*Ethical Principle 5.* A social worker should choose the option that promotes a better quality of life for all people, for the individual as well as for the community.

*Ethical Principle 6.* A social worker should make practice decisions that strengthen every person's right to privacy. Keeping confidential information inviolate is a direct derivative of this obligation.

*Ethical Principle 7.* A social worker should make practice decisions that permit her to speak the truth and to fully disclose all relevant information to her client and to others.

## Application of Ethical Decision-Making Screens

Let us try to apply these ethical decision-making screens to one of the ethical dilemmas that the social worker of Debbie Roberts (Exemplar 3.1) faced. This social worker, you may recall, had to decide whether or not to contact the parents of twelve-year-old Debbie even though she had stated specifically that she did not want her parents to know that she was pregnant. A search of the *Code of Ethics* does not reveal any one paragraph that is directly applicable to this dilemma. We will therefore use the EPS. Ethical Principle 6 indicates that a social worker should not invade a person's privacy by involving others without that person's consent. Ethical Principle 3 stresses the ethical requirement to foster a person's autonomy. Both of these ethical principles direct the social worker to respect Debbie's request to refrain from contacting her parents. But Ethical Principle 1 requires decisions that protect a person's life and survival. This social worker felt that Debbie's pregnancy involved immediate danger to her health and welfare. Since Ethical Principle 1 has the highest priority, overriding any decisions required by lower-ranking principles, she decides that she must contact Debbie's parents immediately.

The two ethical decision-making screens will now be used to analyze several additional exemplars.

### ➤ 3.3 Starting in Private Practice

Cliff Baxter is an experienced social worker who recently resigned his agency job in order to devote all of his time to private practice. Before he left the agency, Dennis Norton, a colleague in the agency, told him that he would be willing to refer clients to him for a "finder's fee."

As in many beginnings, Cliff is having a difficult time making ends meet. His income last month was not even sufficient to pay the rent for the office. Should he give Dennis a call?

We will use the ERS and examine the NASW *Code of Ethics* to determine if there are any rules relevant to this situation. Section I-1 states: "The social worker shall not divide a fee or accept or give anything of value for receiving or making a referral." This rule provides such clear and unambiguous guidance that no further screening seems necessary. Cliff may not take advantage of Dennis's offer.

In the next example we will apply the EPS.

### ➤ 3.4 The Wrong Man Sits in Prison

Raul Lovaas has been enrolled in a drug rehabilitation program in order to break his cocaine addiction. The program's treatment routine includes pharmacological treatment, group therapy, and individual therapy. You are his social worker. You have succeeded in establishing a positive and meaningful relationship with Raul in the daily treatment sessions.

One morning Raul tells you that some years ago he accidentally killed a bank guard during a holdup. He was never caught by the police, but another man was convicted for this crime and now sits in prison on a life sentence.

For several days you have been trying to convince Raul that he should talk to the police in order to free an innocent man from prison. Raul not only refused to listen to your suggestion but has told you that he expects you to keep in complete confidence what he has told you. What should you do?

These are some of the thoughts that you have:

1. Raul has neither a legal nor a moral right to have another man serve a life sentence for a crime that he did not commit.
2. The "wrong" that you may cause by breaking confidentiality is hardly of the same importance as the wrong inflicted on an innocent person who is now imprisoned for life.
3. On the other hand, the effectiveness of the entire program may be compromised if it becomes known that social workers do not always keep confidential the information they receive from clients.

Let us focus our analysis on the latter two considerations since the first point, though obvious, does not relate directly to what you, the social worker, should do, but rather to what the client is ethically required to do.

At least two ethical principles are involved in the second consideration; these are:

*Ethical Principle 3.* Principle of autonomy and freedom, specifically the freedom of an innocent man who is now imprisoned.

*Ethical Principle 6.* Principle of confidentiality, specifically respecting the confidence of the information that your client, Raul Lovaas, gave you.

Some may also base their decision on Ethical Principle 2, the principle of equality and inequality. An innocent man in prison is obviously not in an equal situation and requires additional resources in order to regain access to equal opportunities.

Since EP 6 (Principle of Confidentiality) is of a lower order than both EP 3 and EP 2, the second consideration leads to the decision that this social worker is ethically justified to break confidence and report to the police what she has learned from Raul.

From a practice point of view the third consideration may be especially important since in most situations we would hesitate to do anything that might impede the effectiveness of an intervention. It might be argued that a program that can improve the quality of life (EP 5) of many addicts should receive preference over the quality of life of one individual, even if that person is falsely imprisoned. But it is likely that such reasoning involves a number of fallacies, including:

1. We have no information on the effectiveness of this rehabilitation program. How effective is it in improving the quality of life of all/most/some participants?
2. We do not know what impact, if any, breaking confidentiality will have on the effectiveness of the program. It may well be that other participants will be happy that the worker was instrumental in freeing an innocent person from prison.

3. Statistical probabilities are never a permissible substitute for ethical screening.

In other words, the quality of life principle (EP 5) is not relevant in this situation, but even if it were, it would be of a lower order than EP 3 and EP 2. Consideration 3 is therefore not relevant and should be ignored in making an ethical decision. We would, therefore, conclude that the social worker is obligated to inform the police unless Raul himself is willing to talk to the police.

In this chapter, we have examined a series of guidelines and decision-making processes that social workers can use when making ethical decisions. We noted that every social worker is confronted by ethical dilemmas and that these always require choices which must be made before action can be taken. As a test of one's ethical decisions, Iserson (1986) has suggested that the social worker ask herself three questions regarding impartiality, generalizability, and justifiability; these can serve as a final "check out" before moving to the action phase:

1. Would you be willing to act the way you have chosen if you were in the other person's place? This question asks the social worker to consider the effect her action would have if she or a member of her family or other loved ones were the recipients of the action. The purpose of this question is to correct for partiality and self-interest and to minimize or prevent the possibility they will play too dominant a part in the decision.

2. Are you willing to undertake this action in similar circumstances? Generalizing a particular decision may reduce bias and partiality but also may blind one to the unique qualities of a situation which demands a unique response, one which would not generally be used in many other situations. When one evaluates a particular action in light of its general applicability to similar situations, one is concerned with both the breadth and range of effects and the short and long-range consequences. The purpose of this question is to make the social worker think of the consequences of an action beyond the short term and to consider it not as a particular instance but justified as a general practice in similar circumstances.

3. Can you explain and justify your decision to others? The purpose of this question is to make certain that you have consciously and planfully considered the options and have made certain the client's rights and best interests are served by your professional actions in the context of the values and standards of the profession.

## EXERCISES

1. The legislature of your state has been alarmed by the sharp rise in the number of children born to young adults with mental retardation. Even when these infants are not defective (and many are not), most of the parents with retardation are not able to give their children the care that they need. As a result, most of these children must be placed in foster homes at great expense to the public. A bill has been introduced by a group of powerful state senators, calling for mandatory sterilization of all men and women with mental retardation. The senators argue that this is an effective, efficient, and painless way of taking care of this problem. You have been asked by your local NASW chapter to prepare testimony in opposition to this bill. In your testimony you should be mindful that considerations of efficiency and effectiveness cannot be dismissed out of hand in these days of shrinking welfare budgets. Yet you might argue that ethical considerations are sometimes even more important. Remember, however, that you are trying to convince legislators, not social workers.

2. Organize a class debate on the proposition: "A true professional must be willing to give up some of his autonomy and some of his rights as a freely functioning individual, especially when there is a conflict between personal and professional values."

3. Tonight's forecast is for below-freezing temperatures. The mayor has ordered the police to pick up all homeless persons and to deliver them to the city shelter. The police have asked the shelter social workers to help them to locate the homeless and to persuade them to come to the shelter. You are one of the shelter social workers and know that many homeless persons will refuse to go to the shelter. What are the ethical implications of the police's request? What should you do as a professional social worker?

## SUGGESTIONS FOR ADDITIONAL READINGS

Rachels (1986) provides an introduction to moral philosophy and ethics; written by a professional philosopher, it is eminently readable since it is intended for nonspecialists. Fleck-Henderson (1991) draws on social psychological research on moral reasoning and behavior and applies them to moral reasoning in clinical practice. Reamer (1993) in *The Philosophical Foundations of Social Work* provides a chapter on moral philosophy and social work. Imre (1982) presents a thoughtful discussion of philosophical issues in social work; values and ethics occupy a prominent role in this thin book. One of Imre's more recent publications (1989) is also relevant to this chapter. The relationship between religion and morality is discussed by Himes (1989).

Loewenberg (1992) illustrates some potential conflicts between personal and professional values. Glassman (1992) presents a series of personal and professional dilemmas that emerge when social workers attempt to implement feminist values in a practice setting. Wodarski, Pippin, and Daniels (1988) examine the effects of social work education on personality, values, and interpersonal skills. Roberts (1989) asks some very searching questions about social work ethics, questions that arose in connection with a review of value conflicts between different professions.

# PART TWO

# Ethical Dilemmas
## in Professional Practice

# 4. Confidentiality and Informed Consent

A person's right to privacy is a first-order value in our culture. Every person has a right to determine for himself *when, how,* and *to what extent* he wants to share (or have shared) information about himself with others. Even though the Constitution does not explicitly mention a right to privacy, Chief Justice Richard B. Hughes of the New Jersey Supreme Court wrote that "Supreme Court decisions have recognized that a right of personal privacy exists and that certain areas of privacy are guaranteed under the Constitution" (*In re Quinlan,* 170 N.J. 10, 1976).

The professional ethical principle of confidentiality is derived from this societal value. This principle is not a modern invention but was already recognized by Hippocrates. The physician's oath that is attributed to him states, "What I may see or hear in the course of treatment...I will keep to myself, holding such things shameful to be spoken about" (Van Hoose & Kottler, 1985, p. 7). In the NASW *Code of Ethics* this principle appears as a major rule:

> *Confidentiality and privacy.* The social worker should respect the privacy of clients and hold in confidence all information obtained in the course of professional service (1993, Paragraph H).

Five subparagraphs explicate this ethical rule and some of its limitations. The professional relationship between practitioner and client is based on the social worker's acceptance of this rule and its derivatives.

## PRIVACY AND CONFIDENTIALITY

Confidentiality means that a social worker will not reveal to anyone information that she has received on a confidential basis. However, it is not always easy for a social worker to implement this rule. The *Code* itself already recognizes the possibility that "compelling professional reasons" may lead a social worker to reveal information received in confidence. The nature of some of these "compelling reasons" will be discussed later in this chapter. Observing confidentiality has become a major ethical problem since no social worker can guarantee that information received by her will always remain confidential.

Confidentiality is an ethical principle rather than a legal one. It affirms "an explicit promise or contract to reveal nothing about an individual except under conditions agreed to by the source or subject" (Siegel, 1979, p. 251). An ethical dilemma occurs whenever a practitioner has to find the correct balance between (1) a client's right to privacy and (2) the right of other people and of society to certain information.

It is generally assumed that a client's reliance on confidentiality promotes trust in the social worker. Many think that this relationship with the professional would be harmed if clients were aware that there are limits to confidentiality. They believe that the confidentiality principle is crucial for maintaining a professional relation. Without observing confidentiality, there is a great risk that:

1. People who need professional help may be deterred from requesting this help.
2. People who have already begun a relationship with a social worker may not engage fully.
3. The trust relationship that has already been developed may be destroyed; clients who have disclosed confidential information may feel betrayed by the professional whom they trusted.

In this spirit one New York family court judge ruled that "it cannot be seriously controverted that essential attributes of the [social worker/client] relationship include confidentiality, trust and reliance" (*Hector M.* v. *Commissioner of Social Services of City of New York et al.*, 102 Misc. 2d 676, 1980). But an empirical study by Muehleman and colleagues (1985) does not support the assumption that limiting confidentiality necessarily endangers the client/social worker relationship.

In considering confidentiality and its limits, we must consider the difference between (1) information received directly from a client and (2) information received about the client from others, such as a hospital, an employer, or another social worker. In both cases, the person who supplied the information wants to restrict its dissemination. In the first case, the client does not want others to receive the information; in the second case, the party supplying the information does not want the client to have knowledge of it. The question in the latter case is whether the client who has a direct interest in (and perhaps a right to) this information should have access to it. Who has the right to release this information or to restrict its further dissemination? The client or the person who supplied the information? The *Code of Ethics* gives a somewhat ambiguous answer to these questions:

> The social worker should afford clients reasonable access to any official social work records concerning them…[but] should take due care to protect the confidences of others contained in those records (NASW, 1993, Paragraphs H-3 and H-4).

Trying to meet both of these principles may place the social worker before a difficult ethical dilemma.

Confidentiality is an especially problematic issue because this ethical principle is based on an oversimplified practice model, one that includes only the client and the social worker. If this simple model fully reflected reality, observance of this ethical principle would depend almost entirely on the intentions of the worker. The reality, however, is much more complex because most often there are many participants in the social work action system, each of whom makes conflicting demands for confidential information. These participants include:

*Other social workers.*    Often we do not give sufficient thought to the ethical implications of sharing confidential information with other social workers. We are not referring here to small talk at a cocktail party (which is clearly against the ethical rule of confidentiality), but to formal or informal consultations with colleagues or supervisors, as well as to the transmission of such information to other social workers who have a professional interest in the information (such as a social worker who is working with other members of the same family, the social worker who will take over the case while the worker is on vacation, and so on). This type of information transmission is for the client's benefit since it is intended to assure more effective service, but is it ethical to provide this information to others without the client's specific consent? The *Code of Ethics* does state that "the social worker should inform clients fully about the limits of confidentiality" (NASW, 1993, Paragraph H-2), but would the client have shared the information had he known that many other social workers would have access to it? At the same time, the social worker should consider the harm that may be caused by not providing vital information to colleagues who are in a position to be helpful to the client. It is this consideration that led Taylor and Adelman to conclude that "keeping information confidential can seriously hamper an intervener's efforts to help" (1989, p. 80).

*Colleagues from other fields.*   Many social workers work on multidisciplinary teams or in settings where information must be shared with colleagues from other professions whose confidentiality practices may differ from those of social workers. To what extent is it ethical for hospital social workers to reveal confidential information to physicians? To nurses? Is it ethical for a school social worker to share with a teacher confidential information about a child and his family, knowing that this information may be entered on the child's permanent school record and thus be shared with many others?

*Administrative records.*   Social agencies and other employing organizations need information about clients and client contacts for administrative and accountability reasons. The initial request to supply these data may be entirely proper, but once the requested data have been transmitted the practitioner no longer is able to protect their confidentiality. As the use of computerized records becomes more common in social agencies, this aspect of the confidentiality issue has become even more critical. For example, a California court has ruled that social workers have no legal grounds to refuse to enter confidential information about welfare recipients into the agency's computerized record system (*Belmont* v. *California State Personnel Board*, 35 Ca.App. 3d 518, 1974).

*Insurance companies.*   New dimensions have been added to the problem of confidentiality as more and more social workers are required to report diagnoses to insurance companies in order to qualify clients for reimbursement. While clients generally consent to sharing this information because they are interested in having a third party pay for part or all of the services they receive from a social worker, they are not always aware of the diagnosis reported. Many social workers do not report the actual diagnosis, but the mildest diagnosis that qualifies for reimbursement; for example, many social workers routinely report "adjustment disorders," no matter what the problem. But at other times the severity of the diagnosis is overstated in order to qualify clients for reimbursement (Kutchins & Kirk, 1987). This problem will be discussed at greater length in Chapter 10.

*Police.*   In many states the law requires that social workers, as well as other professional practitioners, inform the police whenever they acquire information about criminal activities that have taken place or that are being planned. For example, a social worker who is present when an adolescent street gang plans a holdup should have no ethical qualms about reporting the gang's intentions to the police. But when she is told about such a plan by a third party (such as a parent or a neighbor), she must ask herself several questions: How reliable is the report? Can the information be used without revealing the source? How might such revelation affect the helping relationship? All of these and other questions have factual, professional, and ethical implications. Often it is difficult to separate these aspects.

Many social workers are perplexed by ethical dilemmas arising out of various other kinds of law violation, particularly delinquent acts which do not seem to harm others. The following exemplar describes one such situation which raises a number of ethical questions:

➤ **4.1 Suspected Fraud**

Social worker Jean Fisher is a marriage counselor and family therapist in the Old Town Family Consultation Center, a nonsectarian United Way agency. Sue and Dean Kern have been coming to her for family therapy once a week for the past two months. Though their problem is not critical, they came to seek help while their marriage was still salvageable. They have made good progress toward reaching their goal.

During today's session Dean Kern mentioned that he has continued to receive SSI support payments for his aged mother, who lived with them until she moved overseas two years ago. She now makes her home with his sister, who lives in England.

Should Ms. Fisher report this case for possible fraud? Or is this communication covered by client/worker confidentiality? What will happen to the client/therapist relationship if Ms. Fisher does reveal what she learned today? Should she consider the possible consequences to the treatment before she decides what to do? What other criteria should she use to resolve the ethical issues posed here?

What would be Ms. Fisher's obligation if she had learned that Dean Kern had escaped from jail some years ago? Or that Sue Kern was pushing drugs? Does the seriousness of the offense change the ethical considerations? Does the degree of harm the offense might cause make a difference?

*Relatives.*    Are the relatives of a client entitled to confidential information that might affect them? A terminally ill patient asks that his relatives not be told how ill he is. His son asks the social worker, "Is my father dying?" How does the social worker decide whether to keep the confidence or tell the truth? This is a type of ethical dilemma which may be especially acute for social workers who are engaged in genetic counseling and who are privy to genetic information that may be relevant to the health of other relatives (Sammons, 1978; Schild & Black, 1984).

Are parents entitled to confidential information about their children? Does the age of the child make a difference? Does it make a difference whether the information came from the child or from another source? Should parents be told about their teenage daughter's pregnancy (see Exemplar 3.1)? Here is another exemplar that raises similar questions.

➤ **4.2 Drug Abuse in the Ninth Grade**

A group of ninth graders approached the school social worker and offered to share with her details about the extensive use of hard drugs in their school. However, they are ready to do this only if the social worker will promise not to tell the principal or their parents that they were the ones who told her.

The social worker knows that she cannot keep this information confidential. Should she tell the young people that she cannot meet their request of confidentiality, even if as a result she may be blocking this information channel? Or should she agree because it is important to obtain this information—and later break her promise? What is the ethical thing to do?

*Client.*    What are a social worker's obligations when a client wants information about himself? How should a worker respond to a client who wants to read his own case record? The NASW *Code of Ethics* states, "The social worker should afford clients reasonable access to any official social work records concerning them" (1993, Paragraph H-3). However, where can a social worker learn what constitutes "reasonable access"?

Those who argue against sharing confidential information with the client, especially against granting him access to his own record, offer the following reasons:

1. The case record may contain information supplied on a confidential basis by a third party, such as another social worker, teacher, neighbor, or relative.
2. The case record may contain "raw data" which have not yet been checked or evaluated.
3. The record may include test results or other data that may be misinterpreted by a lay person.
4. The social worker may use the case record to explore various options or to ask herself questions that need further clarification; when the client reads such material, his trust in the worker may be impaired.
5. The client may be hurt by reading or hearing negative information about himself.

6. The client may use these data for purposes for which they were not intended, including making legal claims against the worker and the agency.

Other social workers argue in favor of giving clients access to their own case records. They make the following points:

1. Reading this information gives the client an opportunity to correct mistakes.
2. A client can give informed consent to share information with others only if he knows what this information is.
3. Knowledge of information may lead to change, while ignorance will result only in maintaining the present unsatisfactory situation.
4. Opening the case record will demonstrate the efficacy of client/worker cooperation and will be followed by even greater client participation in the social work process.
5. The Federal Privacy Act of 1974 (PL 93–579) requires that every citizen have access to his or her records.

We have presented many of the arguments for and against the opening of case records to clients in order to help social workers arrive at an ethical decision. Admittedly, this is a decision that few social workers have to make alone since generally agency policy and directives on this point are specific and clear. But what would be your position if the staff of your agency is asked to make a recommendation to the agency board of directors?

Clearly there are limits to confidentiality. It is generally recommended that these limits be explained to a client at the beginning of the intervention process, but in what detail should these limits be explained? Some explanation is important in view of the fact that most clients assume that everything they tell their social worker will remain confidential. Miller and Thelen (1986) report that 69 percent of the respondents in their study of clients thought that confidentiality was complete and permanent. Yet stressing the limits of confidentiality too early in the developing client/worker relationship may be harmful rather than helpful.

## CHILD ABUSE AND CONFIDENTIALITY

Social workers (and other professionals) are required by law to report all cases of suspected child abuse and neglect to the child protective agency or another designated authority. Though details vary from state to state, such reporting is required in every jurisdiction in the United States and in many other countries. As the growing incidence and the harmful consequences of physical and sexual abuse have become better understood, more and more social workers are filing these reports, as required by law. Simultaneously there is somewhat less concern with the ethics of breaking confidentiality in case of child abuse and neglect; instead the ethical concerns focus on ways to assure the safety of the abused child. Nowadays the question whether reporting will enhance or endanger the child's safety is *the* critical ethical and factual issue. A protective agency worker is required to investigate the reported abuse and is supposed to take any action necessary to protect the child. The question is whether his or her activities will enhance or endanger the child's safety. A news story appearing in the *Philadelphia Inquirer* (January 10, 1988) reported the death of three children, two and three years old, whose deaths occurred despite the "intervention" of the child protective agency. The investigating reporters revealed that the agency had violated state requirements and procedures. The paraprofessional workers who investigated these cases had been inadequately trained. In each of the three cases, there was a pattern of missed home visits and repeated failures to recognize that these children were in life-threatening situations. Similar tragic incidents have been reported from many other cities and rural areas.

In Barksdale's study (1989) of child abuse reporting, eight out of ten social workers responded that they would report suspected child abuse, one indicated that he would persuade the client to file a report himself, while the tenth social worker indicated that he had never reported a case of child abuse. Few of these social workers were concerned that their reporting might have an impact on their relationship with the client. In another study of 202 family therapists (including many social workers), 68.3 percent responded that they would report to the authorities a father of a family in treatment who had physically abused his children several times during the past year, even though he now promised never to do so again. An additional twelve therapists reported that they would make sure that the family itself reported this abuse (Green & Hansen, 1989).

Yet many social workers continue to be uneasy about the ethical and practice implications of reporting suspected child abuse that involves one of their clients. Possible options that such social workers might want to consider include the following:

1. Work to change the law that requires social workers to report all cases of suspected child abuse—but given the strong societal support for this law, any such change is unlikely.
2. Ignore the law and risk the legal consequences that may ensue— there are no known reports of criminal prosecution for failure to report, though civil suits may be possible.

3. Report the suspected child abuse, but do not tell the client that you have done so.
4. Obtain the "consent" of every client at the beginning of treatment to make such reports if the occasion arises—but this procedure may destroy any possibility of establishing a trust relationship.
5. Report the abuse, but arrange for cooperation with the child protective worker in order both to reduce the trauma of investigation and to protect the abused child's welfare. While this option may seem to be desirable, is it really practical?
6. Report the suspected child abuse and tell the client that you have done so (or are about to do so).

## PRIVILEGED COMMUNICATIONS

Privileged communication is a legal right granted by legislative statute. It guarantees that certain information will not be revealed in court without the consent of the person who originated the communication. The rules of evidence define this "privilege" as follows:

> Where persons occupy toward each other certain confidential relations, the law, on the ground of public policy, will not compel, or even allow one of them to violate the confidence reposed in him by the other, by testifying, without the consent of the other, as to communications made to him by such other, in the confidence which the relation has inspired...(97 C.J.S. Witnesses, Section 252, cited by Albert, 1986, pp. 172–73).

Privileged communication is a rule of evidence that allows one party in a legal proceeding (in this case, the client) to limit the admissibility of statements originally communicated in confidence, thus rendering the witness (that is, the social worker) "incompetent" to testify regarding a particular matter.

The common law principle that the public has a right to every person's evidence is followed in the absence of a statute of privilege. No person can refuse to testify in court when called to do so. Persons reluctant to testify can be subpoenaed or commanded to testify by the court; failure to appear and testify in response to a subpoena can result in a citation for contempt of court. Historically, privileged relationships have been limited to husband/wife, attorney/client, and priest-confessor/worshiper. Any other relationship is privileged only when so defined by a statute enacted by a state legislature.

Wigmore's criteria for privileged communications (1961, vol. 8, p. 52) are generally used to determine whether the privilege should apply. Wigmore believed that a privilege status exists only when all four of the following criteria are met:

1. The communication must originate in the belief that it will not be disclosed.
2. The inviolability of the confidence must be essential to achieve the purpose of the relationship.
3. The relationship must be one that society should foster.
4. The expected injury to the relationship through disclosure of the confidential information must be greater than the expected benefit to justice if the witness were forced to testify.

The physician/patient relationship, according to Wigmore, does not qualify because it does not meet the fourth criterion. Social workers who practice psychotherapy appear to meet all four of Wigmore's criteria for privileged communications, but it is doubtful whether other social workers do so. Yet statutes generally cover an entire profession, no matter what specific activities any one practitioner performs (VandeCreek et al., 1988).

In 1994 all fifty states, the District of Columbia, Puerto Rico, and the Virgin Islands had adopted social work licensing or regulatory laws. Forty-two states, the District of Columbia, and the Virgin Islands specifically recognize the privilege for social worker/client communications (American Association of State Social Work Boards, 1995).

The privilege "belongs" to the client, not to the social worker. When a client waives the privilege, the social worker must testify in court even if the client does not know or is not certain what information is included in his case record and even if this testimony may harm him. Other interested persons do not control the privilege. For example, a father or husband cannot suppress or waive testimony of a social worker who is treating his child or wife, even when he pays for the treatment (VandeCreek et al., 1988).

The privilege is not applicable and ceases to exist in a number of situations, including the following (this list is not exhaustive and may differ from state to state):

1. When the client is dangerous and plans to harm another person or himself.
2. When there is a serious risk of suicide or other danger to the client's life.
3. When there is serious suspicion of child abuse or neglect.
4. When information is mandated by a court.
5. When a social worker is appointed by a court to make an assessment (but if one of the attorneys requests a pretrial examination by a social worker, then that social worker is "covered" by the attorney/client privilege).
6. When the client plans to commit a crime.

7. When the social worker determines the client is in need of hospitalization for a mental or psychological disorder.
8. When the client sues the social worker for malpractice.
9. In child custody cases since the interest of the child is considered paramount.
10. When the client has already introduced privileged material into the litigation.
11. When the client threatens to harm the social worker.
12. When a social worker needs a court order in order to collect fees for professional services rendered.

The New York State privilege statute was amended in 1985 to state that a client is not deemed to have waived the privilege in general if he has authorized the disclosure of specific information for purposes of obtaining insurance (Schwartz, 1989).

In many states the privilege ceases to exist when a third party was present at the time that the client communicated the confidential information to the social worker. However, some state laws specifically extend the privilege of communications to situations that involve group, marital, and family therapy, that is, to situations where third parties are present. These states include California, Idaho, Kansas, Louisiana, Maryland, New York, Oklahoma, and Virginia (VandeCreek et al., 1988). In several other states the courts decide whether or not the rule of privilege applies. The Minnesota Superior Court addressed this question in *Minnesota* v. *Andring* (10 FLR 1206, 1984) and ruled:

> The participants in group psychotherapy sessions are not casual persons who are strangers....Rather, every participant has such a relationship with the attending professional, and in the group setting, the participants actually become part of the diagnostic and therapeutic process for coparticipants.
>
> An interpretation which excluded group therapy from the scope of the psychotherapist-patient [privileged communication rule] would seriously limit the effectiveness of group psychotherapy as a therapeutic device.... [T]he confidentiality of communications made during group therapy is essential in maintaining its effectiveness as a therapeutic tool....

In the absence of a privilege statute, a social worker who is forced to testify in court about confidential information that she has received from a client may face a "double bind"—if she testifies, she may be sued by the client for revealing confidential information; if she refuses to testify, she may be cited for contempt of court.

In summary, privileged communication is a legal and not an ethical concept. Questions arising out of privilege communications require legal consultation, while questions about confidentiality require ethical resolution. Admittedly, the line between these two areas is often blurred.

## INFORMED CONSENT

The professional ethics rule of informed consent is derived from the moral principle of autonomy. Informed consent means that a social worker or another professional will not intervene in a client's life or release confidential information concerning him unless the client has consented. Informed consent involves issues of *knowledge, voluntariness,* and *competence.* Problems involving any one or all of these issues make for difficult ethical dilemmas in social work practice.

It is generally agreed that confidential information should be released only with the consent of the person who supplied the information. The problem arises most often when another agency needs information originally supplied (directly or indirectly) by the client. Generally social work agencies require the client's written consent before they will release such information. In order not to delay the transmission of vital information, some agencies routinely ask clients to sign a release form at intake. While observing the technicalities of consent, such a routine does violence to the concept of informed consent. Often clients do not understand what they are signing nor is their signature always voluntary since they are left with the impression that signing the form is a condition for receiving service. Many of the routine forms used by social agencies are either very difficult to understand or are so general that they are practically meaningless. A journalist who investigated this problem concluded that "there is good reason to believe that many, perhaps most, who sign the [consent] forms are displaying trust more than understanding when they pen their signatures to the forms" (*Los Angeles Times,* June 8, 1980, p. 1).

NASW's "Policy on Information Utilization and Confidentiality" (1975) does not spell out clearly the criteria for informed consent. The American Red Cross did address this issue by insisting that "before the 'Release of Confidential Information' form is signed, the service-to-military family worker must be assured that the client or responsible representative understands what information is to be given, to whom, and for what purpose" (ARC 2049, October 1974). The problem may be that many of the forms in use today were designed primarily to protect the agency and the worker from malpractice suits rather than to guarantee the client's informed consent. The challenge facing ethical social workers is to develop a form which is both readable and sufficiently specific, but which does not scare the client.

Ethical problems around informed consent are often difficult to resolve, as will become evident when we consider the following exemplar.

➤ **4.3 Archie Walker's Golden Years**

Muriel Palmieri is an outreach worker of the Downtown Elderly Program (DEP). She has organized a group of volunteers who regularly visit with homebound older people. These volunteers have been trained to identify older people who need additional help, so that they can report their names to the DEP. One of the volunteers recently told Ms. Palmieri that she had discovered a bedridden older man in a cold and dirty fourth-floor walk-up apartment.

Archie Walker was probably not as old or as feeble as he appeared, but the volunteer thought that he required more care than the occasional help provided by his seventy-nine-year-old neighbor, who brought him food whenever he thought of it. When this neighbor forgot to come, as happened not infrequently, Walker subsisted for days on cold water and bread. It had been years since Walker last saw a doctor. He seemed delighted with the volunteer's visit and begged her to come again soon.

Ms. Palmieri told the volunteer that she would see what could be done to make Mr. Walker more comfortable. When she visited Mr. Walker, he welcomed her warmly. Ms. Palmieri verified the volunteer's observations. Mr. Walker seemed relatively alert. The worker thought that his dissatisfaction with his present condition was realistic and a hopeful sign, indicative of a capacity to participate in developing plans for his future. Walker explained that his only income came from Social Security. He had never heard of the federal Supplemental Security Income program (SSI). Ms. Palmieri suspected that he qualified for it. He said that he could not afford to hire someone to look after him or to clean his apartment. Nor could he afford to move to another apartment. But he insisted that he did not want to go to an old folks' home.

Ms. Palmieri, in the course of her visit, explained to Mr. Walker many of the programs which were available to help persons in his situation. She listed the advantages and disadvantages of each and indicated the time it might take before each program or service would start for him. She also noted how she could help him qualify. Among the programs and services she discussed were SSI, Meals-on-Wheels, health visitor, homemaker, Title 8 housing, and The Manor Apartments.

Mr. Walker seemed bewildered by the many programs from which he could choose and by the many decisions he had to make. He asked Ms. Palmieri to do whatever was best for him.

If you were in Ms. Palmieri's place, what would you have done? Here are some of the ethical issues that she thought about as she tried to help Mr. Walker:

1. What did Mr. Walker mean when he told her to do whatever was best for him? Did this mean that he gave his consent for her to make arrangements on his behalf? Is this a satisfactory way of giving informed consent? If not, in what ways did it fall short?
2. Instead of overwhelming him with so many choices, should she have simplified the decisions he has to make by presenting only a few options at a time? Perhaps it would have been better to have Mr. Walker decide first whether he really wanted to stay in his

present apartment or move somewhere else. But can he make this decision without having a full knowledge of all options? Do social work ethics require that a client have *full* knowledge of *all* the relevant options?

3. Ms. Palmieri tried to present all of the advantages of every option. But did she really know *all* of the consequences? And does Mr. Walker really care about *all* of the consequences? Is he not much more interested in what will happen to him in the next few months? How much knowledge must a client have before the social worker can be sure that she has met the demands of the *Code of Ethics*?

4. Would it be ethical for Ms. Palmieri to design a package of relevant services on the basis of her assessment and on the basis of Mr. Walker's wishes—and then ask Mr. Walker whether or not this package was acceptable?

Additional questions could be asked, but it is already clear that in social work practice "informed consent" is beset with many difficulties and that these difficulties often lead to ethical dilemmas.

## Knowledge, Voluntariness, Competence

The three components of informed consent, as noted already, are (1) knowledge, (2) voluntariness, and (3) competency. We will discuss briefly the ethical aspects of each of these components.

*Knowledge.*    A person can be considered sufficiently informed to give consent only if he knows what will occur during the intervention or treatment, what the results of the intervention will be, and what will happen if consent to the intervention is not given. He should know how much better (or worse) he will be if he agrees to the intervention than he will be if he does not agree. He should also have full knowledge about alternate options. Some of this knowledge can be provided by the social worker, but even she may not be cognizant of many of the outcomes. In fact, the nature and consequences of any option are never entirely clear and may be interpreted differently by different experts. Ms. Palmieri might explain to Mr. Walker how Meals-on-Wheels operates, the type of food this program provides, and how much it costs. However, she does not know whether Mr. Walker's stomach will tolerate warm food, how long the present cook will stay, or whether this program will survive the next budget cuts. In fact, Mr. Walker may lose the "help" of his neighbor (inadequate as it is) if he joins Meals-on-Wheels and be in a worse position if that program is terminated. Ms. Palmieri might point out all the benefits and risks, but there are always secondary and unanticipated consequences which, though unpredictable, may be equally if not more important.

There is also evidence that people often do not pay attention to information presented to them. Whether this is a case of selective listening or of suppressing unpleasant information is not always certain. In one study it was found that most patients were unable to recall accurately what they had been told by their surgeon twenty-four hours earlier, no matter how carefully the details of surgery and the possible risks had been explained to them. Lest it be thought that the patients in this study were not given adequate information before signing the "consent for surgery" form, the informed consent explanations were videotaped and later reviewed by independent judges. Many of the participating physicians told the researchers that they had provided their patients with all available information, but they gained the impression that most patients simply did not want to know what might go wrong in surgery (*Los Angeles Times*, June 8, 1980).

Social workers differ in many ways from surgeons, but many social workers also report that their clients really do not want to know all the details. They have a problem and want help from an expert whom they trust. Yet the social worker is ethically committed to the principle of informed consent. One of the dilemmas around informed consent that has ethical implications occurs because a social worker (1) does not want to overwhelm the client with too much information, yet (2) wants to provide sufficient information so that the client can make a meaningful decision. Should the worker proceed when the client gives permission, even though the social worker knows that this client's consent is less than informed? Or should the social worker delay help in order to give the client additional information (which the client may not even want)?

*Voluntariness.*    Consent is meaningful only when it is given freely. Though there is wide agreement with this ethical rule, some social workers practice in settings where the client has little or no freedom. Prisoners and hospitalized mental patients are classic examples of involuntary clients. In the *Kaimowitz* decision (42 USLA 2063, 1973) the court ruled that persons whose privileges and eventual discharge depended on their cooperating with the custodial staff cannot give legally adequate voluntary consent. Is it ethical for a social worker to practice in prisons or mental hospitals, settings where consent cannot be given voluntarily? A social worker who does accept employment in such settings faces serious ethical problems almost constantly. The usual practice, giving as much choice as possible under the circumstances, may be the only feasible option, but this does not completely resolve the ethical dilemma facing the social worker who practices in an involuntary setting.

Consent may also be less than voluntary in other settings. Voluntariness is often presented as a dichotomous value—a decision either is or is not voluntary. But closer inspection will suggest that there is a wide range of possibilities between the two absolutes. For example, how voluntary will be the consent of a "voluntary" client who believes it important to gain the worker's goodwill? A destitute single mother may agree with almost everything her social worker suggests because she desperately wants to qualify for assistance. The man who is eager for a reconciliation with his estranged wife may agree with everything his social worker mentions because he believes that in this way he may be able to salvage his marriage. These people are not forced to come to a social agency or to agree with the social worker, but is their consent fully voluntary?

Another ethical dilemma facing social workers arises out of the desirability of client trust. Research has shown that trust or faith in the practitioner is a key component in effecting change. Yet frequently, faith or trust results in a surrender of decision-making participation. Instead of giving voluntary consent, the client who has "blind faith" will agree to everything his worker says. How to develop and encourage trust, yet at the same time strengthen voluntary consent, is a challenge for every social worker.

The problem of voluntary consent takes on special significance when a client wants to harm himself, either by wishing to commit suicide or by wanting to engage in other self-destructive behavior. There are those who have argued that a social worker has no right to interfere with a person who really wants to harm himself. Every person has a right to make decisions which affect only himself or herself. But there are others who have suggested that intervention, at least temporary intervention, may be justified in order to determine whether the contemplated action is fully voluntary and whether the decision maker is indeed knowledgeable and competent. Gewirth held that "the conditions of voluntary consent are never fulfilled in such cases [since] only abysmal ignorance or deep emotional trauma can lead persons to extreme measures like these" (1978, p. 264). He no doubt would suggest that a social worker must always intervene in cases of threatened suicide or other self-destructive behavior in order to protect that person's welfare.

There is still another aspect to voluntary consent. Social workers often work in settings in which clients are served by using authority and where their participation is nonvoluntary. Such settings include corrections, juvenile justice, child protection, involuntary commitments for mental health treatment, and court-ordered treatment for substance abuse. There may also be subtle coercion for employees to obtain specific services. In addition to issues of voluntariness, issues of trust, privacy, relationship, and the efficacy of treatment may all arise.

Recently, the Group for the Advancement of Psychiatry reported on the findings of research which suggest that forced treatment can be successful, perhaps even more successful than voluntary treatment (Group for the Advancement of Psychiatry, 1994). Social workers have reported mixed effectiveness for individual interventions with those involved in the criminal justice system (Ivanoff, Blythe, and Tripodi, 1994). Another review of the literature on the effectiveness of social work with legally mandated clients found that clients can have more successful results than had earlier been thought to be the case. These positive results, however, also found that coerced intervention often produces *time-limited* benefits that do not last beyond the use of external pressure (Rooney, 1992). In addition to the long-standing belief that successful mental health treatment must be voluntary and uncoerced, the use of involuntary treatment modalities also raises many ethical questions which social workers must face.

*Competence.* Informed consent presupposes that the person who gives consent is competent to do so. However, many social work clients are less than fully competent. Young children, senile persons, the seriously emotionally disturbed, and many retarded people are generally considered less than competent to give informed consent to some or all decisions. However, Robertson notes that even though "competence appears to be a binary process,...on closer examination its binariness dissolves and vanishes" (1985, p. 555). In other words, it is not a question of classifying clients as those who are competent and those who are not; instead, persons will be located along a full range of possibilities, ranging from those completely competent to others who are somewhat competent to still others who are barely competent or not at all competent. This conceptualization has many implications when we consider professional ethics and practice.

Only a court of law can declare a person "incompetent," but there are many situations where a social worker must make an informal assessment of a person's competency to participate in decision making. The ethical problem is complicated because ostensibly the issue of competency is raised only when a client disagrees with his social worker's recommendation; rarely do we consider him incompetent if he agrees! Ethical problems arising out of the issue of competence are well known to social workers in many fields of practice, especially to those who are working with adoption, foster placement, custody, abortion, contraception, and euthanasia.

The social worker's ethical dilemma may become a difficult one, especially when young children are involved. While there is no agreement how old a child must be before he or she is considered competent, everyone agrees that an infant is never competent. Children, like adults, may not always mean what they say or say what they mean. Stated preferences may not reflect actual preferences. One social worker reported, "Children always want to stay [with their families]. No matter how badly they have been abused, they feel they belong to mom and her habit or her boyfriend who brings her the stuff and hits them or rapes them" (*Boston Globe Magazine,* February 5, 1989, p. 33). Can such a request by an abused child be considered a competent or informed decision? The situation is not very different when working with older adults. How senile must a person be before a social worker can ethically ignore the older person's wishes? What are acceptable indicators of senility? Michael Heinrich may be old and may present some evidence of senile behavior, but does his renewed interest in sex with a much younger woman "prove" that he is no longer competent, as his children contend?

➤ **4.4 Michael Heinrich's Girlfriend**

Michael Heinrich is seventy-seven years old and has been living alone ever since his wife died four years ago. When he became seriously ill several months ago, his married son and daughter arranged for round-the-clock nursing care in his apartment. One of these nurses, forty-year-old Lisa Nunn, has now become his girlfriend. She has moved into the apartment and is telling everyone that she and Michael will be married soon.

Heinrich's children are very upset by their father's behavior. They think that he is senile. They have engaged an attorney to have him declared incompetent. They have also arranged for their father's admission to a retirement home. They told the home's social worker not to pay any attention to his ramblings since he was senile and no longer knew what was best for him. They indicated that his sexual fantasies about his "girlfriend" were only one indication of his senility. Obviously he was no longer competent to make decisions and they were now making decisions for him.

When visiting Mr. Heinrich for the preadmission interview, the social worker was able to speak with him only in the presence of Ms. Nunn. He gave the appearance of being very old and participated only rarely in the conversation. But he stated clearly that under no circumstance did he want to leave his apartment or his girlfriend.

The decision to intervene in a person's life must never be taken lightly. To limit a person's freedom by removing him from his home and placing him in an institution is a very serious decision, a decision which ordinarily should not be taken without that person's consent. What are some important criteria that are relevant for waving aside the need for informed consent?

At the same time, it may be a mistake to always accept a client's consent or refusal at face value. A client may be temporarily depressed, may change his mind upon further reflection, or may be reacting to a situational fear or misunderstanding. Robertson warned that "the alacrity [to accept the first response] may stem from a superficial sense of legal and ethical duty" (1985, p. 569).

The issue of informed consent takes on special significance when the client is a community or a neighborhood. A social worker involved in a neighborhood renewal program must consider whether the elected representatives really represent all residents. Does their informed consent suffice, or must every resident consent? What is the situation when the initiative for intervention comes from the outside? It will not be possible to obtain informed consent if the social worker's first objective is to raise the residents' consciousness to the fact that there is a problem. Requiring every person's consent in this latter situation may be tantamount to ruling out any intervention activity, yet intervening without informed consent is a violation of the professional ethics. What should a social worker do in these circumstances?

## Ways of Consenting

Oliver Goldsmith (1764) wrote that "silence gives consent," but social workers have learned that silence and other nonverbal signals, such as a nod or even a verbal yes, may be deceptive and may indicate something other than consent. Clients may be ashamed to withhold consent or simply not understand to what they have been asked to agree. Though clients often do not seem to listen, a social worker is still obligated to offer a full explanation of what the intervention involves, what the projected benefits and risks will be, what other options may be available, and what might happen if the client does not consent. All this must be presented in a language that the client can understand.

Aside from questions of knowledge, voluntariness, and competency, the various forms of consent also make for ethical problems. Consider the following possibilities:

1. *Direct or tacit.* "Direct" refers to the client's verbal response, while "tacit" means that the client remained silent. But when can his not having said no be interpreted as "consent"?
2. *Oral or written.* Written consent is often preferred, but is the use of oral consent necessarily unethical? Does using written consent forms automatically eliminate all unethical behavior?
3. *Past/present.* Does current dissent invalidate all past consents? Is this a case of "change of mind," of "diminished competence," of "situational fear," or of something else? To state this dilemma differently, how much credence should a social worker give to a

person's present consent when she knows that in the past he consistently expressed a contrary view?

4. *Present/future.* Can a social worker assume that the client would (or will) agree with her decision if he were (or when be becomes) more aware of what is involved?

5. *"Forced" consent.* One way to obtain a client's consent is to frame options in a way that the client will "consent," no matter what the response. For example, the social worker may ask: Do you want to move to the nursing home this week or next?

As we have already said, each of these forms of consenting presents ethical problems and dilemmas which require resolution. One thing though is certain, involving the client in providing informed consent is not a one-time activity but an ongoing process.

Some have suggested that good clinical practice will resolve all of the problems around informed consent. If a client is fully involved in the decision-making process, questions of consent will not arise. Yet it is a fact that even formal contracting does not resolve all the problems involved in obtaining informed consent. The power gap between client and worker often results in contract negotiations between unequals. Some unintended coercion may be brought into play and this may lead the client to agree to choices that are not entirely of his choosing.

## DUTY TO WARN

One legal case that received wide publicity concerned a young man who told his therapist that he intended to kill his former girlfriend just as soon as she returned from an out-of-town trip. When the girl was killed shortly thereafter, the girl's family charged the therapist with neglect. The therapist argued that he was not guilty because his relationship with the client/killer was confidential. However, the judge held that

> Public policy favoring protection of the confidential character of patient-psychotherapist relationship must yield in instances in which disclosure is essential to avert danger to others; the protective privilege ends where the public peril begins.
>
> When a therapist determines, or...should determine, that his patient presents a serious danger of violence to another, *he incurs an obligation to use reasonable care to protect the intended victim* against such danger. [This duty] may call for him (1) to warn the intended victim or (2) others likely to apprise the victim of the danger, (3) to notify the police, or (4) to take whatever other steps are reasonably necessary under the circumstances (*Tarasoff* v. *Regents of the University of California*, 1976, 551 P 2d 334 at 340; emphasis added).

We have cited at length from the *Tarasoff* ruling because it has had such a wide impact on social workers. Yet 64 percent of a sample of social workers believed that the *Code of Ethics* does not offer them sufficient guidance if they faced a problem similar to the one faced by the therapist in the *Tarasoff* case (Weil & Sanchez, 1983).

A subsequent court decision explained that under the *Tarasoff* doctrine, a social worker or other professional (1) must be able to predict "pursuant to the standards of his profession" that the client is violently dangerous and (2) must be able to specify one or more clearly identifiable victims (*Brady* v. *Hopper*, 1983, 751 F 2d 329).

In another decision the California Supreme Court extended the *Tarasoff* doctrine beyond the identified intended victim to others who also might be in danger; in this case, the victim's minor children were murdered and their father successfully sued. In the same decision the court ruled that a therapist's failure to use reasonable care to protect a third party from harm constituted "professional negligence," rather than "ordinary negligence." This definition allows suits to be initiated for as long as three years after the injury occurred, rather than the usual one-year limitation (Butz, 1985, p. 87, citing *Hedlund* v. *Superior Court*, 1983, 669 P 2d 41). But the *Tarasoff* doctrine has not been accepted by all states. Some state courts (including those of Pennsylvania and Maryland) have not accepted this doctrine.

The *Tarasoff* doctrine, however, has made a wide impact on all helping professionals. Conte and colleagues (1989) report that 70 percent of their respondents believe that failure to warn a potential victim is grounds for a malpractice suit. Pope and colleagues (1987) found that 88 percent of their respondents consider it "unquestionably ethical" to break confidence when a homicidal client threatens to injure another person. But it must be noted that the California court did *not* establish an absolute duty to warn an intended victim. Warning is only one possible option, as a careful reading of the decision (cited above) suggests. Yet 90 percent of the psychiatrists surveyed by Givelber and colleagues (1984) thought that they had no choice and that it was their legal duty to do so. So do most social workers.

In recent years the "duty to warn" has been further explicated, but its practice applications still are not entirely clear. For example, more psychiatrists consult the American Psychiatric Association legal consultation service about the *Tarasoff* duty than any other issue (Egley, 1992). New decisions by various courts clarify some questions. Yet other important issues remain open, undecided, or ambiguous. Social workers must become aware of the current laws in their states. The duty to warn may be ill-defined in states where laws regulating professions do not define the *Tarasoff* duty. Some professions may receive the benefit of immunity from liability for breaches of confidentiality while others do not. Some state laws create legal confidentiality as a right of the client but do not provide liability waivers for mental health practitioners. There is no wide agreement on what is meant by "serious threat of physical violence," nor on the meaning of "intended" or "capable of being carried out." Different states vary in their requirements in regard to how the warning duty may be discharged: warning the potential victim or someone close to the victim, notifying the police, starting commitment proceedings, informing mental health evaluators of the nature of the threat. But each of the alternatives may present new ethical dilemmas. Reporting to the police, for example, may fulfill the duty to warn but the police may have different values in regard to the uses of this information (Egley, 1992).

Admittedly, the prediction of violence is not a "hard" science. Newhill (1992) in a review of the literature found that "...current empirical evidence suggests that certain characteristics are associated with a higher probability of violent behavior...." Nevertheless, "...the research concludes that mental health clinicians cannot definitively predict potential violence. However, short-term hospitalization or other interventions based on emergency assessments of dangerous states seem justified."

Certain ethical problems arise in regard to the *Tarasoff* duty, the answers to which are not readily found in the NASW *Code of Ethics*. A social worker should only reveal a confidence "for compelling professional reasons" (II, H, 1). Many but not all professionals would consider a threat to a third party "compelling" reason for taking action; yet, there remains much ambiguity about the definition of threats to injure. As Kopels and Kagle suggest:

> ...although the code of ethics supports a duty to third parties, it provides little guidance in deciding how to discharge these duties or how to balance obligations to clients with other social responsibilities. The code simply states that "the social worker's primary responsibility is to clients," and that social workers are also responsible for "promoting the general welfare of society" (Kopels and Kagle, 1993).

The *Tarasoff* decision has not only produced new ethical dilemmas but has also led to changes in practice and to new ways in which professional organizations deal with clients. Clients are now routinely informed about the limits of confidentiality and of informed consent in situations necessitating the prevention of violence. Some practitioners and agencies may avoid accepting potentially dangerous clients because of the possible liability problems which may arise. Some may not explore sufficiently issues of dangerous intent so that charges of negligence can be avoided when no stated specific threat was actually heard. Others have used mental hospitals for preventive detention, sometimes appropriately and at others inappropriately. Such "defensive" practices may be considered "safe" because they may help the social worker avoid legal problems, but are such practices ethical? Are there more ethical ways to comply with the *Tarasoff* duty?

Egley, as a result of his review of the *Tarasoff* decision and subsequent court rulings and legislation, concluded that legislatures offer a better opportunity to define the duty to warn than do the courts. Currently, there exists no statute or model law which provides a complete definition of all the components. The major question is whether or not social workers have a duty to protect the victims. Because there is so much activity in this area of the law, even social workers who practice in states where there is no clear precedent would be well advised to proceed as if they have such a duty (Egley, 1992; Kopels & Kagle, 1993).

But there are those who hold that the *Tarasoff* doctrine should not present social workers with any new ethical problems because the requirement to break confidentiality and warn the intended victim applies only in specific instances. When it does apply, the ethical decision screens provide clear guidance since the saving of human life from direct and immediate danger is a higher order ethical principle than confidentiality. The issue becomes problematic only when the risk to life is ambiguous. An example of this dilemma will be raised later, in Chapter 12 on social work with clients who have AIDS.

## EXERCISES

1.  Investigate the laws of your state (or of neighboring states or of your home state) concerning confidentiality, privileged communications, and the duty to warn, as they apply to social workers.
2.  Prepare a brief to be presented to your state legislature, urging that the privileged communication rule be extended to the client/social worker relationship and that it include group therapy, couple therapy, and family therapy.
3.  Divide the class into groups of two. In each small group have one person assume the role of the social worker, the other the role of an applicant who is seeking help for coping with an alcoholic mate. The specific task is for the social worker to inform the applicant/client of the limits of confidentiality. Try several different approaches and report to the class the one you think is most effective and best meets the demands of the *Code of Ethics*.
4.  Confidentiality is a first-order professional ethical principle to which all social workers are committed. Yet Halleck (1963) spoke of "the lie of confidentiality." What did he have in mind? Indicate in what ways you agree and/or disagree with his position.

5. Your agency is reviewing its policy on giving clients access to their case records. Almost all staff members agree to abide by the *Code of Ethics*, which states that "the social worker should afford clients reasonable access to any official social work records concerning them" (NASW, 1993, Paragraph H-3). But there is a sharp difference of opinion on how to define "reasonable access" and "official social work records." Try to define these two terms in ways that are congruent with both professional ethics and clients' rights. If there are differences of opinion in your class, try to convince the rest of the class of the correctness of your position.

## SUGGESTIONS FOR ADDITIONAL READINGS

Abramson (1989) reports on her research on ethical problems faced by social workers in protective services with the aged, especially on ethical dilemmas arising out of the conflict between autonomy and beneficence. Butz (1985) reviews the issues social workers face around reporting suspected child abuse and neglect. This problem is also discussed by Barksdale (1989).

The difficulties of observing confidentiality that face social workers in group psychotherapy are discussed by Roback, Purdon, Ochoa, and Bloch (1992). Lindenthal et al. (1988) provide a relevant hands-on article on managing problems of confidentiality in social work practice. Another approach appears in Schwartz (1989). Basic considerations and legal dilemmas for family therapists are analyzed by Watkins (1989). Basic considerations of the legal aspects of privileged communications are analyzed by Perlman (1988). VandeCreek et al. (1988) also discuss how social workers are covered by privileged communication statutes.

Egley (1992) reviews the legal evolution of the *Tarasoff* decision, the current status, ambiguities, and state of legislation nationwide. Kopels and Kagle (1993) explore whether social workers have a duty to protect third parties and, if so, how best to discharge this duty. Newhill (1992) summarizes the literature on defining and predicting dangerousness to others as well as correlates of violent behavior as they relate to clinical social work practice.

# 5. Client Rights and Professional Expertise

Social workers believe that every person has a right to make his or her own decisions. Veteran social worker Charlotte Towle noted that "the client's right to self-determination was one of the first, if not the first, of our beliefs to become a banner around which we rallied" (1965, p. 18). Similarly the NASW *Code of Ethics* states, "The social worker should make every effort to foster maximum self-determination on the part of clients" (1993, Paragraph II-G). This rule seems clear and unambiguous. But there is also an ethical rule which requires that social work practice be based on professional knowledge, professional values, and professional skills. Social workers are obligated to utilize these when asked to provide professional help. The *Code of Ethics* states, "The social worker should serve clients with...the maximum application of professional skill and competence" (NASW, 1993, Paragraph F-1). These two ethical rules may at times conflict and thus create a serious ethical dilemma for the social worker who tries to abide by both.

At one time this ethical problem was less severe because there was a great deal of uncertainty about the adequacy of social work knowledge and about the effectiveness of social work intervention. In more recent years, studies by Reid and Hanrahan (1982), Thomlison (1984), Rubin (1985), and others have shown that the application of professional knowledge and appropriate professional skills does result in positive client outcomes. The practice problem with potentially critical ethical implications is how to combine client self-determination with the use of professional knowledge and skill. Is it ethical for a social worker to refrain from using professional knowledge if the client chooses an option with which the social worker cannot concur? The practitioner's ability to help will be severely limited when the client makes decisions that are contrary to the strategy suggested on the basis of professional knowledge. The social worker may know what strategy will best achieve the objectives that the client has chosen, but is it ethical for the social worker to implement this more effective strategy when the client prefers another? Or the social worker may understand what it is that the client needs or wants even before the client is aware of this. Again the ethical question arises: May the social worker follow the strategy suggested by her knowledge and insight when the client has made another, less beneficial decision, based on ignorance or partial knowledge?

Some social workers do not hesitate to give priority to their professional knowledge and skill even when this means ignoring a client's input. Halmos observed that a therapist cannot be helpful "unless we mean therapy to be therapeutic and, therefore, determining and directing in important ways" (1965, p. 92). This view follows the tradition that professionals "profess to know better than...their clients what ails them..." (Hughes, 1965, p. 2). But others hold that a social worker should never make decisions for a client, even if the client's decision does not seem congruent with the worker's understanding. This position is based on a number of principles, including (1) the primacy of the client self-determination rule, (2) the philosophical principle that no one can change a person but that person himself or herself, and (3) the practice principle that change efforts without the participation of the person to be changed will not be effective.

Often a social worker can follow the best of practice knowledge and professional skills and still fully respect a client's right to self-determination. One of the reasons for this is that social workers believe not only in the right but also in the therapeutic effectiveness of client participation in all phases of the social work process. They have moved a long way from the traditionally negative attitude toward clients, such as the one expressed by the 1847 *Code of Ethics* of the American Medical Association, which declared that professionals have "a right to expect and require that their patients should entertain a just sense of duties which they owe to their medical attendants." Early social workers may not have been as blatant in their public statements, but they too expected that clients follow their good advice without too many questions.

The conflict between client self-determination and the worker's use of her professional knowledge and skills need not result from any

Machiavellian desires. Even when a social worker cares about her client's interests and rights, this ethical problem becomes a critical one in many practice situations.

## WHO IS THE CLIENT?

The question "Who is the client?" may be the source of several ethical dilemmas. Traditionally, a client was defined as the person(s) who engaged the practitioner and paid her a fee. Alternately, the client is the person (or the system) whose behavior is to be modified or changed by the professional's intervention. However, most social workers are employed by an organization, such as a social agency, a department of government, or an institution. According to the first definition, the organization that pays the social worker's salary should be considered the client. But is the school really the client of the school social worker? Is the prison the client of the correctional social worker? Nowadays the traditional definition may be too narrow since it was originally devised for clients of the "free" practitioner in private practice.

The alternate definition also is problematic since it is not always correct to say that the client is the person or system whose behavior needs to be changed. Often social work intervention involves changes in systems other than the client system. When a social worker helps a recently widowed woman complete an application for Social Security benefits, the worker does not intend to change the widow, but instead helps the client to change her environment. Until not too long ago a physician was certain that the sick person who came to his office was his patient, just as the social worker automatically considered the person(s) who applied for help as her client(s). Today neither physician nor social worker is certain that the answer to the question "Who is the client?" is quite so simple, as the following exemplars illustrate.

➤ **5.1 Arlene Johnson's Abortion**

Arlene Johnson, eighteen years old and single, is nearly six months pregnant. Yesterday she came to the Women's Counseling Center to request help in getting an abortion. Because of the advanced phase of pregnancy, intake was reduced to a minimum and Ms. Johnson was referred almost immediately to Community Hospital.

The abortion was performed within twenty-four hours after Ms. Johnson contacted the Center. At the time of delivery the fetus was considered viable and was placed in the neonatal intensive care unit as a high-risk premature baby.

Arlene was most upset when she learned that the "abortion" had resulted in a live infant. She refused to look at the baby or take care of it.

Instead, she threatened to sue the doctor and the hospital if the infant survived despite her expressed wish for an abortion.

Arlene asked Robin Osborn, the hospital social worker, to make sure that the baby not be given intensive care, but rather be left alone so that it would die quickly.

Who is Robin Osborn's client? Arlene Johnson? The premature infant? Or who? Whose interests should be accorded priority? The next exemplar is entirely different, but raises some of the same questions.

### ➤ 5.2 Mrs. Linden's Classroom

Mrs. Linden is a fifth-grade teacher in the Abraham Lincoln Elementary School. The school is located in a neighborhood into which a large number of Central American families moved recently. Mrs. Ramirez is the social worker assigned to this school.

Yesterday Mrs. Linden asked Mrs. Ramirez for help in keeping her pupils quietly in their seats. She told Mrs. Ramirez that never in her twenty years as a teacher has she had as much trouble as this year. She thought that her troubles were caused by the many children who recently transferred from foreign schools. Surely Mrs. Ramirez could advise her how to handle these children so that they would be quiet and stay in their seats.

Again, who is the client? Mrs. Linden? The pupils? Their parents? The school? Whose interests should be accorded priority? The two problem situations seem quite different, but in each case the expectations of the applicant for service create for the social worker a dilemma that has ethical implications. Arlene Johnson does not want to have a baby, but once a live infant had been born, her expectations of the obstetrician (and later of the social worker) conflict sharply with the rights of the infant and with what society expects from these professionals. Similarly, Mrs. Linden's expectations are different from those of her students. Both teacher and students (and their parents) have differing expectations from Mrs. Ramirez. The social worker in this instance is not at all sure that the problem is with the pupils; perhaps the teacher is the real problem.

One of the reasons why the "Who is the client?" question causes so many ethical dilemmas is that the question itself is based on an oversimplified and not entirely accurate model of the professional relationship. The traditional model included only the practitioner and the client. But an updated model should include the applicant, client, target, beneficiary, practitioner, agency, community, and others. Each of the four positions noted in Figure 5.1 can be occupied by one or more persons or institutions. Sometimes one person is the applicant, as well as the client, target, and beneficiary. At other times or in other situations, different persons occupy each of these positions. The applicant may not be the client and the

---

**Figure 5.1   Some Participants in the Social Work Process**

APPLICANT   The person(s) or system that requests help with a defined or felt problem.

CLIENT   The applicant who enters into a formal, contractual, goal-focused relationship with the social worker.

TARGET   The person(s) or system that must be modified in order to achieve the desired outcome to which client and worker have agreed.

BENEFICIARY   The person(s) or system that will benefit from successful goal achievement.

---

client need not be the target, nor is the client necessarily the beneficiary of the intervention. When these positions or roles are occupied by different persons, we can be almost certain that each one will have a slightly different expectation from the social worker—and often these differing expectations are in conflict, thus creating an ethical dilemma for the social worker. Whose expectations should receive priority attention? Arlene Johnson and Mrs. Linden are the applicants, but Robin Osborn, the hospital social worker, and Joan Ramirez, the school social worker, face dilemmas around the question of identifying the primary client, target, and beneficiary. But who is the applicant and who the client in the Pomer case, which we shall soon consider (Exemplar 5.3)? Is the "welfare" of Eleanor's brothers and sisters less important (or more important) than Eleanor's welfare? To whom does each of these social workers have a primary ethical obligation? These are practice dilemmas that also involve ethical issues because they are based on conflicting value assumptions.

Social workers who engage in genetic counseling are constantly faced by difficult problems that involve ethical issues. Modern medical procedures, such as the amniocentesis test, make it possible to detect as many as sixty different genetic disorders (including Down's syndrome and Tay-Sachs disease) as early as the fourteenth week of pregnancy. When there are positive findings, the social worker must help parents think through all of the implications so that they can make a wise decision. However, some physicians expect the social worker to persuade the pregnant mother to abort whenever there are indications of a genetically defective fetus. Should the best interest of the as-yet-unborn child play a part in the decision? What is the best interest? Should the social worker stress arguments in favor of abortion, even if it is evident that the parents do not want to terminate this pregnancy? What is the ethical stance that the social worker should adopt? A different ethical dilemma occurs when relatives want access to genetic information that may be of importance to their health or to the future of their children. When the welfare of other people is at risk, does their right to such information take precedence over your client's right to privacy?

Social workers in the criminal justice system face similar ethical issues. In the probation service social workers regularly prepare reports for the juvenile court judge. The judge takes these reports into consideration when making a final disposition of the case. The ethical dilemma here is that the social worker is both helper and judicial fact finder. The client/worker helping relationship starts during the very first contact with the juvenile, long before the social worker has completed her evaluative assessment or presented her report to the judge. From an ethical point of view, to whom does the social worker owe priority consideration, to the juvenile detainee or to the judge—Who is the client? Note that often the ethical issues may not coincide with the legal issues.

## SELF-DETERMINATION

Immanuel Kant, one of the early giants of modern philosophy, insisted that a person's right to determine his or her own destiny is an unconditional right. In his theory, persons are viewed as ends in themselves and are never treated as means. Self-determination is also a first-order principle in American society. Though not specifically enumerated in the Constitution, the Supreme Court in a series of due-process cases, equal protection cases, and, more recently, privacy cases, has developed the position that self-determination is a fundamental right that is protected by the Ninth and Fourteenth Amendments (Jordan, 1985).

A person's right to make his or her own decisions is the source for the social work value of self-determination. Self-determination is an absolute right, yet most social workers would agree with Rothman (1989) that when used as a practice principle, its application is limited. Bernstein (1960) writes that self-determination is "not supreme, but supremely important," while Perlman (1965) suggests that self-determination, though important, is nine-tenths illusion. No wonder that Rothman states "self-determination is accorded utmost esteem in the profession [but] its meaning and application are clouded" (1989, p. 598). The right of self-determination has become the source for "one of the most common and most perplexing dilemmas for social workers" (Abramson, 1985, p. 387). How can a practitioner respect and uphold client self-determination when working with a client whose conception of what is good for him or her differs from that of the social worker?

These ethical dilemmas become more frequent and increasingly perplexing as more and more major decisions about life involve highly technical and specialized considerations that often are beyond the comprehension of lay people. Reliance on professionals who have the necessary expertise has become increasingly common. Under these circumstances directiveness as a helping technique seems to have become more acceptable. But the more frequent use of directive methods raises many ethical questions, such as whether the results achieved by a social worker are more important than the methods used. Should a client be pressured into doing things he does not want to do even when his worker is certain that this will contribute to solving or reducing his problem? Is it ethical for a social worker to deceive a client in order to have him participate in a technique that he would reject if he knew all the facts?

The ethical dilemma arises out of a conflict between two principles: (1) the self-determination or autonomy principle that states that the person most affected by a decision should make that decision, and (2) the benefit principle that posits that the professional social worker has the knowledge and skill necessary to best assure a positive outcome and is, therefore, responsible for making the decision that will secure the optimum benefit for the client.

Some do not hesitate to use their superior professional knowledge and power to move the client in the "right" direction. Thus Gillis writes that "all modern psychotherapists, whether they know it or not, engage in maneuvers and manipulations that add to their power over the patient" (1974, p. 91). Dworkin (1985) adds that control of the client by the worker occurs in all professional relationships, no matter what theoretical framework is utilized. Usually this control is not manifest but occurs in an implicit or unconscious way; Dworkin suggests that it would be better if this control were acknowledged and exercised on a systematic and explicit basis.

*Control* and *manipulation* are concepts that social workers once avoided but which in recent years have entered into the professional vocabulary. This has forced social workers to reassess the meaning and practice of client self-determination. Several years ago Glasser wrote that "self-determination [has] been misinterpreted in many ways that were never intended. As now used [it leads] to practice that at best is not helpful to our clients and at worst can be quite harmful to them" (1984, p. 8).

What are the ethical considerations that should guide a social worker who is convinced that an older adult client (who can no longer cope alone at home) should enter a home for the aged very soon, but who knows from past experience with this client that every worker suggestion elicits a "no" response? If this client has close relatives, should they be asked to make the decision? If there are no close relatives, should the worker make the decision without fully involving the client? Or is it more ethical to involve the client, but frame the choice in such a way that there is no opportunity to say "no"? For example, the client might be asked whether he prefers to enter the East Side Home or the West Side Home? Or he might be asked whether he wants the intake worker from the Home to come to his apartment or prefers that the social worker drive him to the Home for the intake interview? Or must this social worker respect the client's "no," even though she knows that this client can no longer live alone?

Stereotypes should never be used to limit client self-determination. There is some evidence that class-related or age-related criteria are sometimes used to assess the capacity of different client groups to make autonomous decisions. Those who work with aged clients are very much aware of this problem, but this ethical quandary is not limited to the aged. Freedberg (1989) cites as an example an "expert's opinion" that a majority of lower-class unmarried mothers "are incapable of making their own decisions" and therefore should not be expected to make autonomous decisions.

A somewhat different situation, involving both the problem of "Who is the client?" and the problem of self-determination is illustrated in the following illustrative case situation:

### ➤ 5.3 Should Eleanor Pomer Come Home?

Eleanor Pomer is eight years old, the youngest of six siblings. She has been a resident in a special school for the last three years because of a diagnosis of Down's syndrome. According to her cottage parents, psychologist, teacher, and social worker, she functions on a moderately retarded level.

Both of Eleanor's parents are employed. They rent the downstairs apartment of a two-family home in a working-class neighborhood, about one hour's drive from Eleanor's school. The Pomers visit Eleanor once a month. For the past year Eleanor has also spent one weekend a month at home. Eleanor's home visits have been successful. Both Eleanor and her family look forward to these monthly visits.

The school's staff feels that Eleanor now is ready to leave the school and live again at home. The social worker has acquainted Eleanor's parents with this staff assessment, has told them about the community resources which are available in their city, and has urged them to take Eleanor home. However, the Pomers do not agree with this recommendation. They are satisfied with the present arrangement; they feel that it would be too much of a strain on their other children if Eleanor again lived at home.

The social worker is convinced that it would be best for Eleanor to leave the school and resume a more normal home life. Eleanor is excited about the possibility of again living with her parents and brothers and sisters. The ethical problem in this situation arises out of the conflict between applying professional knowledge and respecting the client's right to make decisions. How much weight must the social worker give to the Pomers' wishes? To Eleanor's wish? Should the most important criterion in reaching a decision be what is best for Eleanor? Who decides what is best for Eleanor? What about the welfare of the other Pomer children? Does the social worker have an ethical right to manipulate the environment (for example, by raising the tuition fee) in order to "help" the Pomers reach the decision which staff thinks is best for Eleanor?

Another basic ethical dilemma in social work practice arises out of two, at times contradictory, professional principles that all social workers have accepted. These are (1) the principle to provide professional help when needed or requested by a client in order to assure or improve that person's welfare, and (2) the principle not to interfere with a person's freedom. These two professional principles are almost identical with Gewirth's basic or generic rights of "well-being" and "freedom" (1978, p. 64). Ideally, a social worker should not experience any conflict between these two rights (or principles). But what if a person's well-being can be achieved only at the expense of his or her freedom? Who defines well-being? Who defines the need for professional help? Who can legitimately request professional help for another person?

Unless there are serious indications to the contrary, no social worker will want to interfere with another person's freedom, even if that person is her client. Some go so far as to declare that every person should have "the freedom to make a shamble of his life" (Miller, 1968, p. 30). But there are occasions when intervention becomes necessary even if it is at the expense of freedom. Most people agree that a person's right to self-determination should be limited when its exercise will result in harm to another person, but what if the harm is only to the person himself or herself? It may be that too much attention to freedom and autonomous decision making in situations where the client faces an immediate danger may be a cop-out for the social worker's inactivity. Coercive intervention may be justified when (1) there is a grave threat to basic social values or to fundamental social institutions or (2) when there is a clear and present danger that very great or irreversible harm will be done or will occur unless prompt preventative action is taken. This is why Abramson suggests that "paternalism takes precedence over autonomy" whenever the value of client autonomy comes into conflict with the value of securing a client's safety (1989, p. 105).

Though the conditions which justify coercive intervention seem clear, a social worker who tries to follow them will discover many ambiguities. What is *clear and present danger*? How can it be demonstrated? When is harm sufficiently grave to warrant coercion? Who may coerce? How certain must the social worker be that her intervention will prevent the harm before she is justified in curtailing a person's freedom? Is it ethical for a social worker to initiate involuntary commitment procedures for a mentally ill person if that person's chances for recovery will be only slightly better (but not very great) in an institution than if he were to remain in the community? How much better must be the chances before the social worker can proceed? Is this ethical problem the same when the client is a teenage drug addict or an incontinent older person?

An additional dimension of this ethical problem arises from the social worker's obligation to do more than merely observe the negative injunction of not interfering with a person's freedom. This obligation demands positive action designed to strengthen or promote the client's freedom. If promoting and not interfering with a client's freedom is to be more than empty rhetoric, social workers must understand that a person is truly autonomous only when all of the following conditions prevail:

1. The environment provides more than one option from which a person can make choices.
2. There is no coercion on the person from any source to choose one or another option.
3. The person is aware of all the available options.
4. The person has accurate information about the cost and consequences of each option so that he can assess them realistically.
5. The person has the capacity and/or initiative to make a decision on the basis of this assessment.
6. The person has an opportunity to act on the basis of his or her choice.

No extensive research is needed to discover that the freedom of most social work clients is quite limited. Though these limitations usually do not result from practitioner activities, social workers must be concerned when anybody's freedom is limited. Americans enjoy more freedom than the residents of many other countries, but the structural conditions of most contemporary societies (especially those conditions that reinforce inequality, racism, sexism, and ageism) limit some of the freedom of most people. Social workers are committed to use their professional skill and know-how to help all people gain full freedom. This ethical commitment may explain why many social workers have been in the forefront of those struggling for more freedom and greater equality for all people. But this ethical concern for greater autonomy must also find expression in the day-by-day practice of social workers.

Access to self-determination also varies with the dependency of the client on the benefits he receives from his social worker. The more valuable the goods or services received, the greater the client's feelings of dependency on the worker and the less likely it is that he will choose an option which he believes his social worker will disapprove. In one study it was found that clients who received only "talking" goods (such as advice and discussion) felt relatively free to reject their workers' advice, while others who had received cards from their workers that made them eligible for medical treatment felt much more dependent on their workers and no longer felt free to reject their advice (Handler & Hollingsworth, 1971).

The limited knowledge and/or capacity of many clients to engage in autonomous decision making places a particular ethical obligation on the social worker to help them make a reasoned choice so that they can maximize their benefits. Yet in the final analysis the center of gravity in the helping process remains with the professional. Or as Rothman stated, "The prime responsibility for making professional decisions about means of helping the client falls to the practitioners" (1989, p. 608).

## AMBIGUITY AND UNCERTAINTY

Professional decisions about client rights (self-determination, as well as other rights) would cause fewer ethical problems and dilemmas if there were less ambiguity and uncertainty. Three types of ambiguity and uncertainty make for ethical problems in social work practice. These are (1) uncertainty about values and goals, (2) uncertainty about scientific knowledge and about the facts relevant to any specific situation, and (3) uncertainty about the consequences of the intervention.

These uncertainties occur in a world characterized by a general disillusionment with authority. The infallible guides and granite virtues of yesteryear have been discarded like last season's fashions. Even faith in science and progress, characteristic of the belief system of previous generations, has moved from center stage and has been replaced by a pervasive sense of uncertainty. For many, the pursuit of personal happiness and individual fulfillment has become more important than following any established ethical imperatives. It has become more and more difficult to know what is right. As a result, some have suggested that right is whatever one thinks is good. But even those who accept this approach find that they must cope with ambiguity and uncertainty, like their colleagues who are still searching for ethical imperatives relevant in modern society.

Ambiguity may be more critical a problem for social workers than for many other professional practitioners. The reasons for this include the following:

1. The issues with which social workers deal are often nonspecific and vague.
2. Social work does not offer its practitioners the same comprehensive knowledge base that many of the more established professions have been able to provide.
3. Social workers generally have less control over the outcome of their intervention than do practitioners in some other professional fields.

So many different factors impinge simultaneously on a person that it is often difficult for a social worker to assess the specific impact of her intervention. An unsuccessful outcome may be (but need not be) due to something that the social worker did or did not do. The same intervention activity in two seemingly identical problem situations may lead to two entirely different outcomes because of factors over which the social worker has no control. Nor will a social worker ever know what might have happened had she not intervened or had she utilized a different strategy.

For example, in a case of suspected child abuse, a social worker cannot predict with certainty what will happen if the child continues to stay with his parents, nor will the worker know for certain what might happen if the child is forcibly removed. Similarly, no social worker can predict with any accuracy whether helping a neighborhood council obtain a grant for restoring dilapidated houses is the best or the worst help that she can offer.

One such situation with many ambiguities is explored in the next exemplar.

➤ **5.4  A Victim of Child Abuse**

Several months ago Ms. Gillis told her public welfare social worker that she suspected that an upstairs neighbor, Mr. Hill, regularly and brutally beat his two-year-old son, Leroy. She heard the most frightful noises several evenings each week. When she saw the boy at rare intervals, he always wore bandages and looked so sad. The worker noted these remarks in her case report, but took no further action.

Last month Mrs. Hill brought Leroy to Lakeside General Hospital emergency room. Leroy suffered from multiple fractures which, according to his mother, occurred when he fell down the front stairs. The attending physician did not believe her story since the X-ray revealed a large number of previous fractures in addition to the current ones. As required by law, he notified the public welfare department that he suspected child abuse.

André Conti, an experienced child protection social worker, was sent to the Hill home to investigate. He talked at length with both parents. They admitted beating Leroy occasionally when he misbehaved. This, they explained, was their way of disciplining him. Conti suggested that there were other ways to teach a boy to behave properly. But he concluded that the boy was in no immediate danger. Two weeks later, another social work-er made a follow-up visit to the Hill home. This worker, Millie Walker, agreed with Mr. Conti's assessment that for the time being there was no need to re-move Leroy from his home.

Ten days after Ms. Walker's visit, Mrs. Hill called for an emergency ambulance, saying that her son was having difficulty breathing. When the ambulance crew arrived, they found Leroy unconscious. Twelve hours after he was brought to the hospital, he was pronounced dead. He had not re-covered consciousness. The postmortem confirmed that death was caused by a severe beating with a blunt instrument.

This exemplar gives rise to a number of questions with ethical im-plications, including the following: Did Ms. Gillis's social worker pay sufficient attention to the report of child abuse? Are a neighbor's suspicions sufficient cause to warrant interfering in the Hill family? How can Mr. Conti or any social worker know for certain that "a clear and present danger" exists for Leroy's life? When does parental disci-pline become child abuse? Under what conditions is the removal of a child from his family justified? How certain must a social worker be of the consequences before deciding to leave an endangered child with his family?

It should be noted that there are two sets of ambiguities in the Leroy Hill exemplar: (1) ambiguities resulting from a lack of clarity of societal norms (e.g., What are the limits of parental discipline?) and (2) ambigu-ities resulting from a lack of knowledge (e.g., What evidence is sufficient to warrant intervention? What will be the consequences of intervention?). The social workers involved in this case made professional judgments that Leroy was not "at risk." As a consequence of their mistaken judg-ment, Leroy is now dead. But the mistake could also have gone the other way—identifying a risk when there is no danger to the child's welfare and thus removing the boy from his home needlessly. Every social work-er in this situation faces a critical ethical dilemma since both types of mistakes cannot be avoided at the same time. Ambiguities and uncer-tainties are endemic conditions in social work practice. The test of an effective social worker is that she should retain the ability to function even while coping with the ethical dilemmas that result from ambiguity and uncertainty.

## EXERCISES

1. Role play the situation described earlier in this chapter where the social worker has determined that her older adult client is no longer able to live alone in his home. We know that this client

responds negatively to every worker suggestion. Try various approaches to this problem situation. Keep in mind the ethical aspects!

2. Rothman (1989) and others have stated that the primary responsibility for making professional decisions falls on the social work practitioner. On the other hand, many social workers argue that the client has the exclusive right to make decisions about his life. Organize a debate around these two professional positions.

3. Assume that you are the child protection social worker sent to investigate the report of Leroy Hill's abuse (Exemplar 5.4). What criteria would you use to arrive at a decision to remove or not to remove Leroy from his parental home? Keep in mind the ethical aspects!

## SUGGESTIONS FOR ADDITIONAL READINGS

Abramson (1985, 1989) analyzes the dilemma of social workers who face at one and the same time both the autonomy rule and the beneficence rule—How can a social worker encourage client self-determination and at the same time take full responsibility for delivering the professional services that the client needs? Another aspect of this ethical problem is examined by Kapp (1988).

Freedberg (1989) and Rothman (1989) review the development of the self-determination principle in social work practice and its impact on practitioners. Weick and Pope (1988) also raise important questions about the self-determination rule. Bernstein (1993) explores self-determination in group practice.

A thoughtful analysis of the place of power in the social work relationship is presented by Hasenfeld (1987). Szaz (1986) raises troubling questions about the ethics of professional intervention in suicide prevention. Schild and Black (1984) discuss the ethical dilemmas faced by social work practitioners in genetic counseling.

# 6. Value Neutrality and Imposing Values

The separation of objective facts from subjective values is a basic characteristic of modern society. The "good" is no longer an absolute value; it is rather something relative that cannot be derived from objective data but only from subjective information. Scientists try to avoid all questions of values and morals because they attempt to derive knowledge only from empirical facts. Similarly, professional practitioners who aim to base their practice on scientific principles try to avoid values. Though the *Code of Ethics* does not contain a specific provision which requires professionals to suspend value judgments, one of the traditional expectations is that practitioners do not impose their personal values on clients and that they suspend judgment about clients' behavior and actions even when their own values or societal values demand a judgment.

But in the real world of social work practice, things are not always so simple. Crucial professional decisions always involve value choices—if not worker values, then values of clients or of society. Professional decisions "are not simple choices of technical means to ends, and even choices of means have a value component" (Bayles, 1981, p. 67).

## VALUE NEUTRALITY

The practice principle of value neutrality has found wide acceptance among social workers. Thus Siporin notes that "a value-free science, especially a value-free social science, has been an ideal model for social workers" (1975, p. 63). This principle is encountered repeatedly in the professional literature. For example, one writer urged social workers who work with pregnant teenagers to maintain a neutral position about the girls' behavior if the workers want to be really helpful (Cain, 1979). One reason for suspending value judgments, according to many, is that in our pluralistic society there is no longer any absolute *right* or *wrong*. What might seem wrong to me will seem right to the next person. What is right today may be wrong tomorrow.

Yet there are critical questions about this value-neutral stance that must be considered. Many have asked whether value neutrality or value suspension is a realistic option for social workers. They point out that social workers are human beings, not robots. What are they to do with the values they hold when working with clients who hold contrary values? Can they really avoid imposing their own values by either subtle or non-verbal communications?

There are no easy answers to these questions, yet they need to be considered by every practitioner. *Suspension of judgment,* a basic concept in social work, has in the opinion of many been so misinterpreted that it has caused rather than prevented much unethical professional behavior. Siporin writes that "in being of help to people, there is need to make moral ethical judgments, and to help clients do so as well" (1985b, p. 202). Value neutrality may actually be causing damage. Rhodes suggests that "the idea of value-free counseling is impossible and dangerous" (1986, p. 87). Siporin adds, "The inability to make moral discriminations and decisions is evident in the increased difficulty that many social workers have in distinguishing between what is functional or dysfunctional, normative or pathological behavior" (1985a, p. 5). Siporin concludes, "The assessment, planning, and intervention processes of social work therapy are centrally and necessarily concerned with moral/ethical issues" (1985b, p. 202). Maslow indicates that a science that is "morally neutral, value free, value neutral is not only wrong, but extremely dangerous" (1969, p. 724). When a social worker does not challenge a client's behavior, that client may think that she approves of what he does. The worker may intend her silence to be an expression of value neutrality, but in fact her silence may signal acceptance of that behavior!

Value neutrality is itself a value. Social work has "a kind of de facto ideology—one that is insidious because [it is] unacknowledged, one that permits moralistic judgments by the very caseworker who eschews 'judgmentalism'" (Salomon, 1967, p. 30). The contemporary social worker who bases her practice on value neutrality may judge a compulsively tidy housewife as critically as her colleague a hundred years earlier judged a slovenly one.

Two studies of Carl Rogers' nondirective psychotherapy concluded that a value-free therapy is not possible. In his earlier years Rogers placed supreme value on client freedom and gave priority to promoting each client's self-actualization. However, these studies show that unknowingly he systematically rewarded or punished client verbal expressions according to whether he agreed or disagreed with them. His own values significantly regulated the structure, content, and outcome of the therapeutic sessions that were analyzed (Murray, 1956; Truax, 1966). Rogers himself became aware of this and modified his psychotherapeutic methods at a later date.

The notion that social workers not only are judgmental but must be so received its strongest support from Pilseker, who writes that "social workers cannot be nonjudgmental and they should not attempt to be so. They are merchants of morality and should acknowledge this fact openly..." (1978, p. 55). Value suspension became a professional characteristic in response to the moralistic paternalism of the Friendly Visitors, the volunteers who preceded professional social workers in the last decades of the nineteenth century. Originally suspension of judgment meant that the social worker related to the whole person and to his strengths, instead of only to his weaknesses and problems. It meant trying to understand this person in terms of his personal history, environment, culture, and community. If the client's behavior was problematic, then the social worker was ready to help him change that behavior without condemning him. This was often expressed by, "I accept you, but not your behavior." More recently this stance has been changed so that now many social workers seem to say, "I love you and your behavior, no matter what you have done." But can we honestly say that we do not care what a client does? Can we accept cheating, stealing, or lying? Dare social workers *not* condemn physical and sexual abuse, rape and beatings, irresponsible sexual activities, and similar antisocial behaviors?

## IMPOSING VALUES

Much of what social workers do involves helping people choose between available options; ethical principles are one important consideration in this choice. How can a social worker provide this help without imposing her values? This question takes on special urgency because social workers often grapple with strategies that are designed to modify or change the beliefs and values of clients.

Some approaches to helping people with problems hold that it is desirable to systematically change their values, especially their irrational beliefs, and substitute for these more sensible and more rational values, such as those held by social workers. The rational/emotive therapy developed by Ellis is one school of therapy that urges this view. The therapist's values always influence client values. Those following this school suggest that these values be used in a conscious and controlled manner (Ellis, 1974; Frank, 1974). But many others disagree with this approach.

A social worker may actually impose her own values when she tries to "suspend" value judgments and offer instead a range of value choices. Covert value messages are often more powerful than overt ones. A social worker may define the goals and outcomes of the treatment without once saying what it is that she deems appropriate. How can one ethically justify such unilateral worker control? Some have suggested that an explicit communication of the social worker's values would safeguard the client against any potential misuse of power by the worker (Lewis & Walsh, 1980). Such self-disclosure of the worker's values may enhance the client's comfort with and sense of trust in the practitioner. But value self-disclosure may also be harmful when used inappropriately or at the wrong time (Anderson & Mandell, 1989), Spero (1990), who considered the advantages and disadvantages of value disclosures, concludes that there are short-term advantages, but that these may be canceled by long-term harmful effects.

The problem facing the social worker of Bess and Todd Moore illustrates the range of ethical dilemmas around the issue of imposing values.

### ➤ 6.1 Saving a Marriage

Bess and Todd Moore have agreed to seek help to "rescue" their marriage. Bess recently discovered that Todd has been having sex with several women over the past few years. Todd has told the social worker that his sexual relations with other women are only physical. Since he has greater sexual needs than Bess, he cannot give up these relations. Yet he loves his wife and wants to continue this marriage.

Bess is ready to forgive the past, but cannot bring herself to live with Todd, knowing that at the same time he has sex with other women.

Different social workers hold different values about marriage and extramarital relations. Should the social worker keep her own values to herself so that she will not influence the decision of the Moores? Is this possible? Or should the social worker openly state her own values and then let Bess and Todd work on a solution of their problem? Which is the more ethical approach?

Do social workers have a responsibility to examine together with the client the ethical nature and quality of the problems which people bring to them? Or do they help, while overlooking the moral aspects of the situation? The following exemplar raises these ethical questions in a relatively uncharged setting.

➤ **6.2 A Smoking Lounge for High School Students**

Kate Collins is a school social worker. She is a member of the student-faculty council which recommends policy in the local high school. At a recent meeting several student members proposed setting up a "smoking lounge" to eliminate the safety hazard of students' smoking illegally in the bathrooms and in the locker rooms.

Kate is convinced that smoking is extremely dangerous to one's health. Her reading on the subject has led her to the conclusion that it is most important to discourage young people from smoking. But she also knows that as a professional she must not impose her values on others.

How can she be a party to a recommendation that she considers harmful? But how can she let her values interfere with democratic and autonomous decision making?

Some think that smoking, although injurious, is not immoral, yet they condemn suicide because they believe it to be highly immoral. What are the ethical implications for a social worker who believes suicide to be immoral when she is assigned to a committee charged with preparing a guide to help people commit suicide? Would it make an ethical difference if the distribution of this pamphlet were to be limited to persons with a terminal illness?

Society, with near unanimity, condemns incest. Yet the number of incidents of incestual relationships that come to the attention of social workers is on the rise. This may be due to the fact that nowadays people feel freer to talk about all types of sexual activities, including incest, or it may reflect an actual increase in cases of incest. Many ethical questions face a social worker who receives information about incest. Should she assume a value-free stance and listen to her client's report of incestuous behavior with the same equanimity as she would to any other problem he may raise? Should she communicate the community's valuation of incest? Does it make a difference whether the abuser or the victim is the worker's client? Are there cultural factors which might make a difference in assessing the ethical implications of this type of behavior? What if the client's ethnic culture does not proscribe father/daughter relations which do not involve penetration? What if the incestuous relations occur between consenting adults?

The three types of "deviant" behavior that have been discussed in this section form a matrix of ethical intensity. The discussion suggests that beyond a certain point almost every social worker will abandon any attempt to maintain a value-free stance. But the ethical dilemma is more serious than these "unusual" examples suggest because, in fact, ethical quandaries involving the social worker's judgment occur at every step of the social work process. The social worker who "suspends" her judgment when a client relates a promiscuous episode or an aggressive behavior incident may be as judgmental as her colleague who does not hesitate to indicate disapproval. When a client feels guilty about a certain behavior but the worker addresses only the problem of guilt, the client may conclude that the worker considers such behavior acceptable.

It has been suggested that in these and similar situations a social worker can avoid making judgments by letting the client decide what he wants—whether he wants help with his "guilt" or with the "deviant" behavior. At first glance this appeal to the principle of client self-determination seems to solve all ethical problems. But on second thought it may turn out that this is an irresponsible and perhaps even an unethical response to a client who desperately seeks help. Even when the client's request for help is specific, the worker may have a societal responsibility that she dare not shirk. Should a social worker help a client reduce his guilt so that he can continue to enjoy an incestuous relationship with his teenage daughter?

It seems that suspension of judgment is an impossible demand. Some have tried to avoid the ethical dilemma by suggesting to a client that they disapprove only of a specific behavior, but not of the client. This is a fine, almost legalistic distinction which may seem to avoid the ethical issues posed here. But such a solution creates other practice problems and does not really avoid the ethical issues raised. Perhaps a more realistic way of phrasing this ethical obligation is to demand that the social worker's own value judgment never become the sole criterion for making a decision. There is no relationship that is free of values. At the same time we must remember that in the final analysis, it is the client's responsibility to identify the values that will guide his behavioral choices; the social worker can never assume this responsibility (Frankl, 1968).

## CLIENT/WORKER VALUE GAP

A significant gap between worker values and those of a large proportion of social work clients is characteristic of many settings in which social work is practiced. This gap is another potential source for several ethical problems and dilemmas. A major discrepancy between the religious beliefs and practices of many clients and the nonreligious values held by many mental health professionals has been noted by Siporin and Glasser

(1986) and Loewenberg (1988). This gap in religious values is only one area of value discrepancy, reflective of the discrepancies that exist in many other value areas.

Shared values may optimize the chances for successful outcomes. Goldstein writes that "the initiation of any substantial relationship (including the helping relationship) depends on the extent to which its members can share, complement, or otherwise resolve their moral differences" (1987, p. 181). Though matching of client and worker values may be desirable, this is not always possible in the world of practice. Various problems can arise when there is a significant client/worker gap, but here our concern will be limited to the ethical aspects of these problems. These relate primarily to the possibility of value imposition when there is a major difference between client and worker values. Because of the power imbalance between client and worker, this ethical problem is often very real.

Typical of the client/worker gap is the following exemplar.

➤ **6.3  A Drug Addict Has a Baby**

Jeff Butz, public welfare worker, received a call from the Community Hospital social worker. Mona Koss, a single mother and a known drug addict, gave birth to a baby girl two days ago. Mother and baby are due to be discharged tomorrow, but the hospital social worker does not think that the infant will be safe if she goes "home" with her mother. As far as is known, Mona Koss has no permanent home. Currently she shares a bed with a drug pusher who has been involved in the past in physical and sexual abuse situations.

The world of Jeff Butz is as far from Mona Koss's world as the North Pole is from the South Pole. Their values are diametrically opposed. This, incidentally, is a situation where value matching is neither possible nor desirable! One way for social worker Butz to respond to the telephone call he received is to initiate legal proceedings designed to remove the infant from her mother. This may seem congruent with his own personal values and with what he believes to be societal expectations. But Mona Koss, though a drug addict, is also a human being with her own personal values. Can these be ignored? And what is best for the newborn infant? Jeff Butz feels that he should explore these questions with Mona Koss before making any decision.

In this case, as in many others, a client/worker value gap is often unavoidable. Social workers must therefore develop ways to deal with these value differences. Some have found the following approach useful:

1.  During the intake/assessment/diagnostic stage the social worker should determine if there is a relationship between the value

differences and the presenting problem. The marital problem for which Bess and Todd Moore sought help (Exemplar 6.1) may very well be related to value differences between themselves and their social worker.

2. The social worker should discuss her finding with the clients if they are able to participate in determining whether these differences might complicate the social work process. No prior assumption should be made that a client is not ready and able to participate in such joint decision making. Though Mona Koss holds values that are quite different, Butz must not assume that she cannot participate in making decisions for herself and her newborn baby.

3. A joint decision should be made whether to continue the social work process or whether to refer the client to another social worker with more congruent values, if such a worker is available.

Some have suggested that the social worker should always disclose her own values during the first session so that the client can protect himself against overt and covert value imposition. Yet routine disclosure of the worker's values too early in the social work process may actually harm clients since they may feel that the worker is challenging their own values even before a working relationship has been established between them (Anderson & Mandell, 1989; Beit-Hallahmi, 1975; Spero, 1990).

## EXERCISES

1. It has been said that even when a social worker does not declare her values publicly, her life-style and her nonverbal communications will usually indicate the values that she holds. Identify ways in which your own life-style and nonverbal messages will inform a client of the values you hold. What problems might this create for maintaining a professional relationship?

2. The risk of catching AIDS from sexual activities has been compared with the risk of fatal automobile accidents (Gochros, 1988). Does such a comparison communicate a value or is it an example of value neutrality? Defend your answer.

3. Your client feels very guilty about engaging in a certain behavior. Assume that this behavior is not illegal. He asks your help, but does not specify whether he wants help (1) in dealing with his guilt, or (2) in extinguishing the behavior. Discuss the ethical implications of choosing either approach. Will the specific behavior make a difference in your ethical assessment? Try to assess the two approaches with the following types of behavior: smoking,

masturbation, eating high cholesterol foods, having an extramarital affair.

4. How would you respond to the telephone call that Jeff Butz received (Exemplar 6.3)?

## SUGGESTIONS FOR ADDITIONAL READINGS

A classic paper on the place of values in social work practice was written by Siporin (1985a). The impact of various religious and spiritual values (including Shamanism and Buddhism) on American social work practice was examined by Canda (1988).

Glasser (1984) analyzed what happens when a social worker's values conflict with those of her clients. The impact of differing values about sex is discussed by Gochros (1988).

Anderson and Mandell (1989) review various problems associated with value self-disclosure. Spero (1990) presents another view of this issue. For two views of the impact of gender on ethical decision making see the comments of Dobrin (1989) and Rhodes (1990).

# 7. Equality, Inequality, and Limited Resources

Every person has an equal right to obtain social benefits and an equal duty to carry social burdens. This principle is based on the first-order societal value of equity (Frankena, 1973; Rawls, 1971). From this societal value social workers have derived the professional rule that obligates them to distribute available resources on an equal basis to all of their clients.

## COMMITMENT TO EQUALITY

An ethical problem occurs when available resources are so limited that an equal distribution is not possible. For example, when a county has only twenty beds for the chronically ill aged, these cannot be distributed on an equal basis to thirty clients who need this service. The equity value may create ethical problems even with respect to goods and services that lend themselves to an equal division (such as the social worker's time or the department's budget) since another rule obligates a practitioner to meet the specific needs of each client.

### Time

Time is a very limited and precious resource in the social work process. For example, a social worker in a family agency may be available thirty hours a week for direct service to clients. Is each of her thirty clients entitled to a one-hour interview every week? For some clients an hour a week may be more than they need, while for others it may not be sufficient. Client Peter Barr needs many hours of counseling this week to help him cope with an unexpected and sudden family crisis, but his social worker can meet this need only if she allots less time to other clients. Is such an unequal division of time ethical?

Many strategies are ruled out because sufficient staff time to implement them is not available. Every social worker recalls situations when a client could have received more effective service if only there had been more time available. The attempt to observe equity in the allocation of time to clients results in several ethical dilemmas, one of which is illustrated in the next exemplar.

### ➤ 7.1 Incest in the Schild Family

Donna Schild is a cute thirteen-year-old with a history of school truancy, alcoholism, drug experimentation, and several attempts at running away from home. Her parents appear warm and accepting, but the family agency worker who has been meeting with Donna for the past four weeks suspects that the real problem is Donna's home.

Today was the fifth session with Donna. The conversation was routine and little of significance was said until three minutes before the next client was scheduled to appear. Suddenly Donna started to relate some very important and emotionally charged material. Both her father and older brother have tried repeatedly to have sexual relations with her, but thus far she has not let them go all the way. When she told her mother about this, she was told to forget it had ever happened. As Donna related this information, she became noticeably more upset.

The social worker realized that this interview could not be terminated just because time was up now. But how long could she keep the next client waiting? Donna could easily use all of the next client's hour. But that would not be fair to the other clients scheduled for today. Furthermore, if Donna was not exaggerating, immediate arrangements would have to be made to remove her from her home. This might take many additional hours of the worker's time, hours already scheduled for other urgent assignments.

What would you do? What other ethical issues, in addition to the equity issue, does this worker face? What are the social worker's obligations to Donna? To her parents? To the community?

## Inequality

Americans have accepted as a self-evident truth that all persons are created equal (even though the signers of the Constitution claimed this right only for white men). From this first-order value social workers have derived the ethical rules of "equal distribution of resources" and "equal access to opportunities."

Equality is popularly equated with democracy. Those raised in this tradition often find it difficult to understand how some people can raise questions about it. They are upset when it is suggested that an equal distribution of resources is not always ethical and may lead to injustices. For example, some have asked whether it is right that medical resources, especially scarce and expensive life-extending technologies and instruments, are distributed equally, regardless of a patient's age. Daniel Callahan, a philosopher and medical ethicist, does not seem to think that such an approach is ethical. He writes that medicine should "resist the tendency to provide to the aged life-extending capabilities developed primarily to help younger people avoid premature and untimely death" (1987, p. 24). Instead he suggests that age be used as a decision-criterion for allocating life-extending therapies. What does this mean? Perhaps open-heart surgery should be available only to people under a given age, such as eighty. But is not the life of an eighty-four-year-old person as important and valuable as that of a seventy-four-year-old? Some would argue that the chances of a successful operation decrease rapidly as people grow older. Others avoid this statistical argument by noting that it is preferable to use limited resources to add twenty years of life rather than one or two years. This is particularly so when the younger person can still make a contribution to society while the aging person may be entirely dependent on the efforts of others.

Deciding for and against the allocation of societal resources on the basis of possible returns gives rise to other serious ethical problems. The social contribution of high-intelligence people may be more valuable than that of people with a lower intelligence and certainly more significant than that of persons with mental retardation. Does this give society the ethical right to limit open-heart surgery to people whose IQ is above 150? Or above 98? Or to people with a college degree? Or with a certain income? This diabolic argument can be pushed even further by arguing for the "elimination" of all undesirables, a policy implemented by Nazi Germany in the 1940s. While few will maintain that the "final solution" was ethical or moral, the implication of this approach for the unequal distribution of resources needs further careful thought.

It is a fact that many social work resources are not distributed equally. Lower-class and minority persons are less likely to be accepted for psychotherapy and, if accepted, are often seen for briefer periods of time or treated by less qualified personnel. This differential allocation of resources is often justified by alleging insufficient motivation, lack of readiness, and verbalization difficulties by these clients (Rabkin & Struening,

1976). It is urgent that wherever such unequal distribution of resources exists, this issue be reexamined and, if necessary, corrected.

But as noted in Chapter 3, "Guidelines for Ethical Decision Making," there is another side to inequality. Those who are not equal should receive special (and therefore "unequal") help (both services and resources) in order to gain equal access to life opportunities. It is this consideration which often justifies the unequal allocation of resources. Children with disabilities, for example, will receive more attention and greater resources than other children in order to compensate for disabilities. A blind child will not have the same access to education as a sighted child unless we provide the blind child with extra resources, including talking books and/or a reader.

## RACISM

Despite the efforts of many social workers and other citizens, racism continues to exist in America. In what has become increasingly a multiracial, multiethnic society, intergroup competition for various resources undoubtedly exacerbates conflicts between groups, especially during times of recession, economic changes, increased international economic competition, and diminished purchasing power for many employed persons.

For social workers, racism is a societal problem that impacts directly on their practice, on the availability of resources, and on the delivery of social services. One recent study found that few social workers in Massachusetts were aware of such problems as racism in their work settings, and that even when they did become aware of it, they did not act. ("People in the News," *NASW News*, 1990). Social workers must do more than they are doing now to prevent and oppose racism. There is a whole range of activities that are necessary, ranging from individual interactions to confrontation of institutional and societal racism. Some have suggested that one must differentiate between the individual social worker's obligation to fight racism and the obligation of the profession to fight racism. These two aspects are interrelated, but they are not the same (Bayles, 1981).

The *Code of Ethics* makes explicit the ethical stance toward racism by providing both negative (Thou shan't) and positive (Thou shalt) standards. The *Code* first forbids racism and other discriminatory acts when it states that "the social worker should not practice, condone, facilitate or collaborate with any form of discrimination on the basis of *race*, color, sex, sexual orientation, age, religion, national origin, marital status, political belief, mental or physical handicap, or any other preference or personal characteristic, condition or status" (II, F, 3). The *Code* also includes a more active, positive standard when it states that "the social worker should act to prevent and eliminate discrimination against any person or group on the basis of *race*, color, sex, sexual orientation, age, religion, national origin, marital status, political belief, mental or physical handicap, or any other preference or personal characteristic, condition, or status" (VI, P, 1).

The situations described below suggest some of the ways in which racism expresses itself in situations in which social workers may be involved. Hogan and Siu (1988) provided a historical perspective on child welfare and minority children. They concluded that

> ...the treatment of minority children in the U.S. child welfare system has been marked by racism manifested in inequitable policies and in insufficient and inadequate services.... The system responds more slowly to crises in minority families; such families have less access to support services such as day care and homemaker services; black and Hispanic children receive less comprehensive service plans; and parents of color have been viewed as less able to profit from support services.

Minority children are overrepresented in substitute services, and there is a discrepancy between the services recommended and delivered for minority children and nonminority children. The child welfare system is more tolerant of certain problems in minority families; at the same time assessments and interventions are harsher once situations are defined as problematic. To the extent that these conclusions are warranted, Hogan and Siu suggest that some social workers have been guilty of serious ethical breaches. Even though they did not necessarily engage in deliberate unethical activities, their behavior was unethical when they remained silent in the face of systematic institutional racism. The single child welfare worker may not have been able to change the system, but this is hardly an acceptable excuse to continue working in an unethical setting. Is "doing my best to fight racism" enough? What are the ethical obligations of social workers who encounter such ethics violations by systems or institutions?

Dilemmas about race and racism occur in different situations, not always as serious as the system problems in child welfare noted above. For example, what do you suggest the social worker do in the following situation?

### ➤ 7.2 Al Tabrizzi Is Fragile but Makes a Racist Comment

You are a clinical social worker seeing Al Tabrizzi, an elderly somewhat irrational and very depressed client in a family service agency. This client has been making progress on dealing with a number of tasks—getting out of the apartment more, seeking social life, improving his eating habits, and taking care of his affairs, but he has much further to go. Often he has spoken to you about how comfortable he feels with you as his worker and how he has been growing more trustful of your relationship because you have been so fully accepting of him and not judging him. In today's session, he has just spoken slurs about Hispanics.

Should you ignore these slurs? What is the ethical thing to do?

What do you do if you are on the staff of a training program for young adults whose funding will be cut unless the program serves both white and black persons? At present few whites are enrolled. In order to meet the demands of the funding agency, the staff is making strenuous efforts to recruit qualified white applicants, even though there is a waiting list of qualified black candidates. In these circumstances, should you condone giving a preference to whites? Is this ethical? Weigh the alternatives. If you report the situation publicly, the program will lose its major funding base. If you do not serve more white young adults, funding will stop and even black young adults will not receive the service they now receive. If you do comply, the program will serve fewer black young adults.

## LIMITED RESOURCES

The ethical problems resulting from the equality-and-inequality rule are often aggravated by the fact that available resources are always limited. If they were unlimited, there would be no problem in providing all persons with the help they need. But in the real world there is never enough for everything that should be done. Life is like a zero-sum game. Allocating a scarce resource to one person means that another will not receive it.

But the concept *limited resources* may be a manipulation of language used to conceal certain decisions. Often it merely means that available resources have been allocated elsewhere or that commitments or priorities have been shifted. For example, at the beginning of the 1960s decision makers in Washington decided to give highest priority to landing a human being on the moon by 1970, no matter what the cost. While there undoubtedly was a great deal of waste and even loss of life in pursuing this goal, the first astronaut did land on the moon in the summer of 1969. But this success was made possible only by assigning a lower priority and by making fewer resources available to other important programs, including social programs, such as eradicating poverty, eliminating discrimination, battling illiteracy, and so on. In other words, even while overall societal resources are limited, it is possible to assign almost unlimited resources to one particular program if such a policy decision is made at the highest level and if there is a wide consensus that this program deserves the very highest priority, even at the expense of limiting allocations for other important projects.

If this is the meaning of limited resources, the focus of ethical decision making shifts from the micro to the macro, from the specific case to societal allocations. On one level the ethical problem facing the social worker practitioner will be how to allocate the resources she controls. But on another level the profession as an organized group, as well as individual social workers as citizens, have an ethical responsibility to become involved in the societal allocation process, that is, the political process. Much of what social workers can and cannot do is determined by political decision makers. When the legislature passes budgets, it determines to a large extent the resources available both for public and voluntary agencies and institutions. Other political decisions have major impact on the nation's economic health, rate of economic growth, availability of jobs, and so forth. Are social workers merely passive observers of these political processes? Or is there an "ethic of responsibility" that obligates social workers to take an active part in these societal processes?

We agree with Siporin that social workers are moral agents who have a responsibility to influence organizations and communities (1985a). Priorities and commitments determine resource allocations. Significant resources have been allocated to drug rehabilitation programs, while considerably less monies have been allocated to solve the problems of the homeless. What are the ethics of such decisions when in many areas there are more homeless persons than drug addicts? More funds have been allocated to find a cure for AIDS, while considerably fewer funds have been allocated to develop a diabetes cure, even though the latter disease is a much more prolific killer. What are the ethical responsibilities of social workers when it comes to such decisions?

## Ethical Problems in Allocating Limited Resources

Many allocations are made at the highest political level in Washington or at a state capitol, settings where most social workers do not feel at home. But at other times such decisions are made much closer to home. Consider the decision facing the social workers of the Centro Latino, a United Way agency in Westport, a community which has always had a large concentration of Spanish-speaking immigrants. Centro Latino was started as an indigenous self-help group in the 1960s by immigrants from Latin America. Nowadays its budget is met largely by the United Way and supplemented at times by specific state and federal grants. Though volunteers are still used, most assignments are now handled by professional staff members. The decision-making powers are vested in the agency's board of directors, made up largely of veteran Spanish-speaking residents of the community. At a recent staff meeting the staff discussed an issue which many felt had ethical implications.

➤ **7.3 Refugees in Westport**

Early last year more than four hundred new Central American refugee families arrived in Westport. Centro Latino was able to generate a special one-time $100,000 grant to help in the adjustment of these refugees. The board of directors decided after lengthy discussion to allocate 20 percent of this grant to employ two more part-time social workers and to distribute the remaining funds directly to refugee families to help them in their adjustment. The detailed rules for distributing these funds were to be developed by the agency's staff.

This staff meeting was devoted to developing criteria for distributing the funds. The agency's director, Sandra Lopez, argued that equity demanded that each of the refugee families receive an equal cash grant of approximately $190, which each family could use as it wished. Several staff members agreed with Ms. Lopez. But others urged that the limited funds be used where they could do the most good. Since the basic needs of these families were already met, the new monies should be earmarked for special needs where an intensive use of resources could best achieve the desired objective. Each staff group believed that its proposal was most in line with professional ethics.

If you had been participating in this staff meeting, which position would you have supported? Why? What other ethical considerations should be weighed before making a decision?

## ETHICAL DILEMMAS IN ADVOCACY

The NASW's Ad Hoc Committee on Advocacy has suggested that a social worker "is ethically bound to take on the advocacy role if he is to fulfill his professional responsibilities" (1969, p. 16). A social work advocate "identifies with the plight of the disadvantaged. He sees as his primary responsibility the tough-minded and partisan representation of their interests, and this supersedes his fealty to others" (Brager, 1968, p. 6). The objective, according to Pincus and Minahan is "to help an individual or system obtain a needed resource or service or to obtain a policy change or concession from a resistant or unresponsive system" (1973, p. 113).

The Ethical Principle of Equality and Inequality provides the ethical justification for engaging in the advocacy role. Empowerment techniques are necessary in order to give deprived groups and individuals a chance for equal access to life opportunities. However, this ethical justification does not mean that social worker advocates can avoid all ethical dilemmas. Suppose there is only one bed available in the only home for the aged in your community. Your client needs to enter this institution because he no longer can cope at home. You also know that there are other elderly people (not your clients) whose situation is even more desperate. Should you become an aggressive partisan on behalf of your client, knowing that if you are successful his admission will be at the expense of other oldsters who need this service? Should you advocate his admission even if you are fairly sure that your success will cause irreversible harm to others? What might be other ways in which you can meet your ethical obligation to all the older persons who need this service?

Another ethical dilemma a social worker advocate may encounter is illustrated by the following exemplar.

➤ **7.4 No Winter Clothing**

Three children in a family receiving public aid are sent home from school because they are not adequately dressed. There is no money available at home because their mother has used every last cent she has to pay off more pressing bills. You, the family's social worker, have no emergency funds available for such purposes.

What should you do? Should you become an advocate to press for institutional changes, such as more adequate public welfare allowances or special clothing allowances? Or should you mobilize your volunteer network to locate suitable clothing donations so that the children can return to school as quickly as possible?

What are the ethical implications of causing short-run harm to your client (by ignoring a client's request for immediate help) in order to gain an ultimate benefit? The use of a cost-benefit analysis in this instance (as in so many others) is complicated by the fact that in one strategy the cost is certain (not attending school), while the benefit is uncertain (modification of policy). The other strategy may result in immediate benefits for your clients, but other children most probably will face the same problem sooner or later.

Social worker advocates will encounter many ethical problems when their practice role is not fully-supported by the employing agency. The case of the Apple Hill Young Adult Social Club (Exemplar 9.5) provides one example of this problem. The following exemplar provides another illustration.

➤ **7.5 Traffic in Shady Hill**

Shady Hill was a quiet residential neighborhood until last year when a new expressway exit brought a great amount of nonlocal traffic into its streets. As a result there are now several very dangerous intersections. Last month three children on their way to school were seriously injured crossing one of these intersections.

Parents and neighborhood residents are enraged and have demanded that the city close the exit or put up traffic lights. A meeting with the mayor has led to no results.

Lou Seward is the neighborhood worker who for the past two years has been staffing the Shady Hill Neighborhood Council. Since his arrival the council has undertaken several projects to improve the quality of life in the neighborhood. Everyone has been happy with what these projects have achieved. Since the current problem has become acute, Seward has helped council officers organize a coalition of all neighborhood groups interested in the problem, including the PTA, churches, and fraternal organizations.

At last night's meeting of the coalition it was agreed that ways must be found to put additional pressure on City Hall. It was decided to call a news conference tomorrow morning in order to announce that a protest rally would be held across the street from City Hall next Monday afternoon. If no positive response is received, the exit will be blockaded by residents on the following Monday afternoon. Seward participated in last night's meeting by raising a number of questions and by providing technical information and advice.

In this morning's conference with his supervisor, Seward reviewed the Shady Hill situation to see if there were additional ways in which he could be helpful. His supervisor thought that Seward had not done enough to calm the neighborhood. Though the problem demanded attention, his supervisor did not think that an aggressive conflict strategy was helpful. He and the agency expected the neighborhood worker to use his influence to keep the neighborhood quiet. That, after all, was the major reason why the city allocated monies to this department. The message was clear—and so was the problem.

## EXERCISES

1. What would you do if you were the neighborhood worker in Shady Hill (Exemplar 7.5)? What are the ethical problems this neighborhood worker faces? How would you resolve them? Do you think that the supervisor's comments are in accord with the *Code of Ethics*?

2. The director of a drug addiction rehabilitation program faces a difficult budget allocation decision. He has sufficient budget to mount only one of the two programs his agency would like to offer.

   *Program A* is geared to elementary school students. It will serve five-hundred children from some of the city's most difficult neighborhoods. Past experience has shown that without such a program, two-hundred children will be addicted by the time they are sixteen years old. With such a program it is expected that no more than fifty will become addicted.

*Program B* focuses on the rehabilitation of adolescent drug addicts. Fifty teens can be served each year. The success rate of this program is 60 percent.

What ethical considerations should the director examine? What ethical rules and ethical principles can he use to help him make a decision?

3. The East Side Neighborhood Council has received a small grant to mount an educational program for Central American refugees now settling in large numbers on the East Side. The board is considering two projects—one calls for funding supplementary classes in local schools, the other for establishing English classes for adult refugees. There is a need for both projects, but there is barely enough money to mount one. What ethical considerations should the board members keep in mind? Does the social worker who staffs the board have a responsibility to acquaint board members with the relevant professional ethics? Suggest ways that can be employed by this social worker to reach an ethically correct decision.

4. The racist situation described by Hogan and Siu and that of Al Tabrizzi (Exemplar 7.2) are situated at different levels in social work practice. The former is found at a general, institutional level while the latter occurred at the direct service level. What would you do in both cases?

## SUGGESTIONS FOR ADDITIONAL READINGS

Gilbert and Specht's discussion (1976) of professional ethics and advocacy is still relevant. Brager (1968) also deals with problems still current. Ashford, Macht, and Mylym (1987) describe the problems encountered by social worker advocates in a public defender's office.

Callahan (1987) is the source we cited for using age as a criterion for receiving medical treatment. Ethical questions that occur at the beginning of the life cycle are discussed by Kuhse and Singer (1985).

# 8. The Professional Relationship: Limits, Dilemmas, and Problems

## LIMITS OF THE PROFESSIONAL RELATIONSHIP

The client/social worker relationship is not a primary relationship. Primary relationships, especially those within the family or between friends, have few limits. The professional relationship, on the other hand, is focused on a specific area of personal behavior or environment for which help is sought. This relationship terminates once these objectives have been achieved. It is a limited relationship in contrast to the broad primary relations most people treasure. We will not explore here the practice problems that occur because many clients misunderstand the friendliness and informality that characterize their contacts with a social worker; this is a practice problem which arises because most people have become accustomed to a greater degree of formality, impersonality, and even indifference from their previous contacts with other professional practitioners. We will focus instead on the ethical problems and dilemmas that social workers face because of their commitment to certain values within the professional relationship.

One of the major causes for ethical problems in this area arises whenever a social worker determines that the help a client needs requires a relationship that goes beyond what the traditional definition of the limited professional relationship allows. But as the discussion in this chapter will show, this is only one cause; there are others that create equally perplexing ethical dilemmas.

Anomie is a core problem in the contemporary world. Many people have become rootless; they have lost all connections with their sources, as well as with their fellow human beings. The psychosocial symptoms reflecting anomie are well-known and need not be repeated here. Practitioners realize that often they treat only these symptoms without resolving the core problem. In order to strike at the roots of the problem, it is necessary to establish or reestablish more meaningful interpersonal relationships. Some have suggested that the social worker provide a model for this more meaningful relationship. But how can a client learn a new interaction pattern if the limited professional relationship does not permit the social worker to fully invest in this relationship?

Some social workers hide behind the limited professional relationship because they are uncomfortable with their clients' life-styles and cultures. But many more social workers want to identify with their clients by expressing empathy with their fate. Without wanting to imitate a lifestyle not authentic for them, they want to learn about and participate more fully in their clients' lives. They know that they cannot be effective and helpful without such knowledge. But this type of relationship cannot be limited to the 9 a.m.-to-5 p.m., Monday-through-Friday workweek. Yet the conscientious social worker often is not entirely clear about what the correct professional conduct is. Is it ethical for a social worker to accept an invitation for Sunday dinner in the client's home? Or to join the client on Friday evening in the local bar? May a social worker reciprocate and invite a client for supper at her home or in a restaurant? Practice wisdom has given fairly clear and generally negative answers to all of these questions, but increasingly social workers express discomfort with the barriers erected between them and their clients.

Though the relationship is supposed to be a limited one, social workers often have an emotional reaction to their clients. Such feelings may be natural, but the consequent worker behavior may cause ethical problems. When a worker's own needs become entangled with the professional relationship, emotional feelings may become destructive. In such situations the social worker may lose her sense of objectivity; instead of helping the client, she may cause harm.

## CLIENT INTERESTS VERSUS WORKER INTERESTS

Giving priority to a client's interests is one of the cornerstones of every professional code of ethics. The *Code of Ethics* expresses this professional obligation as follows: "Primacy of client's interest: The social worker's primary responsibility is to clients" (NASW, 1993, Paragraph II-F).

This ethical rule is meant to safeguard the client from exploitation since most clients can neither control nor evaluate practitioner activities. Unnecessary surgery is one widely known violation of this ethical principle, but in fact some members of every profession have at one time or another ignored this rule by placing their own self-interests ahead of those of their clients. Some years ago when school populations were dwindling, teachers were charged with failing students in order to assure full classrooms and in this way prevent threatened personnel cutbacks. This charge is no different from the accusations that some social workers failed to recommend the discharge of institutionalized children in order to assure continued state supplementation and thus guarantee their own jobs. This is hardly an ethical problem for the vast majority of social workers who are employed by social agencies. They do not gain any economic advantage by ignoring this ethical rule. Perhaps an occasional social worker in private practice may be tempted to place financial gain above client interests, but do agency-employed social workers face this dilemma? However, this problem touches every social worker when the issue is self-preservation and survival, rather than financial gain. Must a social worker give priority to client interests, even when this may result in physical injury to the worker? Or in severe harm to her children? Do considerations of self-preservation and survival legitimize actions which ordinarily might be considered unethical?

There are other ethical dilemmas of this kind which do not involve a threat to life. A social worker is in the middle of preparing supper for her family when she receives an emergency call for help from one of her clients. Should she drop everything and rush out to help her client, even if this means that her family will once again have a cold supper? Another social worker has a very important date whom she is to meet within the hour when she is notified that one of "her" foster children has run away. What should she do? What is the ethical thing to do?

Gewirth's Principle of Generic Consistency may be helpful when considering these problems. He stated, "Act in accord with the generic right of your recipients [that is, your clients] *as well as of yourself*" (1978, p. 135, emphasis added). Gewirth seems to suggest that there is no need for the worker to abdicate the right to her own welfare, even when this right conflicts with another person's right to professional services. Since Gewirth's principle was not developed to guide professional activities, some people argue that it does not apply to professional practitioners. Instead, they hold that a professional should always be guided by the ethical obligation to give priority to a client's interests, no matter what the consequences.

Those who would follow Gewirth's lead must consider whether ethics are relative. Do ethical obligations change according to their consequences? What must be the degree of potential harm before it is permissible to disregard the ethical rule that demands giving priority to a client's interests? Must social workers serve their clients' interests at all times, regardless of the consequences? Or is it ethical for them to declare that under certain unusual circumstances the professional obligation to serve their clients' interests is no longer primary? Consider in this connection Digg's observation that "there is an important difference between interpreting a rule, or violating it *in special circumstances,* and deciding each individual case just as if there were no rules" (1970, p. 267). This formulation permits retention of the client-priority ethical rule except in special circumstances, such as when the life of the worker is threatened.

Social workers involved in a strike situation also may face ethical dilemmas of this type. Fisher (1987) notes that there are no ready ethical guidelines for social workers involved in strikes. On the one hand, the *Code of Ethics* mandates the primacy of the worker's service obligation to clients and her commitment to the employing organization; there also are severe sanctions against the abrupt withdrawal of professional services. On the other hand, the NASW Personnel Standards support the collective bargaining process and oppose any laws or policies that limit the right of social workers to strike. This conflict in obligations creates an immediate ethical problem: Should social workers cross a picket line when the institution in which they are employed is struck by a labor union?

## DUAL RELATIONSHIPS

Professionals may fill more than one role concurrently or in serial fashion with clients. It is possible that a social worker because of the nature of the community in which she resides and practices may have social, business, financial, religious, or other roles in addition to her professional role with a client.

Here are some examples of dual relationships:

1. You discover that your client Bertha Martins is your dentist's mother.
2. Ms. Olds, your daughter's new teacher, is the mother of Tom Olds, a troubled teenager whom you have been treating for the last year.

In such dual role situations, it is always possible for a person to be confused by the situation, to exploit or harm the person in some manner, or to interfere with the professional relationship.

The 1993 NASW Delegate Assembly approved the addition of the following standards to the *Code of Ethics:*

(II, F, 4): The social worker should not condone or engage in any dual or multiple relationships with clients or former clients in which there is a risk of exploitation of or potential harm to the client. The social worker is responsible for setting clear, appropriate, and culturally sensitive boundaries;

(II, J, 12): The social worker should not use a professional position vested with power, such as that of employer, supervisor, teacher, or consultant, to his or her advantage or to exploit others.

The new standards highlight the issue of dual relationships so that social workers may take steps to set limits on such relationships or to avoid them wherever possible and in this way avoid actions detrimental to clients. The avoidance of exploitation of or of harm to clients or former clients is the major focus of this standard. In addition to the new standards, several other standards also stress the importance of clarity about the potential of dual relationships for unethical behavior: "The social worker should not exploit relationships with clients for personal advantage" (II, F, 2). "The social worker should under no circumstances engage in sexual activities with clients" (II, F, 5).

Must dual relationships necessarily interfere with professional relationships or be conflictual? In modern society everyone fills multiple roles, and there are many opportunities for social workers and clients to participate in dual or multiple relationships. Both may be members of the same political party or church or their children may attend the same schools or be classmates. There is no reason for a social worker to withdraw from these activities simply because the client also engages in them. The issue is to separate the professional relationship from other relationships. On the other hand, a social worker must avoid situations which have the potential for exploitation or harm. For example, the used car salesman who is a client may offer to sell you a car at a discount. Don't accept!

Kagle and Giebelhausen (1994) reviewed research and publications concerning sexual and nonsexual dual relationships and professionals. Sexual intimacy is not simply an ethical breach, but such intimacy with clients is also grounds for legal action in fifty states where the social worker may be sued for battery or malpractice. Some states have defined sexual contact between client and therapists as professional negligence. Seven states make sexual exploitation of a client a felony offense.

In a number of states, potential legal action against the practitioner is not avoided by the formal termination of the treatment relationship. Current as well as past clients are dependent on the social worker; exploiting this dependency for personal gain, sexual or nonsexual, is unethical, illegal, and unprofessional, regardless of whether or not the social worker's action affects the therapeutic or other outcome.

Recently questions were raised about social workers in health care settings who receive gifts from representatives of medical equipment companies and nursing homes. The vendors expect "gratitude" for their gifts. A number of issues are raised by the gifts. The cost of the gifts is passed on to patients and others. The best interests of some patients become less than paramount. The acceptance of the gift creates a dual relationship between the social worker and the donor, a relationship which suggests an obligation for reciprocity. Social workers are in a position to reciprocate through referral of patients who pay either personally or through insurance. As a result, social workers can become enmeshed in a dual relationship which is not known to patients but which has the power to influence what happens to the client.

Is there a difference between the acceptance of gifts for oneself or for patients? Are gifts given to the social work department different from those provided to individual social workers? Do all gifts carry "attached strings" deserving of reciprocation? Since patients are unaware of these relationships, is the acceptance of gifts consistent with fully informed consent (Ross, 1992)?

## SEX AND OTHER SOCIAL RELATIONS WITH CLIENTS

There are many "gray" areas in regard to social workers and their social, nonsexual relationships with clients. Undoubtedly, there are many qualifications, contextual factors, and motivations which need to be considered for many such relationships. But the *Code* is quite clear that "the social worker should under no circumstances engage in sexual activities with clients" (NASW, 1993, II, F, 5). This ethical rule is found in the codes of ethics of most professions.

To be sure, some social workers have questioned this rule, pointing out that nowadays many problems brought to their attention involve problems of sexual dysfunction (Schultz, 1975; Moser, 1980). The professional intervention, they argue, might include sexual techniques and activities unthinkable only a few decades ago. There are therapists who believe and practice the notion that sexual involvement with a client is beneficial. They suggest that this is not a new helping technique; Freud's colleague Sandor Ferenczi already "helped" his clients express their physical affections toward him as a way of compensating for their childhood deprivations (Van Hoose & Kottler, 1985). But those who say there is no problem regarding sex between social work professionals and their clients are underestimating the impact of such behavior on professional relationships and on the lives of clients. Although this problem does not occur frequently, it is quite serious because of the consequences for the persons involved. Pope and Bouthoutsos (1986) reported that 90 percent of the 559 clients they studied, all of whom were sexually involved with their therapists, had adverse effects and suffered some kind of damage. In 34 percent of the cases, the client's personality was negatively affected. Other consequences included problems of identity and self-esteem, mistrust, anger, tension, apprehension, dissociation, fatigue, lassitude, lack of motivation, depression, anxiety, pessimism, deterioration of familial relationships, inability to work, self-blame, self-hate, and even suicide.

There is some evidence that those most vulnerable to sexual exploitation by their therapists are those who have been sexually abused in the past (Coleman & Schaefer, 1986). Far from being helpful, sexual relations with clients are in fact destructive.

How frequently does this problem occur in social work practice? A review of seven national surveys of mental health practitioners, including social workers, found that 3.8 to 12.0 percent of male practitioners and 0.2 to 3.0 percent of female practitioners reported having had sexual contact with a current or former client (Kagle & Giebelhausen, 1994).

Attitudes of practitioners about having sex with clients are changing. Among psychologists it was reported in 1977 that 5.5 percent of male psychologists and 0.6 percent of female psychologists had sexual intercourse with patients (Holroyd & Brodsky, 1977). Most recently Borys and Pope (1989) reported that only 1.3 percent of therapists reported sexual involvements with clients. This marked drop in sexual activity seems to reflect a broad acceptance of the ethical rule prohibiting sexual relations with clients. What is not entirely clear from the data is whether therapists now refrain from having sex with their clients or whether they are less willing to admit that they behave in unethical ways! (See Table 8.1.)

Another recent study which queried 101 therapists (mostly psychologists, but including some social workers) reported that not one respondent thought that it was acceptable or ethical to have sex with a client while that client was still in treatment. Such behavior was thought to be a sufficient reason for a malpractice suit by 80.2 percent of the respondents, while 89 percent answered that it was unethical to terminate treatment for the purpose of having sex with a client. But only 37 percent indicated that this might be grounds for a malpractice suit (Conte et al., 1989).

Of those *Code of Ethics* cases closed by NASW since 1982, a sample of 300 cases was studied. Of the 226 alleged violations of the *Code* included in the study, 72 were substantiated. Of the substantiated cases, 29.2 percent (21) were found to have violated the *Code* in regard to sexual

Table 8.1    Unethical Social Behaviors

| | Belief: Never ethical [%] | Behavior: Never [%] |
|---|---|---|
| Accept client's invitation to a special occasion. | 6.3 | 64.0 |
| Become friends with clients after termination. | 14.8 | 69.0 |
| Accept gift worth over $50. | 44.9 | 92.4 |
| Engage in sex with client after termination of therapy. | 68.4 | 95.3 |
| Go out with client after a session. | 43.2 | 87.4 |
| Buy goods or services from client. | 36.7 | 77.6 |
| Engage in sexual activity with client. | 98.3 | 98.7 |
| Invite client to party or social event | 63.5 | 92.1 |
| | (N=1108) | (N=1021) |

*Source:* Borys and Pope, 1989.
Adapted from D. S. Borys and K. S. Pope, "Dual Relationships between Therapist and Client: A National Study of Psychologists, Psychiatrists and Social Workers," *Professional Psychology: Research and Practice*, vol. 20, pp. 283–93.

activity, the most frequently cited infraction of the *Code of Ethics* (NASW, 1995). This number may seem minute in terms of the total NASW membership, yet at a recent NASW conference, C. W. King, an NASW insurance board member, reported that incorrect treatment and sexual misconduct accounted for the largest percentage of malpractice suits (NASW, 1995).

All states prohibit sexual intimacy between therapists and clients and make this a cause for legal action. In all fifty states clients may sue for battery or malpractice. Four states (California, Illinois, Minnesota, and Wisconsin) define sexual contact between therapist and client as professional negligence, making it easier to bring malpractice suits. In seven states (California, Colorado, Florida, Maine, Minnesota, North Dakota, and Wisconsin), sexual exploitation of a client is a felony. In California, Florida, and Minnesota, formal termination of the professional relationship does not end the liability of the practitioner, especially if treatment ended so sexual contact could begin (Kagle & Giebelhausen, 1994).

The following exemplar raises a number of ethical issues to which all social workers must pay attention.

### ➤ 8.1 Treatment of an Inferiority Complex

Jill Jordan, a thirty-five-year-old divorcée, has been a client of the Family Consultation Center for a number of months. Her presenting problem was that she feels inadequate, unattractive, and stymied in her job career. She feels her negative self-image contributed to her divorce and has become a barrier to advancement on the job. She feels that her career and more fulfilling relationships depend on her being more positive about herself and being more optimistic.

Bob Temple, an experienced social worker, was assigned as her therapist. A contract was established with the presenting problem as the focus. During the course of treatment Temple was very understanding and warmly responsive to Jordan. His objective was to restore Jill's faith in herself. As treatment proceeded, Jill became more and more openly admiring of Temple. At the end of one session, she spontaneously hugged him and said how appreciative she was for all his help. As she experienced more successes in her life, she would ask for a hug as a sign of his support for her. Still later she made it evident that she was attracted to Bob and would not reject his interest in her. Bob was also attracted to Jill. He very much wanted to express further his feelings toward her and have sexual relations with her, but he knew that the professional ethics demanded that he not do so. What is the most ethical way of handling this problem?

1. It is best that he deny his feelings and continue treatment but discontinue the hugs. Chances are that these emotions, if controlled, will not interfere with the treatment.
2. He can maintain a professional relationship in the office and join her church where there will be opportunities for them to meet after hours, outside the office.
3. He can accept his emotional attraction to Jill, but at the same time realize that a professional social worker cannot have a personal relationship with a client. Next time Jill broaches the subject, he should tell her that he likes her and that if he were not her social worker he might become involved with her. But since he is her social worker, his task is to help her professionally; no other relationship is possible.
4. He realizes that he cannot control his emotions. Therefore, it is best to terminate the relationship and refer Jill to another social worker.
5. He realizes that he cannot control his emotions. Therefore, it is best not to deny his attraction for Jill and instead do what comes naturally, that is, have sex with her; at the same time he can continue to be her social worker.

Option 5 is clearly not acceptable. In most jurisdictions this behavior is judged as illegal, even criminal. The NASW *Code of Ethics* prohibits it, as do the ethical codes of all other professions. Though there is no ethical or professional justification for this choice, we mention it because we are aware that a small number of our colleagues do engage in such behavior, a behavior which is blatantly unprofessional and unethical.

Obviously some of the other options are unethical and go against the code. Use the two ethical decision screens to determine which might be the preferred approach in the situation facing Bob Temple.

Some have tried to argue that sexual relations with clients are permissible if they occur outside the office. But there is no evidence suggesting that such after-hours sex is any less damaging than sexual relations on the office couch. Furthermore, there is no known malpractice case where the after-hours defense has been used successfully. For example, in *Roy* v. *Hartogs* (366 N.Y.S. 2d 297, 1975) a client brought a malpractice suit against her therapist, claiming that their sexual relations over a period of months had caused her damage. The therapist responded that their relationship was not part of the therapy since it occurred in the evening. The judge was not convinced that these activities were outside the professional relationship and therefore ruled against the therapist.

### Touching

What about erotic behaviors that do not involve genital relations? Touching became a popular practice technique during the late sixties and early seventies as a result of the popularity of the encounter movement. Clients "touched" by their therapist evaluated counseling more positively than those not touched, particularly if the touching was done by a therapist of the opposite sex (Algana et al., 1979). Some have questioned the ethical propriety of touching, believing that such behavior is only a first step that will inevitably lead to full sexual relations. Others reject this assumption. The available research evidence is contradictory and does not provide an unambiguous answer (Bogodanoff & Elbaum, 1978; Borenzweig, 1983; DeYoung, 1988; Willis, 1987).

### Other Social Relations

While almost all social workers agree that it is unethical to engage in sexual activities with clients, there is less agreement about the ethical propriety of engaging in other social relations. In one large-scale study of psychotherapists, a random sample of over two thousand professional social workers, psychologists, and psychiatrists participated. Half of the sample was asked whether they believed that it was ethical for a professional to engage in various specified behaviors, while those in the second half were asked whether they had ever engaged in such behaviors. This methodology was adopted in order to avoid contamination of answers. There were no significant differences in the responses of members of the three professional groups (Borys & Pope, 1989). Some of the results highlight the lack of consensus about which social relations are deemed unethical. Table 8.1 presents selected data from the Borys and Pope study. In the "belief" column we report the percentage of respondents who indicated that the specified behavior is "never ethical," while in the "behavior" column we indicate the percentage of those who reported that they had never engaged in the specified behavior.

Almost all respondents believed that engaging in sex with clients during treatment was unethical; more than two-thirds also thought that sex with clients was unethical even after treatment was terminated, yet almost no one admitted having had sexual contacts with current or former patients. On this issue there was near unanimity. But with respect to other social relations, only one activity (inviting clients to a party or social event) was rated unethical by a majority of the respondents, yet a majority reported that in fact they never did engage in any of the specified social relations with clients. This may indicate that actual behavior of helping professionals is even more ethical than their belief system. Or the responses to the researchers may reflect what professionals believe is expected of them. Or the absence of social relations may be indicative of the social gap between social workers and most of their clients—a gap that prevents any natural social contact between clients and practitioners, no matter what the ethics rules require or permit.

The confusion about what behaviors are unethical is reflected in the data reported by Borys and Pope (in Table 8.1). While more than 98 percent of the respondents believed that sex with clients is never ethical, less than half believed that accepting a gift worth more than $50 is never ethical. Only one out of twenty practitioners interviewed replied that it is never ethical to accept an invitation from a client to a special occasion. The wide range in responses suggests that there are many aspects of social relations for which the *Code of Ethics* does not yet provide sufficient guidance.

Social workers who do not practice psychotherapy may have somewhat different views about the ethical implications of some of the behaviors studied by Borys and Pope. Group workers and community workers may have no compunctions about going to the local deli or coffeehouse with a group of clients after a session, but may (or may not) draw the line when it comes to doing the same with an individual client. (See Chapter 12 for a discussion of ethics and social work with groups.) Some social work administrators report that their most important contacts with board members occur in social settings. Obviously, the definition of who is a *client* and the purpose of the professional relationship are two factors that affect the ethical assessment of such professional behaviors.

## DOUBLE-AGENT DILEMMA

As long as social workers believe that there is no conflict between agency interests and client interests, double-agent ethical problems do not exist for them. Usually it is suggested that the agency is committed to what is best for the client. But if we examine this proposition objectively, we must realize that this is only the social work version of "What is good for General Motors is good for the country!" In fact, organizational survival interests often do not coincide with what is best for the client.

The ethical issue of the double-agent dilemma arises out of a social worker's attempt to serve at the same time both the best interest of the client and the best interest of the employing agency or institution. A typical example of this ethical problem is familiar to hospital social workers. Hospital policy (often as a result of requirements by the government or insurance companies that reimburse hospitalization expenses) is to send patients home at the earliest possible time, even if this is not in a particular patient's best interest. In this instance a social worker who is the "agent" of both the hospital and the patient cannot meet the best interests of both. Similar problems are faced by social workers in the armed forces, police, prisons, mental hospitals, and schools. Increasingly this problem is faced also by social workers employed in industrial settings and in social agencies. (See Exemplar 1.2, "Blanca Gabelli Costs Too Much," for another example of this problem.)

A somewhat different version of this ethical dilemma is faced by social workers who employ various group strategies: How can they simultaneously serve the best interest of every participant? If the focus is on strengthening the group or family, one or the other participant may not receive the maximum benefit. On the other hand, if the group is the vehicle to help one or more group members with their problems, there may be other group participants who will not obtain any significant benefit.

## TRUTH TELLING AND MISREPRESENTATION

Telling the truth and avoiding deceptions is so basic an ethical obligation that it is not even mentioned in the NASW *Code of Ethics*. Every human interaction is based on the premise that each side in the interaction intends to tell the truth. Deceiving, that is, deliberately misrepresenting facts in order to make another person believe what is not true, violates the respect to which every person is entitled. Telling the truth to a client is an even stronger professional obligation than the generalized obligation of truth telling. This professional ethic is anchored in the specialized client/practitioner relationship and in the obligations that a practitioner owes to her clients. However, this does not mean that we must accept. Bayles's conclusion that the obligation to be honest with clients does not require honesty toward others when acting on a client's behalf (1981, p. 71).

Honesty may not always be the best policy for a social worker. Expressing such a view is, of course, a little bit like attacking home and mother. But Haley raises a number of questions about the efficacy of always being honest (1976, p. 208). These include:

1.  The therapeutic situation itself is not an honest human experience, but a paid relationship. Does the therapist have an ethical obligation to be honest in such a relationship?
2.  Can any therapist, no matter what his orientation, claim that he is willing to share with a client *all* of his observations and understandings?
3.  Must a therapist answer all questions that a client has about the therapy that will be used? Will this patient be better able to achieve autonomy when he fully understands the theory used by the therapist?
4.  Will an "honest sharing" of understanding solve the problems for which the patient is paying his money to get help?

Haley presents one point of view, but not everyone agrees. In addition to Haley's questions, there are other ethical dilemmas that may arise out of the attempt to tell the truth. Consider the ethical problems facing Gail's social worker in the following exemplar:

➤ **8.2 Gail Finds a Job**

Gail Silva is a single parent; she is raising two daughters, ages seven and six. She has been trying to find a part-time job to supplement her meager welfare check ever since her younger daughter started kindergarten. She has been repeatedly refused a job because she has had no prior work experience. By now she has become very frustrated and has developed a very negative self-image. She believes that nobody wants her—neither as a spouse nor as a worker.

This morning she told you excitedly that she thinks she has found a job. As she describes the job, you realize that she is telling you about an employer who is known to exploit his workers and who pays below the minimum wage, when he pays at all. Should you tell Gail the truth about her prospective employer? Or should you share her enthusiasm, hoping that things will work out? What is the ethical thing to do?

Deception has become so common in our world that we hardly pay attention to the little lies and half-truths that everyone uses and knows how to justify. But what are the ethical implications for a social worker who uses "lies"? What is the ethical question involved in telling another person a bit less than the full truth? When a social worker decides to withhold the truth from a client or to deceive him, she usually thinks that she is doing so for the client's benefit. Whether or not this is really so is subject to empirical assessment. But whether or not her decision was ethically justified cannot be assessed empirically.

There are many reasons why a social worker might deceive her client or not tell him the full truth, including the following:

1. To make a client-selected goal less desirable.
2. To create new goals.
3. To obscure options.
4. To increase options.
5. To change the cost/benefit estimate for one or more options.
6. To increase or decrease client uncertainty.
7. To increase or decrease client anxiety.
8. To protect the client from "damaging" truth.
9. To protect the effectiveness of the current intervention strategy.
10. To obtain the client's "informed" consent.
11. To protect confidential information received from a third party.
12. To strengthen the relationship with a client by lying at his request to a third party.
13. To increase the worker's power over a client by withholding information.
14. To make the worker look good by "papering over" mistakes she has made.

Which of these reasons are applicable in the following exemplars?

### ➤ 8.3 A Growth on the Foot

Art Elder, age thirty-four, is a high school teacher. At present he is a patient in University Hospital because he has "a growth on his foot." His physician told him that there are two ways of treating this problem. Both involve some risks. When Art asked what he would advise, he suggested surgery.

Sally Brown is the social worker in the surgical department. From her discussion with the resident she learned that Dr. Kutner, the physician, did not tell the patient all the available choices and that he withheld information about the option with the least risk. Evidently he weighted his presentation in favor of the experimental treatment method that he is just now developing.

Here we are not concerned with Dr. Kutner, but with Sally Brown. Should she tell Mr. Elder the truth? Or should she mind her own business and leave the giving of medical information to the medical staff? Truth telling requires us to note that the ethical problem presented in this exemplar may no longer be as common among physicians as it once was. One study reported dramatic changes in physicians' information-giving practices, at least with respect to cancer patients. In 1961, 90 percent of physicians studied preferred not to tell their patients that they had cancer, but sixteen years later 97 percent did inform their patients (Novak et al., 1979). But Sally Brown still faces a dilemma. On what basis can she decide what the ethical course of action is?

Truth telling is not a problem that only social caseworkers face. An exemplar from the field of social work administration also raises questions about the ethics of truth telling.

> ### 8.4 The Frans Music Appreciation Room

The Frans family contributed a considerable sum of money to the Uptown Community Center to furnish and equip a music appreciation room in memory of their late mother. An appropriate plaque marks the room.

Since accepting the contribution the neighborhood has experienced a large influx of refugees from Southeast Asia. Because of their needs, the room is now used for purposes other than those designated by the donors.

You are the center's associate director. You know how important the music appreciation room is to the family. There is a good possibility of obtaining additional donations for other projects from this family, but if the family discovers that "their" room is no longer used for music appreciation activities they may lose interest in Uptown Community Center.

At the monthly meeting of the United Way Board of Directors you meet Mr. Frans. He asks you how the music appreciation room is doing. How should you reply? Do you tell the truth? Do you try to avoid the issue by shifting the conversation to another area? Do you tell a little untruth, such as "our refugees love music"? Or what? What is the ethically correct response? How do you decide?

The question of truth or deception involves the intention of the speaker and not the factual accuracy of the statement. Knowing the truth does not necessarily result in telling the truth, while not knowing the truth does not always result in a deception. The relations between the objective situation and a speaker's intentions are summarized in Table 8.2.

Some practitioners who abhor lying have suggested that it is possible to deceive without lying by exaggerating or manipulating. One social worker, for example, wanted to dissuade a client from placing his daughter with mental retardation in an institution. She arranged for the father to visit the worst possible institution, but did not mention the availability of other possibilities. This social worker would never lie, but did she tell the truth? A social work administrator exaggerates the benefits that may result from a new program so that the agency will receive a larger budget allocation next year. Are these social workers acting ethically? Or is this yet another version of the ends-justifying-the-means quandary?

**Table 8.2   Intentions and Facts**

|  | The speaker intends to: | |
|---|---|---|
|  | Be truthful | Deceive |
| The statement is factually: | | |
| True | 1 | 2 |
| False | 3 | 4 |

1 = The speaker intended to tell the truth and did so.

2 = The speaker intended to deceive, but unknowingly spoke the truth, while her intentions were not ethical, her actual behavior does not raise any ethical issues.

3 = The speaker intended to tell the truth, but failed to do so because she did not have the correct information. The problem here may be one of lack of competence or lack of skill, or both, but there is no question of professional ethics.

4 = The speaker intended to deceive and did lie. Only this situation involves questions of unethical behavior.

As the U.S. population becomes more culturally diverse, ethical issues such as truth telling become even more complex. For example, you are the social worker in an urban hospital which has a number of Japanese physicians on staff and which serves many Asian-American patients. A Japanese-born woman, now a resident of your city, is on your caseload. She was just diagnosed as having a type of cancer for which the prognosis is very poor. You have learned that in the Japanese culture physicians often do not tell their patients that they have cancer, but indicate a less threatening diagnosis, such as ulcer. This is done in the belief that the patient will be better equipped to fight against the disease if she is not aware of the seriousness of the disease and hopelessness of the prognosis. Your client, who has been given such a false diagnosis, now asks you to confirm what her doctor told her. What do you do? Do you respect the Japanese tradition, or do you follow the professional approach to truth telling which is based on Western culture (Wheeler, 1993)?

## PRACTITIONER IMPAIRMENT

The personal and professional abilities of a social worker can be damaged, diminished, and impaired by extreme mental or physical health difficulties, overwhelming personal/familial problems, psychosocial distress, or by substance abuse. These problems can affect an individual social worker, her family and friends, and colleagues, and may result in a social worker's inability to provide professionally competent services. Social workers are thought to have about the same rates of alcohol and substance abuse problems as members of other health professions and as the general public. The New York City Chapter of NASW reported that 43 percent of the respondents to a study knew at least one social worker with a drug or alcohol problem. A survey of all Indiana Chapter members reported that 53 percent knew a social worker whose performance was affected by emotional or mental health problems, substance abuse, burnout, or sexual misconduct (Hiratsuka, 1994).

As early as 1980, Social Workers Helping Social Workers was formed to provide mutual assistance for social workers with impairments and related problems. By November 1987 the NASW Delegate Assembly approved a policy statement regarding a Colleague-Assistance Program specifically aimed at encouraging the development of programs to serve impaired social workers and the encouragement of national NASW to promulgate a formal policy acknowledging the needs of impaired social workers.

Other professions also confronted the issue of professional impairment in an aggressive manner. Among the ethical issues for the profession is the assurance that all professional social workers are able to provide quality professional services and that such a standard is maintained while respecting all other ethical norms, including confidentiality. It was thought that a new standard in the *Code of Ethics* would enhance professional self-regulation and avoid dependence upon the complaints of dissatisfied or abused clients who might have experienced incompetent professional conduct or other unethical activities by impaired social workers. The ultimate result of such a standard and its utility is the enhancement of the public's trust in the professional competence of social workers.

Impaired social workers may act in undisciplined, insensitive, erratic, unprofessional, and unethical ways. Sometimes they use inappropriate language or behavior with clients and colleagues, pay haphazard attention to job requirements, fail to follow through on assignments, or engage in excessive absenteeism. Impairments can lead to inadequate and even unethical behaviors which can lower the public's estimate and trust of the profession, result in actions detrimental to clients and others, and present ethical problems for other social workers.

The 1993 NASW Delegate Assembly approved the addition of the following standards to the *Code of Ethics*:

(I, B, 3): The social worker should not allow his or her own personal problems, psychosocial distress, substance abuse, or mental health difficulties to interfere with professional judgment and performance or jeopardize the best interests of those for whom the social worker has a professional responsibility;

[and] (I, B, 4): The social worker whose personal problems, psychosocial distress, substance abuse, or mental health difficulties interfere with professional judgment and performance should immediately seek consultation and take appropriate remedial action by seeking professional help, making adjustments in workload, terminating practice, or taking any other steps necessary to protect clients and others.

[and] (III, J, 13): The social worker who has direct knowledge of a social worker's impairment due to personal problems, psychosocial distress, substance abuse, or mental health difficulties should consult with that colleague and assist the colleague in taking remedial action.

The new standard requiring social workers to take action by consulting with and offering assistance when they have direct knowledge of a colleague's impairment makes this an ethical responsibility. But clarification of the responsibility does not provide answers for all the dilemmas which exist in this area.

➤ **8.5  My Friend, Mentor, Supervisor, and Alcohol**

You are a social worker assigned to a satellite unit of a family service agency with Davis Jones, your supervisor, the only other social worker who works in that office. Your relationship with Davis goes back at least fifteen years, and he has been very important in your life at several junctions. He helped you get into social work school; he recommended you for an advanced treatment institute; and once when your child was ill, he helped you obtain medical care from the best specialist in town. Recently, however, Davis—who also evaluates you for pay and possible promotions—has been late arriving for work and has missed some meetings. You have had to cover for him more than a few times with his clients. You are still somewhat in awe of Davis and owe him a lot. He has helped you out of many a difficult situation. You feel that his current erratic behavior is related to alcohol and a family problem.

So far Davis has done little if any harm. At what point must you act? Earlier or later? What about loyalty to a mentor, friend, and colleague from whom you have learned much? What about loyalty to yourself, your career, and your family? What about the risks you expose yourself to by acting? What should you do?

## EXERCISES

1. If there is an NASW chapter in your area, invite the chair of the Chapter Committee on Inquiry to discuss with your class how

complaints about ethical misconduct are handled. You might want to examine with the chair how effective these procedures are.

2. Sexual activities with clients are prohibited by the NASW *Code of Ethics* (1993, Paragraph F-5). Some social workers have argued that there is no scientific evidence that such activities are necessarily harmful. They say that a rule of this kind is no longer relevant in a society which permits a wide variety of life-styles. Present arguments both for changing and for keeping this rule.

3. The "limited professional relationship" characteristic of the client/social worker relationship baffles many clients. It is a relationship that is quite unlike the formal, bureaucratic relationships with which they are familiar, yet it is also different from the informal relations they maintain with friends and relatives. How important is this principle from an ethical point of view?

4. In teams of two, develop two lists: (1) social relations with clients that are ethical and permissible, and (2) social relations with clients that are definitely unethical and therefore prohibited. Compare your lists with those of other teams. Discuss those areas where you find disagreement.

## SUGGESTIONS FOR ADDITIONAL READINGS

The conflict between workers' and clients' interests in a hospital strike situation is examined by Fisher (1987). Kagle and Giebelhausen (1994) examine sexual and nonsexual dual relationships between social workers and their clients, including ethical, legal, and practice issues. Bates and Brodsky (1988) provide a first-person account of a client who experienced sexual exploitation by her therapist. Clients' reactions to touching are investigated in a study by Algana and colleagues (1979).

Adler (1989) analyzes a particularly difficult ethical problem. What is the social worker's role when it comes to telling the truth to a terminally ill patient? Abramson (1990) and Yu and O'Neal (1992) explore the equally difficult issues of confidentiality when working with persons with AIDS.

# 9. Bureaucratic and Work Relationships

So far our discussion has focused on ethical problems and ethical dilemmas occurring in the professional relationship between social workers and clients. In this chapter our attention will be directed primarily to ethical issues arising out of the relationship between social work colleagues and between social workers and their employers.

We already noted in Chapter 2 that one of the functions of professional codes of ethics is to permit colleagues to work together in harmony without bickering and infighting that might lead to professional self-destruction. One complete section of the NASW *Code of Ethics* deals with the social worker's ethical responsibilities toward colleagues, and another section with her ethical responsibilities to employers and employing organizations. In addition, several ethical rules dealing with relationships with colleagues are found in the section devoted to ethical responsibilities toward the profession.

Twenty-nine percent of the sustained ethical complaints received by NASW Chapter Committees on Inquiry during the years 1979 to 1985 dealt with unethical behaviors toward colleagues (Berliner, 1989). However, the total number of sustained complaints during this six-year period was ninety-six, or sixteen per year for the entire country! But this small number of complaints may represent only the tip of the proverbial iceberg since many unethical behaviors of this type are not brought to the local NASW committee but are handled in other ways, as will be discussed later in this chapter.

## RELATIONS WITH PROFESSIONAL COLLEAGUES

What is a social worker to do when she discovers that a colleague engages in unethical or unprofessional conduct? How should she respond when she realizes that a fellow worker provides client services of a poor quality? What are her obligations when she believes that another social worker harms a client? What is her responsibility when she discovers that another worker engages in activities prohibited by their agency?

The ethical rule obligating social workers to treat colleagues with respect, fairness, and good faith (Paragraph III-J) is one of those self-understood rules which ordinarily do not create an ethical quandary. Most people understand that the members of a club do not "wash their dirty linen" in public. Goffman wrote about the backstage area, access to which is restricted to colleagues (1959, pp. 106–40). Whatever happens in this area may not be revealed to those who are not members of the profession. It remains forever a secret among those who work backstage.

Social workers had relatively few ethical problems of this type as long as the rule governing relations with professional colleagues was unambiguous and not challenged by other ethical rules. But as accountability to clients and others became more important, the rule to "protect your own" became increasingly problematic. Today most social workers are no longer willing to overlook their colleagues' unethical behavior. Yet what to do is not always clear. On learning that a colleague has engaged in unethical behavior, a social worker can choose one of the following options:

*Option A.*    The violating behavior can be ignored. Reporting it may be too troublesome. Or past experience suggests that nothing will be done about it, even if it is reported. Or the conduct thought to be in violation of the *Code* may be so widespread that it is unlikely that anyone will take the complaint seriously.

*Option B.*    An informal approach to the colleague may resolve the problematic behavior, especially if the violation is of a minor or technical nature or appears to be the result of lack of experience or lack of knowledge.

*Option C.*    If the alleged unethical conduct also violates agency rules, it may be brought to the attention of one's supervisor or it may be raised formally by utilizing agency procedures established for this purpose.

*Option D.*   The alleged unethical behavior may be brought to the attention of the local NASW Chapter Committee on Inquiry. In order to utilize this procedure, the colleague who allegedly engaged in the unethical behavior must be an NASW member, the complaint must charge a specific violation of the *Code of Ethics*, the complainant must have personal knowledge about the alleged behavior and must be able and willing to provide the Committee on Inquiry with relevant and reliable testimony.

*Option E.*   In states where a State Licensing Board regulates social work practice, unethical conduct harmful to clients can be reported to the Board, which may be in a position to take effective remedial action within a relatively short time.

*Option F.*   The unethical conduct may be brought to the attention of the general public *(whistle-blowing)* with the expectation that an aroused public will demand appropriate action to bring an end to the violation.

There are a number of possible alternatives within each option. Options B, C, D, and E are sanctioned by the *Code of Ethics*, while option F may be itself in violation of this code. Yet undoubtedly there are times and occasions when "going public" is the only way to proceed. However, the decision to "go public" should never be a routine one and should be taken only after careful consideration of all possibilities.

Before resolving ethical dilemmas of this type, the social worker should attempt to clarify what she hopes to achieve by the action she intends to initiate. Elsewhere Loewenberg (1987) suggests the following as possible objectives:

1. Discontinuance of the unethical behavior.
2. Punishment for the offending social worker.
3. Identifying the unethical practitioner so that potential clients and/or employers will avoid this person and turn to another, more ethical practitioner.
4. Preventing others from engaging in this behavior by warning them that it is unethical and will result in sanctions against the practitioner.
5. Protecting the "good name" of the profession by declaring publicly that the unethical behavior is not approved by the profession.

Several exemplars will highlight some of the problems involved in this ethical issue.

➤   **9.1 Sex with Clients**

Your colleague Mitchell Moore has been hospitalized quite suddenly. While he is on sick leave, you have been assigned to cover some of his cases.

You learn from several of his clients that Mitch has been having sexual relations with them. You do not question Mitch's intentions since you know him to be a conscientious social worker. But this behavior is clearly in violation of Paragraph II-F-5 of the *Code*, which states, "The social worker should under no circumstances engage in sexual activities with clients."

The violation of the *Code of Ethics* is obvious, but what you should do is not clear because many conflicting claims are made on you. Let us examine these claims, one by one, but not in any order of priority. The references are to the relevant paragraphs of the *Code of Ethics* (NASW, 1993). (See pages 232–41 of this book.)

1. Your obligation to support the code of ethics of the profession (M-2, 3).
2. Your obligation to protect the interest, character, and reputation of the colleague whom you replace (J-5).
3. Your obligation to protect clients from exploitation, even from exploitation by another social worker (F-2, 4, 5).
4. Your obligation to respect confidential material received in the course of the professional relationship (H-1).

The foregoing obligations are derived directly from the professional *Code of Ethics*. But there are also other considerations:

5. Rumor has it that a number of other social workers also engage in this type of behavior. Making a fuss about it will only result in making yourself ridiculous.
6. Sex therapy may be good practice, even though it is not yet approved by the NASW *Code of Ethics*. What is unethical today may be declared ethical tomorrow.

These latter considerations argue against your taking any action (Option A), while the earlier considerations suggest a more active response (perhaps Option B, C, or even D). How can a social worker order these considerations into the more and less important? Does the Ethical Principles Screen (EPS) help you in unraveling this conundrum?

Let us consider another situation which presents the social worker with ethical quandaries in her relation with colleagues.

➤ **9.2 Failure to Report a Case of Child Abuse**

Jake Dember, a frail five-year-old, was brought to the Emergency Room of Mt. Ebal Hospital, unconscious, covered with blood from head to toe, obviously with serious internal injuries. His father, Hilary, said that Jake fell from their second-floor apartment and landed headfirst on the cement sidewalk. The medical team was able to save Jake's life, though serious brain damage could not be reversed. Now, two weeks later, Jake is still in the hospital's critical care unit. The attending physicians are determined to report this as a case of child abuse. Before doing so, they have asked the hospital social worker, Josie Perry, to appraise the general home environment.

Erica Dember, Jake's mother, did not want to talk to Josie. She said that she and her husband were already in family therapy at the Family Service Agency. If Josie wanted to know anything about them, she should talk to their therapist, Ed Custer.

Josie arranged to meet with Ed Custer on the following afternoon. Ed was willing to share his assessment of the Dember family since both parents had signed the customary consent forms when Jake was admitted to the hospital. In the course of their conversation, Ed acknowledged that he had been aware of ongoing child abuse in this family, but since he thought that it was not too serious, he did not file a report as required by law. He feared that such a report would have interfered with the therapeutic relationship that he was trying to develop with this family.

There are similarities and differences between this exemplar and the previous one. In both cases, one social worker became aware that another worker had violated ethical standards. In the first case, continuation of the unethical behavior (sexual relations with clients) might result in further harm to clients. In the present case, the harm to Jake had already been done and will presumably not be repeated with Jake, but Ed Custer's unethical conduct and his failure to report other cases of child abuse may cause harm to other clients. Are the conflicting claims on Josie Perry similar to those which faced Mitch Moore's colleague? How valid is Custer's fear that reporting a client's child abuse may interfere with the therapeutic relationship? Does this consideration provide a defense against charges of unethical conduct? How should Josie Perry resolve the ethical dilemma facing her? Should she report Ed's negligence to the NASW chapter? Or should she ignore it?

So far our consideration of the ethical quandaries arising out of this issue have focused on relations with social work colleagues. But social workers also interact with practitioners from other professions and with nonprofessional human service workers. While the nature of these relations may be different, the NASW *Code of Ethics* states that the same respect and cooperation that is extended to social work colleagues should also be extended to colleagues of other professions (1993, Paragraph J-8). In one sense, the ethical problems arising out of these relationships will be the same as those that occur in relationships with social work colleagues. But in other ways the ethical dilemma may be more critical because these non–social work colleagues are not subject to the provisions of the NASW *Code of Ethics*. They may follow other norms of confidentiality or may routinely engage in behaviors defined as unethical for professional social workers.

## ADHERENCE TO AGENCY POLICIES AND REGULATIONS

The fact that most social workers are employed by bureaucratic organizations makes for another set of ethical dilemmas. Every organization has rules and policies. Those who accept employment voluntarily agree to abide by these regulations. The NASW *Code of Ethics* considers this commitment to the employing organization a basic ethical obligation: "The social worker should adhere to commitments made to the employing organization" (1993, Paragraph IV-L). But the goals and objectives of many organizations, even of social service agencies, are not always congruent with the objectives of the social work profession. Organization maintenance and survival demands may lead to rules which contradict the primary obligation of social workers to give priority to their clients' interests. Efficiency measures may limit intervention options so that the most effective option for a given client may not be available. Budgetary considerations may result in service cutbacks which will not necessarily be in the clients' best interest. In these and similar situations, a social worker, and especially a social work administrator, must resolve a critical ethical dilemma—whether to give priority to adherence to agency rules or to service to clients.

The issue of loyalty to the employer was particularly vexing to members of the task force which prepared the revised *Code of Ethics*. According to Robert Cohen, the NASW staff member assigned to the task force, "the frequency with which advocacy responsibilities, obligations to clients, and duties owed to colleagues conflict with agency practice or policy" was noted by task force members; but they also expressed concern that this loyalty to the employing organization "too often provides a convenient excuse for failure to act, i.e., 'to blow the whistle,' to 'go public,' to confront" (1980b, p. 10).

Collusion with clients to violate agency policies is often rationalized by the social worker through defining her activities as promoting the client's welfare or contributing toward social justice. But Levy holds that it is never ethical to violate agency policies (1982, p. 52). But are there never any exceptions to this ethical rule? For example, a welfare recipient has an occasional additional income which he is supposed to report to his social worker so that part of this income can be deducted from the following month's welfare check. If the social worker does not report this income, all of the extra money will be available to the client. Keeping quiet may be in the client's best interest. But what about the worker's obligations to her employer? See Exemplar 12.1 on page 195 for another example of this ethical dilemma.

A particularly difficult ethical dilemma is faced by social workers when they discover that their agency's policies or regulations are unethical. A hospital social worker discovers that the hospital administration encourages unnecessary surgery or delays discharges in order to assure additional income. The administrator of a child protective agency hires inadequately trained paraprofessional workers to investigate complaints of child abuse since insufficient budgets have made it impossible for him to hire professionally trained workers for this assignment, one that requires a particularly high skill level. How can these social workers resolve the ethical dilemma they face?

A different aspect of the conflict between agency interests and client interests that results in ethical quandaries is illustrated by the following exemplar:

➤ **9.3 Case of a Hyperactive Boy**

David is a hyperactive child in a residential institution. In the last few weeks he has become very disruptive. The consulting physician has prescribed large doses of a tranquilizer to calm the child and manage him better, but the cottage social worker has refused on ethical grounds to administer this medicine to David. She feels strongly that such pharmaceutical control will interfere with the child's welfare and freedom and will be counterproductive in any therapy attempted. Her social work supervisor has supported this decision.

David continues to disrupt daily routines and has repeatedly injured other children. The institution's physician has now informed the director that he will refuse to respond to further calls to treat children injured by David unless the medication he has prescribed is given to David.

The institution's director supports the doctor against the decision of the social worker. What is really best for David? What ethical issues are involved in reaching a decision?

## Non–Social Work Employers

When a social worker is employed by an organization outside the human services field, the ethical problems that arise may be even more perplexing. Nowadays social workers are employed by industry, police, prisons, the army, colleges, and a variety of other organizations that are not social work–oriented. To whom do these social workers owe their primary loyalty? Who is the "client" of these social workers? Should the employer be informed of client problems that may affect the production schedule of a factory? Or that may have security implications? Should detectives have access to confidential information about prisoners?

In one study of social workers employed by various Illinois police departments, 70 percent of the social worker respondents said that they considered themselves most responsible to their clients, while only 7.5 percent said that their first loyalty was to the police department which employed them. Yet 39 percent of these same social workers occasionally shared confidential information about their clients with police officers; 4.9 percent indicated that they did so often or frequently (Curtis & Lutkus, 1985). Is there an ethical basis that permits social workers to share such confidential information with others when their primary obligation is toward their clients?

From an ethical point of view, this problem may be especially difficult for social workers in military service. Consider the following exemplar:

### ➤ 9.4  A Colonel Outranks a Captain

Pfc. Richard Mozart recently discussed some personal difficulties with Capt. Emilio Pacifico, a social worker on an air force base. Mozart is very concerned about his aged parents who live in a distant state and who find it increasingly difficult to cope by themselves. He has been so worried about this situation that he has started to use drugs intermittently. He told Capt. Pacifico about this in confidence.

Recently, because of some physical complaints, Mozart took a number of tests at the base hospital, including a urinalysis. The results of this test confirmed his use of drugs, but Pfc. Mozart is not aware of this finding.

On this base the base commander does not have access to the medical files of servicemen, but social workers, psychologists, nurses, and physicians have ready access.

Yesterday the base commander, Col. Benjamin Brown, discussed with Capt. Pacifico his concerns about Pfc. Mozart. His work has been less than satisfactory; his behavior suggests that he has serious problems and that he may be on drugs. Col. Brown asked Capt. Pacifico to check out the situation and let him know whether Mozart uses drugs.

Capt. Pacifico is troubled by this request. Must he comply with the order issued by his commanding officer and disclose the results of the medical test or information which he has received on a confidential basis from his client? Or should he refuse and claim privileged communications? What is the ethical behavior expected of him?

Ethical problems arising out of adherence to agency policies occur in all settings. Some of our illustrations are taken from non–social work settings because there the ethical dilemmas may be more evident. But social workers employed by social agencies should not think that these problems cannot happen to them, as the following exemplar illustrates:

### ➤ 9.5  Apple Hill Young Adult Social Club

The Apple Hill Community Center is a group service and recreation agency in a "changing neighborhood." When it was established almost fifty years ago, it served an immigrant population and was instrumental in the Americanization of many thousands of newcomers. It now sees "character building" and "strengthening democratic decision making" as its major contribution to the community. As a matter of policy it avoids all political activities. Neither staff nor groups affiliated with the center are allowed to take a public stand on controversial issues.

Otto Zupan, a social group worker, staffs the Young Adult Social Club. This group is composed of twenty-five young men, ages eighteen to twenty-one, almost all of whom are high school graduates. They spend much time at the community center because most of them are unemployed. Lately they have talked a lot about why there are no jobs for them. Some thought that the recession was to blame, others felt it was because they were black. Otto urged them to do some research and see if they could come up with the real answer to their question. The results of their field study left little doubt that they were the victims of discriminatory hiring practices.

Otto urged them to go public because discrimination in hiring was against the law. Letting the public know about their findings might help them get a better break when applying for the next job. They thought that Otto's idea was great and decided to call a news conference. They asked Otto to arrange for a room at the center for the news conference.

When Otto talked over their plan with the center's director, he was rebuffed flatly. Not only could they not have a room for the news conference, but as a center social club they could not engage at all in this type of action program. Furthermore, Otto must do everything to bring the group back to its original objectives as a social club. The center director added that if he could not do this, he should ask for another assignment.

Loyalty to agency rules or meeting client needs—these are two conflicting professional obligations which create a serious ethical problem for social worker Otto Zupan. Is it ethical for him to abide by the agency's directives and thus abandon the young adults at this critical point in their development? Or should he ignore his obligations to his employer and help group members organize outside the center? What is the ethical stance demanded of a social worker who faces this situation?

Another type of ethical dilemma occurs when an agency channels clients into programs that are not beneficial for them. For example, what are the ethical issues faced by social workers when a large number of unskilled men and women are directed into job-training programs that lead only to dead-end or nonexistent jobs? Should social workers act against agency policy and tell their clients all that they know about these programs? Or is it more ethical to follow organizational directives and keep quiet? How does a social worker make ethical decisions of this type?

What are the ethical implications when a social agency engages in discriminatory practices? There was a time when such practices were blatant and open; nowadays they are less obvious but may be equally damaging. One child welfare agency places white children in adoptive homes and minority children in institutions "because there are no adoptive homes for them." In another agency homosexual AIDS victims receive one type of service, while heterosexual AIDS victims, another. Whatever the reason, discriminatory practices never benefit the client who is being discriminated against. The *Code of Ethics* clearly states that "the social worker should not practice, condone, facilitate or collaborate with any form of discrimination..." (NASW, 1993, Paragraph F-3). What does this mean in practice? Should a social worker refuse to accept employment in an agency that practices discrimination? Must she resign when she discovers such practices? Or should she ignore such agency policies and, whenever possible, not follow them? What would you do if you had Dale Jenkins's job?

➤ **9.6 Social Work in a Bank**

Social worker Dale Jenkins is employed by a large bank as a community representative in a minority neighborhood. Jenkins is black. Part of his assignment is to be visible and become accepted in the community. He has been very successful in meeting this objective. He is accepted by the neighborhood's residents and is liked by nearly everyone. In the past year he has been able to help a number of residents qualify for business loans and mortgages.

Mr. Stamos, vice president of the bank to whom he reports, recently told Jenkins that the bank has decided to direct less money and services to this neighborhood, but his job is "safe." Stamos implied that in a few years the bank might again direct monies to this neighborhood. In the meantime Jenkins should be more "selective" in referring residents to the bank for loans and mortgages.

Jenkins understood this message as meaning that the bank no longer would give mortgages to minority group applicants.

He considered the options he had, including the following:

1. Try to persuade Mr. Stamos and other bank officials to change the new and discriminating policy.
2. Ignore the new policy and operate as he had in the past.
3. Tell community leaders about the new policy and encourage them to apply political pressure on the bank to change its policy.

What are the ethical implications of each of the options that Jenkins is considering?

## ETHICAL DILEMMAS IN SOCIAL WORK ADMINISTRATION AND SUPERVISION

Social work administrators and supervisors have an ethical responsibility to protect clients' rights and to foster an atmosphere in which workers will do the same. At the same time, they are accountable to the agency's sponsors for productivity and for operating within the authorized budget. With diminishing budgets and rising demands this can be a most difficult task. In addition to ethical obligations toward the agency, an administrator also has responsibilities toward his or her employees.

For many administrators the line between ethical and unethical behavior is crossed only when their activities result in personal gain. They feel that it is ethical to do whatever is necessary as long as their activities benefit clients or the agency. If a government contract provides budget for staff training but not for staff supervision, they have no hesitation to "redefine" supervision as training. Or recreation services are renamed "respite services" if government funding for recreation is dropped (Bernstein, 1990). In such cases an illusion of compliance is achieved by playing semantic games, but is this ethical?

The adoption of the success model by many administrators has created another set of ethical dilemmas. While in earlier generations business was always depicted as the antithesis to civilized values, in recent decades the world of Big Business has been presented as the Good Thing. The overriding message is that bigger is better and that profitability is the most important objective, even for social programs. The success model directs social work administrators to do whatever needs to be done to increase the agency's share of the "market." Emphasis is placed on growth. Everything is reduced to time, money, and quantitative outputs. Efficiency becomes the bottom line and at times overrides human considerations (Miller, 1990). Administrators who follow this success model may not even be aware of the many ethical questions they encounter.

Another ethical dilemma that some administrators face occurs when there is a conflict between their responsibility for organizational maintenance, on the one hand, and professional or communal responsibility, on the other hand. Take the case of the director of a children's home that for decades has provided institutional care for infants aged three days to one year. From a professional point of view, there is no longer any justification for continuing this service, yet the director has responsibilities to the sponsors, to staff, and to others for ensuring that the agency continues to function. How would you respond to the ethical dilemma facing this social work administrator?

More generally, both supervisors and administrators have a responsibility to support workers' ethical behaviors and to stop workers' unethical behaviors. But they must remember that workers (as well as clients) are human beings, not robots.

## Dual Relations

Supervisors and agency administrators are powerful persons since they hold power over the social workers and students whom they employ or supervise. They make assignments, evaluate their work, decide on promotions, and at times terminate their employment. They are obligated to use this power in ethical ways. This rule has a number of implications.

To engage in any relation with employees or students in which an administrator/supervisor takes advantage, exploits, or harms persons with less power is unethical, even if the initiative comes from the employee (supervisee). This holds for sexual relations, as well as for other types of relations which create bonds that may negatively affect the professional relationship. Among the newest standards added to the code are two (II, F, 4 and III, J, 12) introduced to provide clearer guidance for social workers in regard to dual/multiple relationships. This area of unethical behavior has received more attention in recent years. Here we wish to highlight the need for social workers to consider seriously the ethical problems that may arise in work settings among persons with different degrees of power.

When you consider the following supervisory situations, how would you assess each of the following situations:

- Your supervisee's husband is an insurance broker. She tells you that her husband will give you a large discount on your automobile insurance. Will you avoid the dual-relationship problem if you place your insurance with him but pay the full insurance rate?
- Your supervisee, a BSW social worker, just enrolled in a graduate school of social work. The school is ready to appoint you as a field instructor and have you supervise your employee's field instruction.
- Your agency is employing your wife as a caseworker and assigns you to supervise her work.
- Your supervisee has a summer home in the mountains. She invites you and your children to use it this summer while she and her husband are vacationing elsewhere.

Each of these situations presents different ethical problems, yet in each the dual relation is the cause of a potential ethical difficulty. Do the new standards (II, F, 4 and III, J, 12) give clear answers to these?

## Other Conflicting Obligations

Social work supervisors are often in the position of the person "in between" with multiple pressures and obligations, as the next two case situations will illustrate.

➤ **9.7 The Ethics of Moonlighting**

The employment contract of the Bay City Department of Human Services (DHS) states:

> Social workers may not work for another employer in their professional social work capacity, even outside of their regular working hours.

Every new social work employee in the department is made aware of this provision and acknowledges her agreement to it in writing.

The other evening Ellen and Bill Stock had to rush their infant daughter Sharon to the hospital because she had a very high fever. While Ellen stayed with the baby in the emergency room, Bill handled the admission routines.

Later on Bill told Ellen that among the people with whom he had to speak in the admissions office was a social worker. He had been very impressed by her warm and sympathetic interest in their sick child. Ellen asked Bill if he recalled the worker's name and was surprised to learn that it was Joan Gilligan, one of the social workers she supervises at DHS.

On the way out of the hospital, Ellen peeked into the admissions office to make sure that this was the same social worker she supervises. It was she. Since Ellen did not use her husband's name at work, she was sure that Joan did not realize that she had been helping her supervisor's husband.

Ellen did not know what she should do about her discovery. On the one hand, Joan's moonlighting was in violation of the commitment that she, like all DHS social workers, had made to the agency. The *Code of Ethics* states clearly, "The social worker should adhere to commitments made to the employing organization" (NASW, 1993, Paragraph IV-L). On the other hand, Joan's moonlighting did not harm anyone. As a matter of fact, her presence in the hospital admissions office benefits many patients at a time when they are in a state of crisis. Yet what about Ellen's obligations to her employer? To her colleague? To the profession?

The next exemplar will deal with yet another aspect of this issue.

➤ **9.8 A Caribbean Cruise**

Wilma Stevens supervises a unit of six social workers. Carla Bick is the most qualified and most effective of the six workers in her unit. Last week Carla was not at work. Her boyfriend called in to say that Carla had a bad case of the flu and would probably be out all week. Today she returned to work, bringing a note from her doctor which stated that she had been sick all week. Aside from the note, there was no evidence of her having been sick. She explained that yesterday she went to the beach; this accounted for her suntan.

Wilma's cousin had been on a Caribbean cruise all of last week. When they had supper together tonight, the cousin told Wilma all about the trip and about the many interesting people she had met on board the cruise ship. One of those people had been a young social worker, Carla Bick. The cousin wondered whether Wilma happened to know her.

As Wilma thought about Carla's absence from work last week, she noted the following points:

1.  Carla's absence was not authorized and was in violation of agency policy.
2.  Carla's behavior was unethical and unprofessional.
3.  Carla harmed her clients by failing to provide them with regular service.
4.  Carla had not told the truth when she claimed that she had been sick.
5.  But Carla was her best worker and Wilma did not want to lose her.
6.  Other workers probably also had misused sick leave, but were not caught. Would making an example of Carla persuade others to desist from this unethical behavior?

It will be difficult to differentiate between Wilma's administrative/ supervisory responsibilities and her professional social work responsibilities. Any decision that she will reach will necessarily include both aspects. But whatever her decision, it will have ethical implications.

One of the assignments of an agency director is to "staff" the board of directors, the agency's policy-making group. Establishing a good working relationship with board members is essential for every successful agency director. But at times the agency director will encounter ethical dilemmas because of conflicting ethical principles. Consider the following exemplar:

➤ **9.9 The Board of Directors of the Alzheimer Association**

The Alzheimer Association is a local, voluntary United Fund agency established about ten years ago to provide a wide range of community services to families of Alzheimer's patients.

At last night's meeting the board of directors voted to eliminate all homemaker services because the insurance carrier had again raised the premium for liability insurance that homemakers must carry.

You, the agency director, know that the demand for homemaker services has always exceeded the staff available. It is not only a popular service, but a resource that has enabled many families to keep their Alzheimer's patient at home instead of placing him or her in an institutional facility.

You know that the agency provides other services for which there are fewer demands; reducing these services could pay for the higher insurance premiums. But these other services are of special interest to several board members; they will do everything to protect "their" services.

What are the ethical problems that this exemplar raises? How can you resolve them?


## ADVERTISEMENTS AND SOLICITATION

In 1988 NASW entered into a consent order agreement with the Federal
Trade Commission which required that NASW amend its *Code of Ethics*
as a result of a complaint the Seattle Regional Office had presented to the
Commission. As a result of the consent order, several changes were
introduced having to do with solicitation of clients, advertisements, and
payments for referrals. The resulting changes in the *Code* illustrate the
power of the state and law in relation to the nature of a profession's code
of ethics.

Among the results of the consent order were three revisions in the
*Code*. The prior standard (III, K, 1) which prohibited the solicitation of
colleagues' clients was deleted. This meant that NASW may not ban any
of its members from engaging in truthful, nondeceptive advertising and
marketing. Members may engage in solicitation of actual or prospective
clients or other consumers and may offer services to clients or other
consumers receiving similar services from another professional. The
order also allows payment of remuneration to a patient-referral service.
NASW may formulate and enforce reasonable principles or ethical guidelines to prevent deceptive advertising and solicitation practices, as well
as guidelines with respect to solicitation of business or testimonials. Finally, the consent order does not prohibit NASW from issuing reasonable principles or guidelines requiring that factual disclosures be made to
clients or other consumers regarding fees paid by any social worker to
any patient referral service.

Article II, F, 2 was amended to read: "The social worker should not
exploit relationships with clients for personal advantage." The deleted
phrase was "or solicit the clients of one's agency for private practice."
Article II, I, 1 was amended to read: "The social worker should not accept
anything of value for making a referral." This wording replaced the earlier
standard which read: "The social worker should not divide a fee or accept
or give anything of value for receiving or making a referral."

The changes in the *Code* make some things clearer and others more
ambiguous. What is truthful, nondeceptive advertising and marketing?
How much real choice does a potential client under stress actually pos-
sess? Does such a stressful situation allow for fully informed consent in
which the autonomy and liberty of the potential client are assured?

Social workers are allowed to pay referral fees to referral organizations; however, they are not eligible to receive payments for referrals

they make to practitioners or organizations. Is this a double standard? What is the ethical difference between payment for receiving referrals and payment for directing referrals to certain services?

➤ **9.10 Payment for Referrals in an Employee Assistance Program**

Libby Rudo, the social worker in the Employee Assistance program of the Colonel Electric Company, worked out an arrangement which meant that the treatment agencies to which her staff refers employees for longer-term treatment will pay the Colonel Electric Company a fee. She made the agreement based on the consent order between NASW and the Federal Trade Commission regarding advertisement and solicitation which allows for payment of remuneration to a patient-referral service. The NASW code, however, states, "The social worker should not accept anything of value for making a referral" (II, I, 1). On the one hand, the consent order allows for such payments. Furthermore, she is not receiving the fee; it is being paid to the Colonel Electric Company. What is the ethical thing to do?

May a social worker solicit payments for referrals so that they are paid not to her directly but to a nonprofit agency or department? If a social worker is a member of a for-profit group, may the group receive payment for referrals and include the payments in the overall income of the group to be distributed to the members as part of their earnings? Does it make a difference if business suppliers provide honoraria, conference expenses, luggage, lunches, or other gifts to an individual social worker? What if the gifts are provided to the agency and the agency distributes them? When a business firm provides free or discounted service for one of your poor clients because of other referrals you have sent to the firm, is this "payment" a fee for referrals in the same way that it would be if you received it directly?

The ruling of the Federal Trade Commission was based upon an economic analysis concerned with market forces. Economic concerns may not always be consistent with ethical concerns. It remains to be seen to what extent social work treated as a business will be consistent with professional ethics. There may also be ethically problematic situations which can arise as social workers engage in active competition with their professional colleagues in a free-market system.

## EXERCISES

1. Consider the ethical dilemmas facing social worker Timothy Land (Exemplar A.11 in Appendix A). How would you resolve the ethical problems that he faces?

2. Some employers make demands that may force social workers to violate the professional ethics (if they do not want to look for another job). But when this happens in the computer age, a new type of ethical dilemma occurs. Exemplar A.9 (in Appendix A) presents such a new dilemma. How would you respond to this ethical challenge?
3. Prepare a list of unethical professional behaviors that you think should be actionable by the state licensing authority. What sanctions or punishments should be available to this authority?

## SUGGESTIONS FOR ADDITIONAL READINGS

Ethical problems facing administrators of voluntary social agencies are discussed by Lewis (1989). Loewenberg (1987) analyzes how a social worker might respond to a colleague's unethical behavior. Ethical decision making by social work supervisors is examined by Congress (1992).

Managing volunteers in social agencies is an activity not covered in this book, but it is one that is becoming increasingly important in many social agencies. Netting (1987) reviews ethical issues encountered in working with and supervising volunteers.

# 10. Private Practice Social Work

Almost one of every three employed NASW members in 1991 was in private practice, either on a full-time or part-time basis (Gibelman & Schervish, 1993). When the NASW Delegate Assembly officially recognized private practice in 1964, few thought that so many social workers would choose to practice outside the traditional agency setting. The thinking of the delegates on this question emerges clearly from the 1964 decision, which states specifically that "practice within socially sponsored organization structures must remain the primary avenue for the implementation of goals of the profession" (Golton, 1971, p. 950).

As more and more social workers engage in private practice, there is growing concern about changing attitudes and behaviors which may no longer be in consonance with the profession's ethics. An "increasing inattention to the needs of the most vulnerable in our society" may be one of the consequences of such a shift, according to Land (1988, p. 87). This problem is especially critical when social workers opt for private practice in order to gain status, prestige, and higher income; when this happens, professional ethics may become a secondary consideration.

A number of ethical problems and dilemmas faced by private practitioners will be discussed in this chapter. Some of these problems (such as misdiagnosis) are also encountered by social workers in agency practice, but are discussed here because practitioners in private practice come upon these ethical problems and dilemmas more often and more acutely than their agency-based colleagues. Many ethical problems discussed in this chapter are problems faced by all private practitioners, regardless of their professional affiliation.

## FEES

Social workers must make sure that the fees they charge "are fair, reasonable, considerate and commensurate with the services performed and with due regard for the client's ability to pay" (NASW, 1993, Paragraph II-I). Some private practitioners who want to practice in an ethical way do not know what "due regard for the client's ability to pay" means. Does it require a sliding scale? Does it mean that varying rates should be charged for the same service, depending on the financial resources of the client? Or is a "reasonable fee" the fee that most private practice social workers in this locality charge? This is one ethical question, but there are other questions concerning fees that also have ethical implications.

### Client Dumping

What is the ethical thing to do when a client's situation changes and he can no longer pay the agreed-to fee? Consider the situation of Larry Firth.

➤   **10.1  A Difficult Family Situation**

Larry Firth came to consult with you about a "difficult family situation." His wife has left him and their two sons in order to live with her boyfriend. He himself has formed a satisfactory relationship with a married neighbor. However, he is concerned what his teenage sons will say and do when they find out the truth about their parents.

You are making good progress in helping Larry Firth come to grips with his problem. But today Larry tells you that he has lost his job and that he can no longer afford your fee. You are not yet sufficiently well established to carry "free" cases. What should you do?

"Dumping the client" is one way that some practitioners have responded to clients who can no longer pay the fee. There are various ways to dump a client. A worker may tell a client that his problem has been solved successfully (when it has not yet been solved) or that no more can be done for him (when, in fact, the worker could still be helpful). Or the worker may cancel appointments so frequently that the client loses interest. No matter what technique is used, the worker's objective is to get rid of the client who can no longer pay. Barker (1988a) considers dumping clients highly unethical. But what can an ethical practitioner do when this situation arises? There are several options a social worker should consider, including (1) continuing treatment on a "free" or a reduced fee basis, (2) continuing treatment with the understanding that the client will pay when his financial situation improves, or (3) making a proper referral to an agency for continued treatment. None of these options is without problems, but each of these options occurs within an ethical frame.

## Double Billing

Double billing occurs when a service provider bills a third party, such as an insurance company or a governmental program, for services not provided or for services already billed to another party. This practice usually occurs without the client's knowledge. It is both unethical and illegal. If detected, the practitioner is liable to criminal prosecution and to malpractice litigation.

## DIAGNOSIS AND MISDIAGNOSIS

The controversy about the place of diagnosis in social work practice has a number of ethical aspects. Many social workers believe that diagnosis is an essential element in every professional intervention, but others reject its use because they consider it an inappropriate application of the medical model to social work practice. Some point to psychologist Carl Rogers, who consistently argued against the use of any psychodiagnosis because he thought that such a procedure unduly interfered with a client's need to experience himself subjectively. Diagnosis, according to Rogers (1951), substitutes an external definition about the problem at a time when it is most crucial that the client gain greater subjective clarity about his situation. Psychiatrist R. D. Laing (1967) also criticized traditional diagnostics because it often leads to a self-fulfilling prophecy. If certain behaviors are expected, chances are that the client will perform them and/or that the worker will detect them.

In recent years the problem of diagnostics has become even more critical for many social workers as use of the series *Diagnostic and Statistical Manual of Mental Disorders* (DSM-IV, 1994) of the American Psychiatric Association (APA, 1994) has spread rapidly among social workers.

Many social workers are required to use DSM-IV even though they do not think that it is an appropriate diagnostic instrument for social work practice. They are required to use it by many government programs (which authorize service or reimburse for service rendered only on the basis of an appropriate DSM-IV diagnosis) and insurance companies (which require such a diagnosis before they will authorize third-party payments) (Denton, 1990). "Diagnosis increasingly provides a mechanism for clinicians to be reimbursed and for clients who cannot afford treatment to get the services they need," according to Kirk and Kutchins (1988, p. 226). Often authorization and reimbursements are limited to certain diagnostic categories, or the amount of reimbursement (or the length of treatment authorized) depends on the diagnosis submitted. All of these requirements put pressure on social workers to use this diagnostic instrument. Often they engage in deliberate misdiagnosis in order to meet the stated requirements. The following exemplar illustrates one of the ethical problems created by this procedure.

➤ **10.2  Let the Insurance Company Pay the Bill**

Cristine Sales has been seeing a social worker in private practice for several weeks. Last week she told her social worker that she hoped her insurance company would reimburse her for these sessions. Today Cristine brought in the insurance company forms and asked her social worker to complete them. The social worker, who was familiar with the requirements of this insurance company, realized right away that she would have to report a more "serious" diagnosis than was clinically indicated if she was to qualify the client for insurance reimbursement.

DSM-IV attempts to codify available scientific information about mental disorders and specify objective criteria for diagnosis. It attempts to provide an atheoretical descriptive approach to the classification of mental disorders along five axes or dimensions. Axis III, for example, involves a medical decision on the physical condition of the individual client. Axis I is based on identifying a range of psychiatric conditions (including organic and neurological disorders). Whether social workers have the legal authority or sufficient psychiatric and medical knowledge to use DSM-IV and similar diagnostic instruments are questions that we will not discuss here, but that are vitally important (see Kutchins & Kirk, 1987).

Kirk and Kutchins (1988) studied a 10 percent random sample of NASW's Register of Clinical Social Workers (which contained over eight thousand MSWs with at least two years of experience, Academy of Certified Social Workers [ACSW] membership, or equivalent state certification) to learn about their experiences with the original DSM-III instrument. Questionnaires were returned by 382 social workers; of these, 25 percent reported that they used this diagnostic instrument daily, another 25 percent used it at least once a week, and an additional 30 percent several times a month. In other words, 80 percent of the respondents used DSM-III regularly. Many of the respondents indicated that they had questions or misgivings about using this instrument, but that they felt that they had no choice but to use it.

Kutchins and Kirk (1988) note in another paper that the practice of deliberate misdiagnosis is very common among social workers. Most justify this practice because they think that it is harmless or in the client's best interest. Generally social workers use "the least noxious diagnosis" (also known as *mercy diagnosis*). Reasons for deliberate misdiagnosis include the following:

1. It minimizes the communication of damaging and confidential information to nonsocial workers, especially to insurance companies and others.
2. It avoids the labeling effects of a more severe diagnosis.
3. It limits the adverse impact on client's self-esteem if the client should become aware of the diagnosis.

The above reasons are used to justify *underdiagnosis* by suggesting that this is in the client's interest. Eighty-seven percent of respondents admit to deliberate underdiagnosis at some time. Most use the category *adjustment disorders* when a more serious diagnosis would have been more accurate.

But 59 percent of respondents also report the use of *overdiagnosis*, that is, they report a more severe diagnosis than the actual diagnosis. They may use an Axis I diagnosis when this is not warranted in order to qualify a client for insurance reimbursement. Though claiming that overdiagnosis is done for the client's benefit, the real beneficiary may be the social worker whose payments are now guaranteed by a third party.

Another ethical problem arises when a social worker reports a diagnosis for an individual when the primary problem is located in the family system. Since DSM-IV allows only the diagnosis of problems of individuals, this deliberate misdiagnosis is also utilized to facilitate insurance reimbursement. This type of misdiagnosis was reported by 86 percent of the respondents.

Most practitioners try to avoid facing the ethical problems associated with misdiagnosis by pointing to the benefits the client gains. Kirk and Kutchins observe, "By focusing only on the presumed benefits to clients, clinicians avoid confronting the broad ethical implications that emanate from the practice of misdiagnosis" (1988, p. 232).

Even under the best of circumstances, social workers, like many other professionals, will make mistakes and err in their diagnosis. These mistakes are unfortunate and regrettable, but probably inevitable. But there are other "mistakes" in diagnostics that have ethical implications.

These include:

1. Lack of sufficient knowledge in using diagnostic instruments such as DSM-IV.
2. Poor professional judgment.
3. Deliberate misdiagnosis, often in connection with third-party insurance reimbursement claims and/or reimbursement by government programs.

Mistakes such as these may involve both illegal and unethical behaviors. Jones and Alcabes (1989) report that 5.8 percent of the 225 malpractice suits against social workers during the years 1981–85 were based on allegedly improper or incorrect diagnoses. Even though diagnosis and assessment are often viewed as professional techniques that are based solely on skill and knowledge, they always involve ethical considerations. Examine the following exemplar and consider the ethical aspects involved in arriving at a diagnosis:

➤ **10.3 Barry Has a Learning Problem**

Barry is a first-grader. He has two older brothers, ages eight and ten. His oldest brother is doing very well in school, but his middle brother has been identified as a "slow learner" and is in a special education class. Barry's teacher reports that Barry also has some learning problems and finds it difficult to keep up with the rest of his class.

The school social worker and the educational psychologist have been discussing what to do with Barry. His tests indicate a relatively low IQ, but within the "normal" range. The social worker knows that Barry would benefit from special attention that his regular teacher cannot give him. However, sending Barry to an ungraded class might label him for the rest of his life.

In this situation, as in many others, the "simple" technical task of diagnosis has a number of ethical aspects which every thoughtful social worker must consider seriously before arriving at a decision.

## OTHER ETHICAL ISSUES

### Fitting Diagnosis to Treatment

An ethical problem occurs whenever a social worker tries to fit the diagnosis to the treatment she plans to use, rather than select a treatment that is appropriate for the identified problem. This ethical problem ccurs in various guises. One such version is illustrated by the following exemplar:

➤ **10.4 Casework or Family Therapy**

The parents and adolescent children in the Martin family have been having their problems. There has been a series of incidents in which everyone involved has been shouting at each other, calling each other names—or not talking to each other for days.

Ms. Martin feels that she has failed as a mother. She has asked Ms. Aberdeen, a private social worker, to help her cope with her feelings. After talking with Ms. Martin the worker felt that the problem went beyond Ms. Martin's feelings, and that family therapy was indicated. Even though Ms. Aberdeen is a competent caseworker, she has had no experience in providing family therapy. However, there are no family therapists in this rural county. Ms. Aberdeen, therefore, diagnoses the problem in such a way that casework intervention is appropriate.

Is it ethical for Ms. Aberdeen to define the problem in a way that makes it possible for her to help Ms. Martin? From an ethical point of view, would it make a difference if this situation had occurred in a city where there were a number of family therapists?

There are other ethical aspects to this issue. Professional ethics demand that the intervention method be selected on the basis of the social worker's best professional judgment. Using other criteria may be unethical. For example, short-term therapy may be indicated for a given case, but some social workers invariably indicate the need for long-term therapy. They do so either because they are uncomfortable with short-term therapies or because they assign priority to building up a steady clientele (Land, 1988).

## Supervision and Consultation

While social workers hold various views about the need for traditional supervision, there is a general consensus that an ethical social worker does not practice without having consultation available. But consultation costs money; skipping supervision may be one way to "cut corners" in private practice. But is this ethical?

## Misrepresentation

The NASW *Code of Ethics* specifically states: "The social worker should not misrepresent professional qualifications, education, experience, or affiliations" (1993, Paragraph B-2). What seems like a simple ethical rule gives rise to a number of questions, including the following:

1. Is it ethical for a social worker to identify herself as something other than a social worker (such as a marriage counselor or psychotherapist)?

2. Is it ethical for a social worker to call herself Doctor when she has not yet earned this degree?
3. Must a student social worker always identify herself as a student in field instruction placements? Or can she present herself as "your social worker"?

Those who engage in one of these practices claim that they do so to give clients greater confidence in their worker and thus increase the chances for a successful outcome. But is this ethical?

## Promises

In an attempt to convince potential clients to enter treatment, a social worker may claim that she can help the client (perhaps even obtain a cure), when she only hopes that she can do so. Is this ethical? What do you think?

## EXERCISES

1. Discuss various ways in which social workers can avoid giving the impression that those who can pay a fee to a private practice social worker will receive better social work services than those who cannot do so; therefore, those who cannot pay will have to use agency services.
2. Some social workers have argued against the use of diagnosis, but most believe that diagnosis is an essential and necessary step in the treatment process. Have every student in the class select a partner. In each group of two, have one student role-play the pro-diagnosis position and the other, the antidiagnosis position. Try to convince each other of the *ethical* problems that the other's position causes.
3. There are many impediments on the road between diagnosis and treatment. Consider the case of Mr. Biao (Exemplar A.16 in Appendix A). How can this social worker be sure that his plan is ethical and correct? Is Paragraph D-1 of the NASW *Code of Ethics* relevant for making a decision in this case? Would the use of one of the other social work codes of ethics make a difference?
4. Consider the case of Barry (Exemplar 10.3). What ethical aspects does this case present? How would you resolve them? Use the Ethical Decision Screens to answer these questions.
5. Did Ms. Aberdeen, the social worker of Ms. Martin (Exemplar 10.4) conduct herself in an ethical way? What other options could she have employed?

6. Consider the ethical questions raised in the Misrepresentation section of this chapter. Instead of simply saying that such behavior is unethical or ethical, note arguments that may be offered by a social worker who does present herself in one of these ways. Then answer these arguments.

## SUGGESTIONS FOR ADDITIONAL READINGS

Kelley et al. (1987) explore a number of ethical dilemmas that arise in private practice, including the professional identity of the private practitioner, quality control of practice, accessibility of potential clients, and relations with social agencies. Land (1988) also raises a number of ethical dilemmas with which practice practitioners and other social workers must deal.

A reasoned condemnation of client dumping by private practice practitioners can be found in an editorial in the *Journal of Independent Social Work*, written by the editor and one of the leading academic experts on private practice (Barker, 1988a).

Ethical and other problems created by the use of the DSM series are discussed by Denton (1989), Kirk and Kutchins (1988), and Kutchins and Kirk (1995). These latter two authors also (1987) raise the possibility of malpractice suits that may occur when social workers use these diagnostic instruments.

# 11. Changing World/ Changing Problems

## TECHNOLOGY

Social work like many other professions has been affected by the impact of the computer and other modern technologies. Many persons, including social workers, hold the belief that things, unlike people, are value-free. However, technology exists within a human context; it reflects and shapes human choices. Human choices go beyond questions of technological feasibility and efficiency, but always involve value choices and ethical priorities.

At first, social workers were concerned that the introduction of information technologies into social agencies and social work practice would result in more critical ethical dilemmas because these technologies were thought to be insensitive to variations in human needs and individual differential values and cultures. Additional problems were expected in the areas of confidentiality and of protecting the ownership of personal data. It was believed that it would be more difficult to protect information from inappropriate prying and from inappropriate control.

On study of forty-eight microcomputer-using private nonprofit agencies in North Carolina found that three-fourths of the agencies maintained computerized client data. The agencies studied successfully transferred appropriate confidentiality safeguards from paper records to electronic records. However, as coordinating agencies, grant-funding agencies, third-party payers, and others seek to obtain data, improved methods for guaranteeing the confidentiality of records will be needed. As multiple agencies become linked in networks in order to promote collaborative case management, to what extent and under what circumstances is client permission needed for one agency and worker to receive all the information held by another agency about a common client? To what extent can agencies successfully limit the client data they have computerized and how can clients actually be sufficiently informed so as to be able to limit the information transferred to another agency? Another question is whether clients or patients understand the realities of the information networks to which agencies and their personal records are tied. To whom do these data belong? How can clients be assured privacy? No agency in this study reported that records were reviewed by clients for accuracy. Nor is there any indication that clients were aware that this information is at times shared with others (Finn, 1990).

Caputo (1991) set forth an ethical framework for information systems which asserts the primacy of clients as citizens. The ethical framework fulfills the following functions:

1. It provides a way to inform clients about the existence of a computerized client-information system;
2. It enables clients to give an informed consent in regard to the uses of information about themselves;
3. It offers an opportunity for individuals to inspect, correct, or add information about themselves, allowing them to expunge all or parts of their records, except where such records are legally required;
4. It develops an information needs matrix to guide unit allocation decisions on the basis of critical success factors; and
5. It holds professionals to a professional practice that is mindful of ethical standards, including respect for clients' autonomy, their right to information and privacy, the need to weigh the efficacy of demands for efficiency against the principle of human dignity, and adherence to confidentiality regarding the use of routinely collected information about clients.

Clearly, the ethical issues around the use of information technology extend beyond the early concerns for protecting confidentiality. In recent years additional technologies have entered the practice arena; many of them have resulted in new ethical dilemmas. These may occur when social workers practice in situations which use genetic counseling; psychotropic medications; various forms of blood, alcohol, and drug testing; DNA tests, various contraceptive, fertility, and abortion means, as well as life-support systems, and others.

Other ethical issues arise out of still newer developments. We are already beginning to see the impact of "second-wave" information technologies on practice (Cwikel & Cnaan, 1991). Among these are databases which can be used for screening and assessment; the selection of practice and service recommendations; expert systems for evaluating various risks such as foster care, parole, and suicide; and interactive treatment games and various forms of therapy. Among the ethical dilemmas which have developed as a result of these are questions of beneficence (autonomy versus paternalism), equity of access to scarce resources (ensuring equality of opportunity), and the promotion of the common good (ensuring that the maximum number of individuals benefit from the introduction of information technology).

The assumption of many advanced software and expert systems is that there is always one "right" decision which should be followed. As a result, problems concerning client autonomy and worker flexibility have become more critical. How is it possible for the worker simultaneously to defend the autonomy of the client, meet the expectations of the agency, and avoid paternalism and control of clients?

The introduction of information systems into social agencies with very tight budgets means that scarce resources must be deployed to pay for the new technology and for staff with specific expertise even while other agency programs and client supports will be reduced or eliminated. Work patterns and organizational structure will change and some resources will not be available for some kinds of client services.

Consider the common dilemma which confronts the social worker in the exemplar described below. The *Code of Ethics* states that "the social worker should act to ensure that all persons have access to the resources, services, and opportunities which they require" (VI, P, 2), and that "the social worker should act to expand choice and opportunity for all persons, with special regard for disadvantaged or oppressed groups and persons" (VI, P, 3).

➤ **11.1 Computerized Information System or Services for Teens?**

Miri Neidig is a member of the Board of Directors of a Neighborhood Service Center which provides counseling and other services, including services for low-income minority teenagers at a local shopping minimall. This service has recently been instituted and is highly valued by community members concerned about sexually transmitted diseases and by teenagers because of the privacy afforded by the location as well as the "simpatico" staff. The local United Way has been pressing the agency to computerize its operation, a project on which it has been making progress with the use of special funds earmarked by the United Way for this purpose. Other grant-funding agencies have also been pressuring the agency to implement a computerized information system. In fact, some funds were expended for this purpose in the past year. Now, however, the agency funding situation has become precarious. The board will meet this evening to review the agency budget since expenses must be reduced. The budget committee indicates that the Board must choose between eliminating services for teens at the mall or discontinuing the computerization program.

Ms. Neidig, a social worker and board member, is faced with a difficult choice. If she votes in favor of continuing services for teenagers, she will deny the agency the possibility of attaining more resources from the funding agency. If she votes for computerization, she denies the community and teens services which they desperately need. How is she to choose? Do the Ethical Assessment Screen (Figure 3.2) (page 61) and the Ethical Principles Screen (Figure 3.4) (page 63) help her decide what to do when faced with this ethical dilemma?

The increasing use of electronic mail makes available unsought information which may confront a practitioner with critical ethical dilemmas. Note the following exemplar:

➤ **11.2 E-mail from Europe and Suicidal Thoughts**[*]

A university student used an electronic mail discussion group to inquire about a drug which could be used for a painless suicide. A professor in Europe who read this request communicated his concern to the sender's university, which forwarded this message to the university's counseling department. The counselor assigned to this case decided to obtain more information before deciding what to do. She contacted the director of the Computer Center who broke into the student's account where additional messages on suicide were discovered. At this point the counselor decided to contact the student's parents.

This exemplar has been presented because it reflects the rapidly expanding use of electronic mail and because it raises some issues that social workers must consider. One issue facing the counselor is whether or not to act on the basis of third-party information, a third-party who is unknown to her. Since the situation was potentially life-threatening, this counselor decided to take the information conveyed by the third-party seriously, but she also wanted to obtain verification of the facts, if possible. Here the worker decided that intervention was justified. But, more generally, questions can be raised regarding the circumstances under which a social worker should seek entry into a confidential electronic file. Is there any issue short of life-threatening situations which might support such an action? Under what circumstances does the Computer

---

[*] This situation was described on a Social Work electronic discussion list and is used with permission of Steve Marson of Pembroke University. The counselor was not a social worker.

Center or a social agency have a right to examine someone's personal computer account? What should the counselor have done if the Computer Center (or agency) stated such an invasion was illegal or against the rules? She felt justified in asking the Computer Center for verification because of the potential life-threatening nature of the situation. Was it ethical for her to enter the student's computer account without obtaining his permission?

Since the student is at the university and the counselor is a university employee, she has some responsibility for his welfare, especially after she gained information about what was in his file. What should she have done if the student's account did not include life-threatening materials?

We do not know the counselor's reasons for contacting the student's parents rather than the student himself. Is telling the parents about their son's behavior an improper invasion of the student's right to privacy and confidentiality? What should the counselor do if—instead of contacting the student's parents—she spoke to the student, and he simply stated that he has an intellectual interest in painless suicide as a chemical problem? Which standards in the *Code of Ethics* provide guidance in this type of situation?

## HEALTH AND MENTAL HEALTH CARE

It seems that almost every day there is a new technology, a new disease entity, or a reorganization of the delivery system in health and mental health care. These changes can create new ethical dilemmas for social workers employed in these services.

The following situation illustrates some of the difficult ethical choices which confront health care social workers at the interpersonal and community levels.

➤ **11.3 To Treat or Not to Treat—At What Costs?**

Jorge Gaudi, an HIV-positive person, has contracted a strain of TB which is virulent and drug-resistant. He is extremely infectious. If he is successfully treated, his life will be only slightly extended and he will no longer be able to infect others. It is estimated he will die within two years. Successful treatment depends on his consistent compliance with the treatment regimen. The cost of treating him will be at least $200,000. He does not comply with his treatment regimen while in the hospital and wanders the hallways where he "bothers" staff and others. He has had to be restrained. He is homeless, lacks family supports, and is drug-addicted. Any possible cure depends on his complying with a difficult regimen, which is unlikely in his current life pattern.

The patient's inability to comply with the demands of treatment create for the health team a number of ethical dilemmas. Since he does not voluntarily comply, the team has to decide whether it can or should force compliance on a patient who cannot or will not comply with necessary treatment of an illness which threatens the health of others. Compliance provides no guarantees, but noncompliance makes it probable that other persons will be infected. The decision to force compliance will be easier if nontreatment endangers the lives of others, as is the case here; however, even here there are limits. Castro isolated all Cuban AIDS sufferers in camps as a public health measure; in the United States such a step would be politically and legally problematic. But is it ethical?

A second ethical issue raised by this case situation is whether or not a patient should receive treatment, even if a cure for all his illnesses is not possible. Given the best of all worlds, the ethical rule would say to treat Mr. Gaudi, even if treatment would add only an hour of life. In this case, the protection of human life (that of the patient and those with whom he will come in contact) suggests treatment is necessary since the alternative is to leave a highly contagious condition uncontrolled and the patient's life may be slightly improved, at least in respect to TB.

The cost of this treatment is high. This raises several additional ethical dilemmas, even if a cure were certain and compliance were assured. Is it fair to expend so many resources on someone who has no chance of a complete cure? Because of budget cuts, public health measures have been reduced in this city; funding for the homeless and for prisoners has been especially hard hit. Rationing health care is a reality as scarce resources have been allocated to other problems. The human and dollar resources which can be provided for treatment of this patient are limited. The critical ethical decisions related to Mr. Gaudi and his illness are made at several levels in society, some at community levels and others at the hospital and treatment team levels. Who decides what Mr. Gaudi and others will get and what resources will be assigned to their needs?

Among the options are (1) to arrange a comprehensive discharge plan which will require coordination among many agencies and persons and motivate Mr. Gaudi through special incentives for compliance, that is, provide housing, drug treatment, and psychiatric treatment while others wait for such resources; (2) to provide monetary incentives, and pay him to comply; (3) to involuntarily confine him and/or let him live in the community but put him on directly observed therapy, having him and all others in a similar situation mandatorily observed while taking their medications; (4) to discharge him and leave him to make his own decisions. Since his optimum life expectancy is in any case very low, dying a few months earlier is not significant; and (5) to provide a specialized foster home placement.

Mr. Gaudi illustrates a major public health problem. TB has always been found among the poor, immigrants, and minorities. He is drug-addicted, homeless, and will die in any event of AIDS. Is it racist and inequitable to single out poor and minority persons for confinement and mandatory programs? If patients are forced into directly observed therapy, what should be done if they are noncompliant? Should those persons be treated in isolation? Under what circumstances can a person's freedom be taken from him? Does this require a special institution for this particular population? Does society need to be protected against such an illness? Because of the exorbitant cost of serving this multiproblem group, people with other problems will have to go without.

As we think about this very complex situation, there are a number of ethical dilemmas and political problems at both the individual and the community levels. If you were the social work member of the hospital team considering what to do, what would you suggest? Why? (Arras, 1993).

Technological advances in neonatology have made it possible to sustain the lives of many newborn infants who in the past would not have survived. But survival for many will mean chronic disabilities, perhaps life-long institutionalization; keeping such infants alive raises questions about the immediate and future quality of life of the child, the parents, and other family members.

There are three ethical issues that are generally involved in these situations: the welfare of the parents versus the welfare of the child; the freedom of choice of the parents versus the life of the child; and the costs to society versus the life of the child. Embedded in these issues is one background issue: Under what circumstances should extraordinary actions be taken to enable the birth of a live fetus or to sustain a newborn child with multiple life-threatening problems? These problems are even more prevalent among aging persons, who often have a number of life-threatening problems simultaneously. But here we focus on newborn infants.

➤ **11.4 One Baby/Many Ethical Dilemmas**

Dr. Jane Newhouse just informed Mr. and Mrs. Lanier that their newly born son has been born with kidney failure, gastrointestinal obstructions, brain damage, and recurrent seizures. A bowel operation, dialysis, and a kidney transplant will be needed. Dr. Newhouse was extremely pessimistic about the immediate survival possibilities and more certain that if the infant survives, he will face survival crisis after survival crisis. The ultimate prognosis will be a child who will require institutionalization very early in life. Mr. and Mrs. Lanier, who must authorize any surgery, ask to meet with you because they trust you.

When should an infant be considered hopelessly ill? Is the life of a severely damaged infant of sufficient quality to warrant being saved by extraordinary measures? Who will pay for such expensive long-term care? Who will go without health care if this infant is kept alive? Who should make such decisions? For many health conditions, it is very difficult to predict with any certainty what will occur in the future. For others, the total situation clearly indicates early death, but miracles do happen. How should you respond when the Laniers ask you what they should do? Who is the client to whom you owe priority consideration: the baby, the parents, or society? In the Ethical Principles Screen, the highest value is the principle of the protection of life. Does this mean any life, even the life of a severely damaged person? Given the cost of saving and caring for Baby Lanier, whose life should be protected? The infant's? The parents'? Those in society who need the resources which will be directed to saving and sustaining this infant?

Following the "Baby Doe" case, Congress passed the Child Abuse Amendments of 1985 and assigned public child welfare agencies the responsibility of policing decision making concerning catastrophically ill neonates. Public child welfare agencies became responsible for assuring that decisions regarding medical treatment which would either end or sustain life would be in the newborn's interest and not be neglectful or abusive. Thousands of disabled children are born each year with life-threatening medical complications. In most cases the parents, physicians, and ethics committees are in agreement regarding how to proceed.

There are at present no clear and effective guidelines, even though states are expected to assign authority to their child welfare systems. Many people believe that the locus of decision making should reside with the parents of the child. Others think that these decisions are best made by physicians, bioethical committees in hospitals, child welfare agencies, or the courts. Still others believe that religious organizations should serve as the chief decision makers.

State and county departments of social services have moved to protect children from abuse and neglect, guided by the child's best interests. One result is that child welfare agencies sometimes find themselves responsible for making such life-and-death decisions when the Department of Social Services has legal guardianship over the child for the following reasons: (1) the mother is dying or has already died; (2) she is incompetent; or (3) the infant is born HIV-positive, has been abandoned, or otherwise has become the ward of the agency.

Hughes (1993a and b) concluded that in our pluralistic society there is no consensus which can provide guiding principles for child welfare workers and agencies. Nevertheless, he suggested a "guiding ethical paradigm" that can serve child welfare agencies faced with these critical and

difficult decisions. This guiding ethical paradigm consists of two principles for those with responsibility for treatment and case management
for catastrophically ill newborns: (1) The *quality-of-life principle* can be
described as the need to assess and consider the future quality of a person's life as an important variable in deciding whether to intervene to
prolong life. This principle suggests that some lives are worse than death;
and (2) The *principle of social transcendence* can be defined as the requirement that decisions not be based upon the potential relative social
utility of a person's life. It requires that treatment not be withheld on the
basis of an assessment of a child's future potential to contribute to society or upon the priorities of social utility. Hughes believes that quality of
life and social transcendence are consistent with the intent of the historical child welfare principle of best interests of the child. Suppose you are
the child welfare social worker assigned to the Lanier infant. Apply these
principles to the situation. Do they help you in making a decision? Would
they do so in another and different case situation? Do the two principles
form a sufficient base for decision making? What limitations can you
identify for each of these principles separately and for the two in combi-
nation? Do you see any conflicts with the NASW *Code of Ethics*? Does the
Ethical Principles Screen suggest a different course of action?

Proctor et al. (1993) found when they studied ethical dilemmas in
hospital social work that most ethical dilemmas involved conflicts
between client self-determination and client best interest; dilemmas were
more likely when a patient's mental status was impaired and decision
making was problematic. They found that these dilemmas related to
delayed discharge, in-hospital mortality, and less than adequate post-
discharge care. A large proportion of these conflicts were connected to
decisions about discharge destinations, that is, going home or going to a
nursing home. When there were disputes among various parties, four out
of five disputes were over the discharge plan or medical care. Families
were in conflict with medical teams or specific physicians; there were
conflicts between patients and staff members; between social workers
and medical staff persons; between patients and everyone else; or among
family members. Ethical dilemmas were found to be more likely when
patients were physically dependent and mentally confused.

What would you do in the following situation?

➤ **11.5 A Friend's Home? Nursing Home? Or What?**

Rochelle Diego is eighty-two years old and has been in the hospital for almost a month and a half. Her discharge has been delayed several times
when discharge plans had to be altered at the last minute. Once a close
friend had agreed to let her be discharged to her ranch-style home. But
after the agreement several of Mrs. Diego's adult children were furious with

her and forced her to back out. Then there was an attempt to discharge her to a nursing home, but other adult children objected. To make matters worse, Mrs. Diego drifts in and out of coherence. When she is coherent, she understands and you feel you can move ahead with assurance; soon after, however, she will be incoherent.

Free and informed decision making requires Mrs. Diego's clarity, but most of the time she is incoherent. There are conflicting values among her family members and no destination seems to be acceptable to all. Family discord has led to abortive attempts at discharge. The friend who offered to take her in is not a relative. The family members are unable to agree on discharge, but also have not offered to care for her in their homes. There has been an endless changing of minds by her family members. At what point is it ethical for the social worker to take a stand?

The following exemplar also raises questions about the role of the social worker and involves several ethical dilemmas.

### ➤  11.6 Our Daughter or Our Lives?

Irma Bream, a social worker at Heartland Children's Hospital, is meeting with Albert and Sorelle Clayton about the forthcoming discharge of their disabled eighteen-year-old daughter, Alice. The options upon discharge are: a nursing home which accepts very young persons; a specialized foster care placement; or returning her to her parents who would have to work twenty-four hours per day to care for their daughter without hope of respite time or any other help. The only real choice for the parents seems to be to give up their lives for the care of Alice or to give up Alice to foster care. After much discussion and several meetings, Albert and Sorelle can't come to a decision. Now they are asking Ms. Bream what she thinks is the right thing to do?

Who is the client in this situation, and to whom is priority owed? Who should make the decision about what will be done? What should Irma Bream say in answer to this question? Can you identify other ethical dilemmas facing the social worker in this situation? Where in the NASW *Code of Ethics* would this social worker find guidance?

## MANAGED CARE

In 1991 13.4 percent of the gross domestic product was spent on health care; this amounts to an average of $2,867 for each American man, woman, and child (OECD, 1994, p. 44). When one dollar in every seven is spent for health care—especially when health care costs have been escalating beyond the rate of inflation—there is increasing demand to control expenditures.

Managed care is one major strategy developed in an attempt to control health and mental health costs; this is done by monitoring access to and the type of health care a patient will receive from a health care practitioner or from a health maintenance organization. The goal is to reduce costs by placing controls on health practitioners and by fostering competition among HMOs. Managed care plans attempt to reduce these costs through controlling the type of health practitioners utilized, limiting access to service, and prescribing the type and length of service provided.

Practitioners from several disciplines have objected to the ways in which cost-conscious managed care plans are limiting patient service. The professional autonomy of practitioners is threatened by the controls exerted by the managed care organization. There is concern that practitioners are selected because they are willing to accept lower fees and more controls over their practice in exchange for high volumes of patients and guaranteed payment. Those not selected fear the loss of income. Further, there is concern that the various controls instituted will result in poorer-quality service and less ability by practitioners to provide what they consider to be high-quality professional service.

Managed care not only has an impact on professional persons in private solo or group practice but also on social agencies as these become ever more dependent on third-party payments. A number of ethical dilemmas are created for social workers by the impact of managed care on their practices, whether in private or agency-based practice.

The *Code of Ethics* has at least three standards which are of special relevance: (1) "The social worker should not participate in, condone, or be associated with dishonesty, fraud, deceit or misrepresentation" (I, A, 2); (2) "The social worker should be alert to and resist the influences and pressures that interfere with the exercise of professional discretion and impartial judgment required for the performance of professional functions" (I, D, 1); and (3) "The social worker should terminate service to clients, and professional relationships with them, when such service and relationships are no longer required or no longer serve the clients' needs or interests" (II, F, 9).

Managed care programs may place the social worker in situations where their compliance with the meaning of standard I, A, 2 may become questionable. For example, in order to provide a "reimbursable service" for a client, the practitioner may have to consider "fudging" the diagnosis in some way. What would you do in the following situation?

➤ **11.7 What Should the Diagnosis Be?**

You are having a first session with Mr. Xavier Anderson who has been referred to you because of an alcohol problem on the job. As you explore his situation and problems you discover that his symptoms—agitation, aggression, and mood fluctuations—may be defined either as psychiatric or as those associated with alcoholism and drugs. At this early stage you estimate that he will need more counseling sessions than his third-party payer usually allows for alcohol and drug abuse. But you also know that additional sessions will be allowed if you diagnose his symptoms as psychiatric.

Should you provide a "psychiatric diagnosis" even though you suspect that this is not indicated in order to guarantee reimbursement for all the counseling sessions that Mr. Anderson will need? Or should you provide an alcoholism diagnosis even though you know that the number of counseling sessions allowed for this diagnosis will not be sufficient for a cure?

Certain ethical dilemmas arise from the need for compliance with standard I, D, 1. For example, in a hospital setting, the managed care provider might declare that the patient should be released at the end of thirty days. But the treatment team may feel strongly that the patient should remain in treatment beyond the length of time allowed by the third-party payer. What should you do? Or what would you do in the following managed care situation which could also be encountered in other situations when a patient has no insurance coverage and cannot afford hospitalization?

➤ **11.8 Suicide Threat and Managed Care Says No Hospitalization**
You have been treating Ms. Adele Lang, a twenty-four-year-old college student who has been seriously depressed because of school failures and difficulties with her family. She has been threatening suicide but the third-party provider does not agree that she should be hospitalized. The claims reviewer has cited recent research on which she bases her decision.

The cost of hospital care is great and in-patient treatment is least desirable for the payer. However, in your professional judgment Ms. Lang should be hospitalized. Who actually will be responsible for the decision not to hospitalize this suicidal patient and for what happens to Ms. Lang? Strom (1992, p. 401) reports that in a recent court case it was found that "clinicians remain ultimately responsible for decisions affecting patients." One is bound by the *Code of Ethics* to practice with the maximum application of professional skill and competence. Under the circumstances, the social worker could agree and seek a "second-best" treatment. After all, the choice is not only between no treatment and hospitalization. On the other hand, the social worker has a responsibility to practice consistently with her best professional judgment, to give priority to her client's welfare, as well as to recognize she is the person who will be open to suit if harm comes to her client.

Similarly, social workers have been confronted with pressures from managed care organizations to provide more group therapy for their clients. The stance of the insurance company may be that group service is time- and cost-efficient. They stress that out-patient services in time-limited groups have been found to be very effective. Since group treatment can result in greater income, the practitioner may be tempted to agree, even though her professional judgment counterindicates this mode of treatment. Here the social worker faces another ethical dilemma: how to juggle the demands of her own professional judgments, of the insurance company, and of the desire for economic security. This dilemma is not limited to workers in private practice, but occurs also in agency practice as the following exemplar shows.

➤   **11.9  What Pine Tree Insurance Company Wants**

Dr. Felicia Montivedeo, director of social work clinical services for Family and Children's Services of Pleasant City, was surprised when she received a letter from the Pine Tree Insurance Company (Managed Care Division) and later a phone call, both of which subtly suggested that more of the agency's treatment services be offered in time-limited groups. When she raised the issue with the agency's administrative executive committee, some argued in favor of complying because the money received from the insurance company made up a substantial part of the agency's income. Others were concerned that such a change in operating procedures would upset the staff. Still others argued that compliance would mean yielding their professional judgment to the Pine Tree company.

Among the options suggested by committee members are the following: (1) to ignore the suggestion since it had not been explicitly stated; (2) to comply as soon as possible with the suggestion; (3) to refuse to comply and to begin to advocate with Pine Tree Insurance for the current mix of service modalities; (4) to begin research as to the relative effectiveness of various treatment methods; and (5) to meet with Pine Tree representatives to explore ways to phase in slowly more group treatment. What are the ethical implications of each option?

Social workers are employed as staff members in managed care organizations in various roles, including utilization management and other administrative capacities. What do you suggest that Ms. Priscilla Johanning, a social worker employed as a claims reviewer by the Claxton Insurance company, do in the following situation? Her job is to oversee the proper use of insurance funds by mental health professionals by ensuring proper diagnoses and treatment plans.

➤   **11.10  Confidentiality or Living with a Little Gossip**

The Claxton Insurance Company demands that clinicians release much information before they can obtain third-party reimbursement. Failure to provide very detailed reports means no reimbursement. Many of the insurance company's employees are not professionals; they are not bound by a code of ethics nor are they respectful of confidentiality. When Ms. Johanning learned that staff members gossiped about confidential information provided by providers, she complained to the manager. He said he would look into this, but the gossiping continued. When she asked again, he said, "Look, my job is to make sure company funds are controlled properly. I'm willing to live with a little gossip but I cannot do without the information."

Ms. Johanning has to choose between accepting management's view of what is best for the company, that is, to control mental health costs, and the professional view of safeguarding the best interests of all persons who receive services. Should Ms. Johanning remain silent or should she "blow the whistle"? Does the NASW *Code of Ethics* help in this situation?

## END-OF-LIFE DECISIONS

In 1993 the NASW Delegate Assembly approved a new policy statement on "Client Self-determination in End-of-Life Decisions." Social workers have been involved in the clarification of the legal, ethical, and other issues and policies concerning the conditions under which life may be ended, but this was the first time that NASW issued a policy statement to guide social workers. NASW's position was based on the principle that client self-determination should apply to all aspects of life and death.

The policy statement contains the following ideas:

The social work profession strives to enhance the quality of life; to encourage the exploration of life options; and to advocate for access to options, including providing all information to make appropriate choices.

Social workers have an important role in helping individuals identify the end-of-life options available to them.

Competent individuals should have the opportunity to make their own choices but only after being informed of all options and consequences. Choices should be made without coercion.

Social workers should not promote any particular means to end one's life but should be open to full discussion of the issues and care options.

Social workers should be free to participate or not participate in assisted-suicide matters or other discussions concerning end-of-life decisions depending on their own beliefs, attitudes, and value systems. If a social worker is unable to help with decisions about assisted suicide or other end-of-life choices, he or she has a professional obligation to refer patients and their families to competent professionals who are available to address end-of-life issues.

> It is inappropriate for social workers to deliver, supply, or personally participate in the commission of an act of assisted suicide when acting in their professional role.
>
> If legally permissible, it is not inappropriate for a social worker to be present during an assisted suicide if the client requests the social worker's presence.
>
> The involvement of social workers in assisted suicide cases should not depend on race or ethnicity, religion, age, gender, economic factors, sexual orientation, or disability.

Though NASW's policy statement is based on the principle of self-determination, many doubt whether meaningful self-determination and voluntary consent prevail in situations in which a person wishes to harm himself or commit suicide since "only abysmal ignorance or deep emotional trauma can lead persons to extreme measures like these" (Gewirth, 1978, p. 264).

The new policy statement raises many questions, among which are the following: Whose quality of life is supported by assisted suicide? Whose life is harmed? What is competence in such a situation? How does one judge competency? Is coercion entirely absent when people are considering suicide? What should one do if the option chosen creates issues for other professionals, family members, significant others, friends? What should one do if there are conflicts among those involved—some wanting to maintain life at all costs, others supporting the person's decision? What does it mean to be present but not participate? Is this just another form of approval of the act?

The NASW policy does not take an explicit position on the legalization of assisted suicide. It cautions social workers that it is inappropriate for social workers to deliver, supply, or personally participate in an act of assisted suicide. But social workers may now be involved in counseling clients on assisted suicide matters. However, the exploration of suicide as an option and the presence of social workers during assisted suicide seem to condone such actions. It is still too early to tell whether social workers in direct practice will back this policy statement.

As this is being written, a bare majority of voters in Oregon made that state the first in the nation to allow doctors to hasten death for the terminally ill. Under the new law, a physician is allowed to prescribe, but not administer, lethal doses of drugs. The patient must make the request in writing several times, must be judged to have six months or less to live, must wish to end unbearable suffering, and must have two physicians agree that the patient's condition is terminal. The patient must take the last steps personally. However, the law has not yet been put into effect because a group of doctors and patients filed a lawsuit in Federal District Court in Eugene to block the law as unconstitutional, arguing that the law violates the Constitution's equal protection and due process guarantees as well as the Americans with Disabilities Act of 1990. The court issued a preliminary injunction preventing Oregon from putting the voter-approved law into effect until the court can decide on its constitutionality, a process which was expected to take at least a year.

The Oregon law as well as the NASW policy statement raise a number of ethical and practice issues. The definition of terminal illness is not always clear. Sometimes even the best of practitioners makes a mistake, and persons judged to be terminally ill live beyond the projected time. Can "comfort care" and the control of pain offset the desire to end one's life? Sometimes "lethal doses" of medications prove not to be lethal, adding to the agony of the patient.

If you look at Figure 3.4, the Ethical Principles Screen on page 63, the principles of autonomy and freedom as well as quality of life are listed below the principle of protection of life. Was NASW correct in approving such a policy? Or should it have opened the discussion to a more extensive exploration of the issues, including ethical issues integral to the policy? What would you do? Would you base your decision on the *Code of Ethics*, the Ethical Principles Screen, or the NASW policy statement?

## EXERCISES

1. In a group discuss the ways in which technologies present ethical dilemmas for your agencies and for social workers. Identify ways in which these ethical dilemmas could be avoided and/or dealt with ethically.
2. You are on a committee to consider the fate of a severely disabled infant whose survival is questionable. Identify standards in the *Code of Ethics* which help you to weigh the welfare of the parents versus the welfare of the child.
3. You are serving on the committee in Exemplar 11.9, "What Pine Tree Insurance Company Wants." Which of the options suggested by committee members would you choose? What standards in the *Code of Ethics* support your choice?
4. If you were confronted as a social worker with the issue of assisted suicide, what would be your position? What justification would you provide for your decision?

## SUGGESTIONS FOR ADDITIONAL READINGS

Caputo (1991) presents an ethical framework for information systems which can be used in a social agency. Cwikel and Cnaan (1991) examine several ethical implications regarding information technologies. Hughes (1993a and b) presents a guiding ethical paradigm for use in child welfare settings in relation to catastrophically ill newborns. Maesen (1991) examines "Fraud in mental health practice: a risk management perspective" in relation to third-party payers. *Social Work Speaks* (NASW, 1994) includes "Client self-determination in end-of-life decisions," the NASW policy statement on this issue. Callahan (1994) presents arguments in opposition to the NASW policy position on end-of-life decisions.

# 12. Social Work with Selected Client Groups

## WOMEN AND SINGLE PARENTS

Does the gender of a client make a difference when it comes to making ethical decisions? The answer to this question is far from simple. A number of aspects that must be considered will be discussed in this section.

It is difficult to locate accurate data on the number of women and men who are clients of social workers, but it is widely believed that the proportion of women is far greater than their proportion in the general population. Thus Walrond-Skinner and Watson write that "the majority of therapy patients in Great Britain and the United States are female" (1987, p. 75). At the same time it is a fact that most social workers are women. The situation is different in many of the other helping professions; for example, most psychiatrists are male. The preponderance of women both among professional social workers and among their clients is a consideration that impinges on the question raised at the beginning of this section.

The dramatic increase in the number and proportion of female single parents among all parents and in the caseloads of most social workers is another consideration that must be kept in mind as we examine the possible impact of gender on professional ethics. Of course, there are also men who are single parents, but the overwhelming majority of single parents are women.

Table 12.1   Selected Characteristics of Household Composition, by Presence of Own Children under Eighteen, 1970 and 1992 (in thousands)

|  | 1970 | % | 1992 | % |
|---|---|---|---|---|
| All households | 63,401 | 100.0 | 95,669 | 100.0 |
| All family households | 51,456 | 81.2 | 67,173 | 70.2 |
| Married couple with children | 25,532 | 40.3 | 24,420 | 25.5 |
| Male householder, no wife present, with children | 341 | .5 | 1,283 | 1.3 |
| Female householder, no husband present, with children | 2,858 | 4.5 | 7,043 | 7.4 |

Source: Steve W. Rawlings, U.S. Bureau of the Census, Current Population Reports, "Household and Family Characteristics: March 1992," Series P20–467, Table A, p. vii, 1993.

Significant changes in the composition of the American family have occurred in the last generation. When we compare the 1992 census data with the 1970 data, we see that for all families the proportion of married-couple families has declined, while the percentage of one-parent families headed by a woman has almost doubled. The change is smallest among white families and largest among black families (see Table 12.1).

In 1970 one out of twenty families with children under the age of eighteen was headed by a woman with no spouse present; by 1992 this proportion had increased to one in every thirteen (see Table 12.1). The differential distribution of single female householders becomes apparent by examining the data in Table 12.2, which presents data by race (see Table 12.2). The proportion of female single householders is more than three times as large among black families as it is among white families. In 1992, 13.5 percent of all white families were headed by female householders with no spouse present, while 46.4 percent of all black families were headed by female householders without a spouse present. Hispanics also have a high percentage of single female householders. The number and percentage of white, Asian, and Pacific Islander female single householders is also increasing. The reasons for female single parenthood also vary for the different racial groups. Among white women the most frequent reason for single parenthood (in 1992) was divorced (38.8 percent), followed by never married (20 percent); married, spouse absent (19.3 percent); and widowed (4.7 percent). Among black women the reasons for single parenthood were: never married (55.9 percent);

**Table 12.2  Family Households by Type and Race, 1970 and 1992 (in thousands)**

|  | All Family Households | | Married-Couples Families | | Female Householder, No Husband Present | |
|---|---|---|---|---|---|---|
| Total | | | | | | |
| 1970 | 51,456 | (100%) | 44,728 | (86.9%) | 5,500 | (10.7%) |
| 1992 | 67,173 | (100%) | 52,457 | (78.1%) | 11,692 | (17.4%) |
| White | | | | | | |
| 1970 | 46,166 | (100%) | 41,029 | (88.9%) | 4,099 | (08.9%) |
| 1992 | 57,244 | (100%) | 47,124 | (82.9%) | 7,726 | (13.5%) |
| Black | | | | | | |
| 1970 | 4,856 | (100%) | 3,317 | (68.3%) | 1,358 | (18.0%) |
| 1992 | 7,716 | (100%) | 3,531 | (47.1%) | 3,582 | (46.4%) |
| Hispanic origin | | | | | | |
| 1970 | 2,004 | (100%) | 1,615 | (80.6%) | 307 | (15.3%) |
| 1992 | 5,177 | (100%) | 3,532 | (68.2%) | 1,261 | (24.4%) |
| Asian or Pacific Islander | | | | | | |
| 1970 | NA | | NA | | NA | |
| 1992 | 1,624 | (100%) | 1,284 | (79.1%) | 237 | (14.6%) |

*Source:* Steve W. Rawlings, U.S. Bureau of the Census, *Current Population Reports*, "Household and Family Characteristics: March 1992," P20–467, Table E, p. xii, 1993.

divorced (17.1 percent); married, spouse absent (17 percent); and widowed (3 percent).

But how do these data relate to the ethical questions that we are examining? An illustrative case study of a specific practice situation may help focus attention on some of the ethical questions.

### ➤ 12.1 Supplementing a Welfare Check

Olga Wilks has two children, ranging in age from four months to six years. This one-parent family lives on Olga's AFDC check. Occasionally Olga supplements this meager sum by babysitting for a neighbor. Olga has not reported this additional income to the welfare department as she is required to do by law. She knows that if she does report this additional income, next month's welfare check will be reduced.

Olga's social worker is aware of this additional income, but is not quite sure what to do about it. In considering what steps to take, she considers the following points, paying particular attention to the ethical implications of each:

1. Failure to report this additional income constitutes fraud against the welfare department; if she fails to report this extra income to her supervisor, she may also bear responsibility.

2. If she reports the additional income, there is a possibility that Olga will be criminally prosecuted.
3. If the department decides not to go to court but merely attempts to recover the monies by reducing the already inadequate welfare payments, Olga would be unable to provide as adequately for her two children as she has done until now.

What are the ethical aspects of this practice problem? Does the fact that Olga is a woman and/or a single parent make a difference as the social worker applies the ethical decision screens? Would a social worker respond differently to this situation if the head of the family were a man? If two parents were present?

The impact of sexism among social workers is a problem of critical ethical concern since stereotypical views of the female role in our society may undermine any effective client/worker relation. There are those who have expressed doubt whether a male social worker who has grown up in this culture can really be helpful to female clients. Research evidence does not support such a generalization, but all agree that sexism, whenever and wherever it exists, does interfere with professional helping. There is still a great deal of sexism in contemporary American society. Blatant sexism that once was acceptable has been reduced, but not eliminated. Some studies report that social workers have become less sexist, but other researchers note that social workers as a group continue to be promale, antifemale, or both. Sexist stereotypes are also found among many social work clients. Some researchers report that women clients prefer female social workers. But other studies indicate that women prefer male social workers, reflecting the common stereotype that men are considered more competent than women.

A special ethical concern arises whenever the client is a woman and the social worker, a man. In this situation there may be a danger that the husband/wife dominant/subordinate relationship will be duplicated. When faced by such a situation, the male social worker must exercise special caution to avoid the possibility of any sexist bias.

What are some of the special concerns that may make for a difference when a social worker's client is a woman? For one thing, the consequences of family breakup and/or single parenthood are usually more serious for the woman than for the man. These may include loss of social role, loss of status, income reduction, and additional child-rearing burdens. Many women feel a greater pressure to resolve family problems because they do not have viable alternate roles or support networks outside the family. For such women continuing family life with a spouse is of critical importance. They have more at stake and therefore may be willing to risk more to maintain the family.

Is therapy for women different from therapy for men? Many social workers answer this question with a resounding yes because they have found that the problems faced by women are so often generated by society's definition of gender, a definition that promotes passivity and dependence. If women in our society are not equal, it will not be sufficient to offer them the same services that men receive. They must receive special attention to overcome their unequal status.

Awareness of the problem of family violence has grown dramatically in recent years, but far greater emphasis has been focused on child abuse than on spouse abuse. Wives who are victims of family violence often minimize rather than exaggerate the frequency and severity of the abuse received. Many will report that their husbands have abused their children, but keep silent about the abuse that they themselves have suffered because they are ashamed and/or afraid. When social workers in one agency routinely asked mothers who reported child abuse, "What about you?" they learned that 85 percent of them admitted that they had also been victims of their husbands' physical abuse. This is another situation where limiting treatment to the client-identified problem may result in avoiding a serious problem and in unknowingly supporting discriminatory practices (Star, 1980).

Some readers may wonder how all the information we have presented about women relates to social workers' ethical decision making. One way to answer this question is to take note of Gilligan's theory, which asserts that gender makes for competing ethical principles. Her theory suggests that men and women follow different approaches to helping. Women emphasize an ethic of care, while men give priority to an ethic of justice. Gilligan does not claim genetic differences, nor does she maintain that every male person follows one ethic and every female person another. Instead she refers to modal differences. According to her theory, most women adopt the ethic of care. Some men also accept this ethic, but most men (as well as some women) follow an ethic of justice. Many question Gilligan's theory and its applicability to the client/social worker professional relationship, but to the extent that Gilligan has captured reality, gender will make a difference in the resolution of ethical issues (Davis, 1985; Dobrin, 1989; Gilligan, 1982; Gould, 1988; Meyer, 1985; Rhodes, 1985). For example, a more recent study of gender differences in the selection of sanctions against wrongdoing found only small differences between males and females, insufficient in magnitude to warrant any broad conclusions about possible gender differences with regard to choosing principles upon which to base ethical decisions (Thomas and Diver-Stamnes, 1993).

A note of caution that every social worker should keep in mind will conclude this section. The egalitarian values and attitudes popularized by the feminist movement may not be equally acceptable to all client groups. Social workers who assume that all women clients really want to be "liberated" may be imposing their own personal values on clients.

## CLIENTS WITH AIDS

Acquired immunodeficiency syndrome (AIDS) has come to be recognized as a global threat. Its impact can no longer be avoided by any social worker. "This epidemic," according to Ryan and Rowe, "is a crisis that demands an immediate and proactive response" (1988, p. 325). All social workers, even those who are practicing with populations or in areas of the country that have so far had a low incidence of human immunodeficiency virus (HIV)/AIDS, will sooner or later confront on their caseloads clients who have AIDS or who test HIV-positive. When this happens, these social workers will be faced by many ethical problems, some of which will be quite different from those with which they are familiar.

AIDS is not an "ordinary" disease. People who have AIDS or who test HIV-positive cannot be discussed in quite the same way as people who suffer other kinds of diseases. This is because AIDS is always fatal; people with AIDS have to come to terms with their own death, frequently at an early age. There is also a very high degree of stigma associated with AIDS, more stigma than is true for almost any other illness. This is because AIDS was first discovered among groups that are traditionally labeled as deviants—gay people, drug users, and prostitutes. Because of this stigma, many people with AIDS do not want others to know that they have the disease. They often go to considerable lengths to conceal the illness, even from those who are closest to them. They need help to ask for the help that they desperately need.

Social workers' concern for persons with acquired immunodeficiency syndrome (AIDS) is not new, but goes back almost to the beginning of the public recognition of this epidemic. Already in 1984, the NASW Delegate Assembly adopted a policy statement on AIDS (NASW, 1985, pp. 2–4). This statement acknowledged the role social workers must play in alleviating the plight of the victims. The 1987 NASW Delegate Assembly adopted a further policy statement, "AIDS: A Social Work Response." When social workers from sixteen countries and thirty states met at the First International Conference on Social Work and AIDS in 1989 they resolved that

> social workers and social work agencies are ethically obligated to provide appropriate services to all people affected by HIV/AIDS. These agencies and social workers are further obligated to ensure that direct care providers,

supervisors and administrators have necessary training, education and support to maintain high standards of service provided with full protection of civil liberties and without discrimination or fear of working with people affected by HIV/AIDS....

But adopting policy statements is only a beginning. Much work needs to be done to make social work intervention with this population effective. Social work with such clients requires a great deal of knowledge and expertise; this places a special responsibility on social agencies that must provide their workers with training and direction for work with HIV/AIDS-infected clients. When agencies are lax about this, social workers themselves have an ethical responsibility to press for this help, even at the risk of being stigmatized and labeled.

People who are infected by HIV/AIDS require a great many services, including medical, legal, employment, housing, and social services. Social workers are particularly well equipped to meet several of the special needs of this population, including:

1. Mental health, housing, entitlements, education, case management services.
2. Advocacy to protect these clients against discrimination and to ensure that they will receive all the services they need.
3. AIDS education for the general public, for the families of infected persons, and even for those with HIV/AIDS themselves.
4. Bereavement counseling for the families and loved ones of those who have died from AIDS.

## Biases about AIDS

Many social workers want to avoid working with HIV/AIDS-infected persons because they are worried that they might "catch" the disease. Medical sources agree that HIV/AIDS is not spread by casual contact. Social workers can be certain that they are not at risk of HIV infection when serving clients who have AIDS. Yet these fears, false as they are, exist and must be overcome if social workers are to provide effective service to people with HIV/AIDS.

There are other stereotypes and biases that interfere in the relation between social workers and HIV/AIDS-infected persons. Many, but by no means all, such clients were infected as a result of having sex with an HIV-infected partner or because they shared a needle with such a partner. Many social workers disapprove of sexual relations outside of marriage and most disapprove of the use of drugs. In working with these clients, a social worker is not asked to approve the behavior that resulted in the HIV/AIDS infection; rather she is expected to provide vital services to a person who needs them. The ethical social worker will do everything to work through her own biases so that they will not interfere with the professional relationship.

The AIDS epidemic has become widespread. Many persons have become infected, including spouses and significant others of infected persons, recipients of infected blood, newborn babies of infected parents, persons who shared needles, and others. Some of these persons may share the general public's biases about AIDS, and the stigma associated with AIDS may keep many of these persons from asking for the help they need when they know they are HIV-positive. Social workers must find ways to open communication channels with all of these people, both those who are diagnosed as HIV-positive and those who have developed AIDS.

## Mandatory HIV Screening

Many have demanded mandatory screenings for HIV so that health care professionals can identify infected people, treat them, and curtail the spread of the disease. Critics of mandatory screening programs argue that the small number of HIV-positive cases that would be identified in low-risk groups does not justify this use of the state's police power, nor the extraordinary expenditures such programs require. They also suggest that there is no evidence that mandatory testing leads to behavioral changes or to a reduction of the incidence of AIDS. In fact, there is some evidence that the threat of mandatory testing has the opposite result. Some infected persons may leave voluntary treatment programs when there is a chance that mandatory testing will make their illness a matter of public record. Nor does "knowledge" that one is HIV-positive necessarily lead to behavior changes. In one recent study 25 percent of those who tested seropositive continued to refuse to warn their casual sex partners that were HIV-positive even though they "knew" the risk involved in such behavior (Ryan & Rowe, 1988).

There are many considerations for and against mandatory testing programs. Social workers have expressed ethical concerns about the way some of the mandatory programs operate. Informed consent, a cornerstone of the social work professional ethics, is not part of a *mandatory* testing program since persons are tested whether or not they consent. Test results may or may not be shared with the person tested. Even more serious is the possibility that a person's privacy is invaded by making test results available to others without the tested person's permission. In some places results of these tests have become available to insurance companies which have denied coverage to HIV-positive persons and to employers who have discharged employees with AIDS. The deficiencies of many of the current screening programs which do not fully observe the rights of the persons tested have led many to oppose these programs. Thus Reamer notes that "social workers oppose mandatory testing that exacerbates discrimination and emotional trauma, and discourages individuals from seeking treatment" (1988, p. 462). Yet a number of state legislatures have or are now in the process of considering mandatory testing for selected populations. In these state social workers must provide leadership in order to ensure the protection of all persons' basic rights.

## Confidentiality and the Rights of Partners

A recent study by Abramson (1990) suggests that the issue of secrecy is a major ethical problem for social workers who have people with AIDS or people who are HIV-positive on their caseload. The ethical dilemmas facing these social workers arise out of (1) the obligation or duty to warn a third party that he or she is endangered by unprotected sex (this will require breaking confidence), and (2) helping infected persons to work through the problems that keep them from informing their partner. Often HIV-positive clients fear rejection, abandonment, and/or loneliness if their partners find out that they are infected. The following exemplar illustrates one aspect of this dilemma:

➤ **12.2 Gary Has Unsafe Sex**

You staff a support group for HIV-positive adults. During one of the group meetings Gary Damian relates that he continues to engage in unprotected sexual relations with his wife. When challenged by a group member, he admitted that he was not fair with his wife but that he was afraid she would leave him if she found out that he was HIV-positive.

What is your responsibility? If you cannot help Gary talk to his wife and/or convince him that he should change his behavior, should you break confidentiality? Does the *Tarasoff* ruling require you to notify his wife of the danger she faces? Whether a social worker is required by law to warn a third party when there is a threat of HIV infection is at this writing not yet certain because this question has not yet been litigated in an appellate court. Among the legal arguments bearing on this question is the proposition that harm from a gunshot is virtually certain, but that there is somewhat less certainty with regard to harm from unprotected sex with an HIV-infected partner. Not every person who has sex with an infected partner will become infected. Yet legal arguments aside, from an ethical point of view the risk faced by the partner of an HIV-infected person may be sufficiently great to require breaking confidentiality and warn the potential victim (Girardi et al., 1988; Melton, 1988).

In the language of our Ethical Principles Screen (EPS), this ethical dilemma can be resolved by determining whether or not Ethical Principle 1 is involved. If the danger to the partner's life is direct and immediate (as most social workers think it is), this principle takes precedence over Ethical Principle 6 (privacy and confidentiality). The medical profession has dealt with this ethical dilemma in a similar way. The Council on Ethical and Judicial Affairs of the American Medical Association (AMA) suggests that if a physician fails to persuade the HIV-infected person to inform a third party, the physician should inform the health authorities or the endangered third party (*Journal of the American Medical Association*, 1988, 259, pp. 1360–61).

A particularly difficult ethical problem occurs when a client has AIDS but has not been told about it, either because his physician feels uncomfortable to do so or because it is felt that a child or elderly person is better off if he or she does not know. The social worker who does know the diagnosis often does not know what the professional ethics expect of her in this situation.

### Diminished Competency

In time many persons suffering from AIDS show signs of progressive dementia, similar to those occurring in Alzheimer's disease. At times this AIDS-related dementia develops even before there is a definitive AIDS diagnosis. Central nervous system dysfunction and neuropsychiatric impairment raise critical questions about a client's competence to make autonomous decisions (Morrison, 1989).

All the ethical problems and dilemmas discussed in Chapter 4, especially those in the section on competency, also apply here. The fact that many HIV/AIDS clients are isolated persons who have lost contact with other family members only serves to exacerbate the ethical dilemmas around diminished competency.

### Other Ethical Problems

There are many other ethical dilemmas and problems that social workers face when working with these clients. For instance, Reamer (1988) asks whether social workers can be morally neutral when a client who has AIDS wants to commit suicide, knowing that such a person faces prolonged suffering and certain death. What do you think?

"Rationing" medical care presents another set of ethical problems where a social worker's advocacy services may be necessary. There are numerous reports of HIV/AIDS-infected persons who have not been offered cardiopulmonary resuscitation (CPR) or ventilator support because physicians presumably think that such "heroic" measures are futile for those patients. Other clients are discouraged by their physicians from seeking treatment because of the very high financial costs associated with caring for an AIDS-infected person. In these instances the physician's values, rather than the client's values, serve as decision criteria (Ross, 1989). Does a social worker have an ethical obligation to protect the rights of these clients?

As we shall see later in this chapter, ethical dilemmas may be encountered at the direct service level or at policy levels. The following exemplar presents such issues at several levels.

> ### 12.3 School Policy, Condoms, and Parental Permission
>
> You are a social worker in a high school, assigned to the school's health team. HIV and AIDS are threatening teenagers, many of whom ignore "safe sex" practices. The school system recently adopted a policy that condoms can only be distributed to students whose parent(s) have given written permission. Because of this rule, the team members can no longer provide condoms even when students who are known to be sexually active request them. This morning such an active student asked you for condoms. How would you have responded? Today's team meeting will discuss the new condom policy and what the team can/should do about it.

This social worker is faced with the ethical dilemma of choosing between agency policy and protection of life in this specific instance. Also, if the social worker helps this sexually active student and additional condoms are not available, would this action be fair to other students who have the same problem? At another level, what ethical dilemmas face the team as they consider the school system's policy? Does the *Code of Ethics* provide direction for this social worker and for the team?

## THE AGING

The aged population, sixty-five and older, is expected to reach 35.2 million by the year 2000. By then, one out of every eight Americans will be sixty-five and older and one in sixteen, seventy-five and older. The fastest growing age group are those eighty-five and older, who comprised only 0.7 percent of the total population in 1970, but who by the year 2000 will comprise about 1.5 percent, more than a 100 percent increase in thirty years. Life expectancy continues to increase at birth and at age sixty-five. At the same time, the number and percentage of those over sixty-five living alone also continue to increase.

Cassel found that as the aging population increases, the rate of people with cognitive and physical impairments also increases. Almost one-quarter (23 percent) of those sixty-five to seventy-four years of age and 45 percent of the eighty-five-plus group have difficulty with activities of daily living such as remembering the social context and standards for eating and toileting. As the size of the aging population increases in the coming decades, communities must prepare for an increase in the size of the disabled population. But it must be remembered that socioeconomic status influences the pattern of disabilities. The patterns of morbidity and the incidence of disease found among the two lower socioeconomic levels already in middle age (forty-five to sixty-four) are not reported for the higher levels until the age group seventy-five and above (Smyer, 1993).

As the number of aging persons increases and the number of such persons with cognitive and/or physical disabilities grows, one can anticipate an increase in the number of ethical dilemmas, some old and some new, that social workers will have to face.

Informed consent is an ethical issue when working with people of any age, but it becomes critical when working with the aged. Informed consent implies a rational process. The person has a right to understand the situation, the choices, and the projected results of the decision to be made. In the case of aging persons who are clearly incompetent, courts may appoint a guardian. But there are many aged persons who have a limited capacity for understanding and decision making, yet they are legally competent and have a right to make their own decisions. Should the social worker do what she thinks is best for such clients? After all, they are aged and there are real limits to the possibility of independent decision making and functioning. Since such persons may have limited understanding and the social workers have limited time, is it fair to use more of their available time to help them understand more completely the implications of their decisions? What is the necessary degree required of informed consent in such a situation?

A study of depression and mortality among nursing home residents showed a significant difference in the mortality rates of residents with depressive disorder and those without (Wicclair, 1993).

The choice facing Rosalind Lippe and her social worker, Teresa Richards, is difficult.

➤ **12.4 Depression, Day Treatment, or the Nursing Home**

Rosalind Lippe, seventy years of age, has been depressed for some time. Teresa Richards has been visiting her at home and helping her in a number of ways, but Ms. Lippe's depression has only slightly lifted even with medication. A psychiatrist has recommended a day treatment program, but Ms. Lippe cannot afford payment for this service. However, Ms. Richards knows that treatment would be available for Ms. Lippe if she were to enter a local nursing home. Medicaid will pay the nursing home because of Ms. Lippe's low income.

Nursing home placement tends to be irreversible, yet in this case placement may be the best option. Ms. Lippe is a young-old person but she is in difficulty. Right now a bed is available in the nursing home, something that does not occur often. A decision will have to be made very quickly; if a mistake is made, it will probably not be possible to correct it. Several ethical issues need to be considered. How can Ms. Richards ensure informed consent by Ms. Lippe? Very few people want to enter a nursing home. Torn among her need for help, her ambivalence, and her depression, how can this be a fully voluntary decision? Given what is known about mortality rates among nursing home residents, what factors must Ms. Richards balance? On the one hand, Ms. Lippe needs help for her depression; on the other hand, there will be a loss of freedom and possible health risks if Ms. Lippe enters the nursing home. In what ways can Ms. Richards resolve these ethical dilemmas?

## SOCIAL WORK WITH GROUPS

The language and concerns of the *Code of Ethics* of the National Association of Social Workers appear to apply primarily to practice with individual clients; they have more limited utility for social workers with groups (Dolgoff & Skolnik, 1992). Social workers with groups will find little direction in the *Code* for certain ethical dilemmas they encounter such as choosing between individuals and the group, agency, or society. The self-determination of one or more group members may run counter to the self-determined decisions of the group and/or of some fellow members. For example, what should the social worker do in the following situation?

➤ **12.5 Releasing the Group Record or Not**

A member of a group of adults requests (at the suggestion of his probation officer) that group records be submitted to the court. If the records show that he has made progress in the group he may be permitted to visit his child. You—the group social worker—insist this request be discussed by the group. One member will not agree under any circumstances to the release of the group records.

In such cases, the *Code of Ethics* does not provide clear guidance. Who "owns" the group record? Does each individual member have a veto over the release of information? Can the record be submitted to the court with the identity of other group members protected? Similarly, how is the social worker to choose between responsibilities toward individual group members, the group as a totality, and others, including society?

In the following incident, the social worker is faced with an issue of confidentiality as well as an issue potentially of life and death.

### ➤ 12.6 A Playful Tussle, a Scratch, and Confidentiality

You are a social worker in a hospital. You know that one member of your therapy group has AIDS, but this is not known by the group members. In a moment of playful tussle he scratches another member of the group and in turn is scratched. The hospital has a rule that members of the staff are not to identify to any other persons those who are HIV-positive or have AIDS.

To inform the group members, including those scratched, is to violate agency policy; but to ignore the scratches denies the person who is not HIV-positive the knowledge that he was scratched by a person who is HIV-positive in a situation where the risk of infection exists. To remain quiet protects confidentiality and the hospital, but deprives the group member of important information which may not save his life but does more fully inform him of facts important to his life. What should this social worker do? How does the Ethical Principles Screen (Figure 3.4) help in this situation?

Confidentiality in groups poses additional challenges and dilemmas. Sometimes ethical considerations must yield to a legal mandate, while in other situations, the legal status of confidentiality is so ambiguous as not to be helpful. The legal protection of confidentiality through privileged communication laws is never 100 percent since a judge may decide that the good of full disclosure supersedes the good of confidentiality. Furthermore, the right to confidentiality is particularly vulnerable when working with more than one individual. Privileged communication usually only covers communication between two people. While group and family therapists may request that their patients keep sessions confidential, the patients have no legal responsibility to do so. The right of therapists to resist subpoenas in regard to issues of confidentiality differs from state to state; the standards for social workers, psychologists, and psychiatrists may also vary.

Another ethical issue which social workers with groups have to deal with occurs when they have to choose between group members.

### ➤ 12.7 Charlie's Special

When Charlie, an emotionally disturbed youngster of ten, joined the group, Emo Wilkommen, the social worker, took an immediate liking to him. Charlie's mother died some years ago and his father is imprisoned. In order to ease Charlie's way into the therapy group, Emo set firm limits on two rambunctious group members and also set up several opportunities for Charlie to shine. Group members claimed that the worker is favoring Charlie.

To what extent is Charlie entitled to unequal treatment in the group in order to make up for past deprivations and difficulties? Should Emo be entirely honest with the group members? What approach would do the most good and the least harm? Is it ever ethical for a social worker to be manipulative with a group?

## MACRO PRACTICE

Some professional social workers hold stereotyped views of their colleagues who engage in macro practice. They believe that practitioners who engage in agencywide change efforts, social planning, neighborhood and community organization and development, social action, and social policy efforts are operating in a highly politicized arena. They think that this practice area is grounded on techniques and methods based on pragmatism rather than on ethical decisions. This perception is fostered not only by the nature of the settings in which macro practitioners practice but also by the language they use, especially the use of such terms as *tactics*, *strategies*, *conflict*, and *advocacy*. Indeed, references to ethics are only rarely found in macro practice textbooks (exceptions include Netting, Kettner, McMurtry, 1993, and Tropman, Erlich, and Rothman, 1995).

Nevertheless, macro social workers also encounter many difficult ethical dilemmas in their daily practice. The NASW *Code of Ethics* applies to all NASW members, including those in macro practice; the *Code of Ethics* states that "the social worker's primary responsibility is to clients" (II, F) and "the social worker should promote the general welfare of society" (VI, P, 1). Further, "the social worker should act to ensure that all persons have access to the resources, services, and opportunities which they require," (VI, P, 2) as well as "act to expand choice and opportunity for all persons, with special regard for disadvantaged or oppressed groups and persons" (VI, P, 3). When trying to comply with all of these standards, many dilemmas are encountered. These dilemmas include determining who is the client to whom primary responsibility is owed and selecting the persons who have access to resources when not every needy person can be supplied because these resources are in short supply. Another type of dilemma occurs when there are several similarly disadvantaged groups. How does the worker choose the one who will receive her priority attention?

In the following social planning situation, the social worker has to choose between many different groups. The choices to be made clearly deal with promoting the "general welfare of society." But in this instance, who is society? Which group deserves priority consideration?

➤   **12.8 Establishing a Cancer Treatment Unit**

You are the director of social work in a large urban community hospital located in a low-income area serving people from various economic levels. You have been assigned to staff the planning committee charged with creating a plan for the future of the hospital. You grew up in the community and have family and long-standing friends who reside there. You also have relationships with many community human service administrators and staff members.

As the planning process proceeds, it becomes clear that most committee members favor the creation of a specialized cancer treatment unit which will gain status and recognition for the hospital and also attract patients from throughout the state. But such a recommendation will not make it possible to recommend improvements for emergency and ambulatory care that are desperately needed by the neighborhood. A recommendation for a cancer treatment unit will change the nature of the available health care, who will get the jobs, use of community space, kinds of housing which will be available, etc.

It becomes clear to you that the local community will gain very little and lose much if a cancer treatment unit is installed. You are torn between loyalty to the hospital, to the community in general, to the social and human service agencies in the community, and to the community's population, including your friends and relatives who need a different type of service.

As a member of the planning group, you are faced with the dilemma of choosing between groups to determine who will benefit from the distribution of resources. What criteria will help you choose between the cancer patients (who do not necessarily come from the immediate community) and the health needs of your family, friends, and neighbors? Choosing between two groups, both of which have real health needs, is a typical ethical dilemma faced by social workers who are social planners. Whose good is primary? As a social worker, you owe first priority to the potential recipients of health services, but which of the groups has a higher priority? In addition, is the hospital's long-term viability a consideration that should affect the ethical decision-making process?

A review of the ethical Principles Screen (EPS) in Chapter 3 can be helpful as one thinks about the dilemma confronting this social planner. We would suggest that a consideration of Ethical Principles 1 and 2 is most compelling in the present case.

*Principle 1—Protection of life.* All medical services ultimately deal with the protection of life. Cancer patients are at a great risk, and inevitably face life-threatening situations which require early treatment, the earlier the better. On the other hand, the emergencies typically treated in a hospital ER range from routine treatments which are far from life-threatening to life-threatening situations which require immediate treatment—for the latter any delay may be a death sentence. Principle 1 does not provide unambiguous guidance, but can be used to buttress either choice.

*Principle 2—Equality and inequality.*   Cancer is today a very high-profile disease. A cancer treatment unit will be established in at least one hospital in the state, no matter what the board of the Neighborhood Hospital decides. For the neighborhood residents, however, the Neighborhood Hospital is the only chance for receiving timely emergency services; transportation to the next nearest hospital would add five to ten minutes' travel time—too much time when every minute counts. Under this principle neighborhood persons have the ethical right to expect preferred consideration. The social worker can therefore with a clear conscience support a recommendation in favor of improving emergency services.

Social workers are expected to be open and honest. Among the very first standards in the *Code of Ethics* is the expectation that "the social worker should not participate in, condone, or be associated with dishonesty, fraud, deceit, or misrepresentation" (I, A, 2). At every step in their education and later in agency practice, social workers are encouraged not to be "manipulative" nor to engage in secretive, hidden, or disguised actions. Much attention has been paid in the literature to efforts to change social agencies, always with the justification that one's efforts are designed to improve services for clients or to attain some general good. In some cases, concealed and unavowed action may be thought necessary to gain a greater good for a community or for clients. In these cases, social workers have to weigh the ethical balance between a greater good and hidden actions.

What is the best way for the worker to respond in the following situation?

➤  **12.9  How to Fight the Half-Truths of the Real Estate Lobby**

Ed Corey is a community organizer, employed by a social agency to develop new housing in a neighborhood. Ed staffs a community coalition which is vigorously working on the new housing. The early activities of the coalition were very successful. But powerful real estate interests who wanted to block the development of the new housing began to spread rumors about Ed's personal history and life. They also used deceptive and distorted facts in advertisements to destroy the coalition's efforts and to undercut Ed's potential influence.

Ed, for his part, knows about the "shady" dealings of some members of the real estate group. He senses there will be no new housing unless aggressive action is taken, but he is unsure what he should do to combat the half-truths and lies of the opponents of the new housing. How should Ed use the information he has? Should he be open and rebut the charges of the opponents? Or should he retaliate and fight "fire with fire" behind the scenes? Should he use the facts he possesses with strategically located opinion molders to undermine the influence of the real estate group?

## EXERCISES

1. If you are confronted by the ethical dilemma which faces the director of social work in Exemplar 12.8, "Establishing a Cancer Treatment Unit," what do you think your decision would be? What arguments support your decision? What arguments exist contrary to your point of view?
2. What are the ways in which aging persons attempt to make health decisions in advance of medical operations? What dilemmas occur which impact on social workers when such arrangements either have not been made or are unclear in some important way?
3. Can you identify ways in which sexism appears in American society and in social work practice? How do these relate to the social work *Code of Ethics*? What can a social worker do to minimize these?
4. Suppose a female or male client says that they do not want a social worker assigned to them who is of the opposite sex. Is it ethical for an agency to comply with their request?
5. The legislature of your state has been alarmed by the sharp increase in the incidence of AIDS among all population groups. A bill has been introduced calling for mandatory HIV screening of all persons applying for a marriage license. The problem is a real one; the solution suggested may or may not be effective. But it does raise a number of ethical issues. Your local NASW chapter has asked you to discuss these questions at the next membership meeting.
6. You are a social worker in a teaching hospital. You have learned that some persons with AIDS who need intensive care have not been admitted to the hospital's intensive care unit (ICU). You know that the number of beds available for AIDS patients has been arbitrarily limited by the hospital administration and that these beds are already filled, even though other beds in the ICU are empty. What ethical obligations, if any, do you have to help those AIDS victims who are waiting for an "empty" bed?
7. Paul Ziff is a fourth grader in PS 19. He suffers from hemophilia and needs frequent blood transfusions. It was recently confirmed that he suffers from AIDS. When word of this got around PS 19, his fellow students shunned him and their parents demanded that Paul be taken out of the school. Soon his teachers informed the

principal that they were afraid to have Paul in their classroom lest they become infected. You are the school's social work consultant. The principal asks you to design an educational program to deal with the concerns of teachers, parents, and students.

8. You are a social worker for a hospital support group of young adults recovering from serious illnesses. The group has been told they can make decisions "within agency policy" in a democratic fashion. When the group is informed that a new member will be joining, one member recognizes the person, says she is disruptive, and the group joins in and says the new member cannot join. What should you do? Support the group or the new member?

## SUGGESTIONS FOR ADDITIONAL READINGS

Dobrin (1989) utilizes Gilligan's theory to discuss ways in which ethical decisions of male and female social workers differ. Taylor-Brown and Garcia (1995) identify issues concerning HIV-affected families as do Andrews and Patterson (1995) in regard to substance abuse during pregnancy. Abramson (1990) and Yu and O'Neal (1992) analyze the issue of confidentiality that faces social workers who work with clients with AIDS. Dolgoff and Skolnik (1992) examine certain limitations of the *Code of Ethics* for social work with groups. Torczyner (1991) examines ethical issues in social action. Howell (1988) explores ethical dilemmas concerning those persons who are both aging and have significant mental and physical disabilities.

# 13. Whose Responsibility
## Are Professional Ethics?

Ethical decision making is often presented in a way suggesting that the social worker who must make a decision is alone and lonely, cut off from every system which might give her guidance, support, and recognition. Many have questioned this view. Frankena cites the philosopher W. D. Walsh, who wrote that "morality is first and foremost a social institution, performing a social role, and only secondarily, if at all, a field for individual self-expression" (1980, p. 33).

Every social worker is, of course, responsible for her ethical decisions. Or as Reamer writes, "Individual social workers have the responsibility to recognize the relevance of ethical considerations to their professional duties" (1987, p. 191). At the same time it must be recognized that every social worker is a participant in a number of networks and social systems which support or which should support her ethical decision making. Decision making always occurs within a social setting which influences, rewards, or guides certain behaviors and which limits, sanctions, or disapproves others. The social agency employing the social worker is one such setting, the service delivery team or office is another, the professional association a third, and so on. No discussion of steps designed to facilitate and strengthen ethical decision making is complete if it does not take these systems into consideration.

While there will never be a time when clear and unambiguous guidelines will be available for every ethical decision that social workers have to make, over the years various societal and institutional mechanisms have been developed to provide guidance and support. Here we want to discuss a number of mechanisms that are particularly promising for further development.

*Peer review.*    Peer review permits a social worker to test her ethical decision making against that of her colleagues. In the past social workers have utilized informal groupings to review their professional practice decisions. Such groupings can also be useful for reviewing ethical decisions. However, informal groups, valuable as they may be, are no substitute for formal disciplined review groups. In this age of consumerism and accountability, formal review mechanisms are a necessity for every professional group that wants to survive.

There are additional considerations for social workers in private practice who are more isolated than workers in agency-based practice and who have less opportunity for interaction with peers. Controls and accountability of private practice social workers depend almost entirely upon the sensitivity and knowledge of the individual practitioner. Peer pressures, which are so immediate in agency practice, are much less in evidence among private practice practitioners. Because of these considerations, social workers in private practice may want to organize peer review systems specifically geared to review their ethical decision making so that they can be certain that their decisions will be of the highest ethical quality.

*Accountability systems.*    Social agencies are accountable for what they do. So are the social workers who work in these agencies. Social agencies that want to implement this responsibility in a positive way must develop and operate accountability systems. These systems are characterized by the following features:

1. A sensing or monitoring system.
2. A method for sampling activities and decisions.
3. Clear indicators of the desired quality.
4. Clear indicators or criteria of the desired quantity.
5. Feedback systems that permit an early alert to problem situations.

These accountability system features, as described by Hoshino (1978), relate primarily to practice performance, but there is no reason why such systems could not incorporate additional indicators also concerned with the ethical aspects of practice.

*In-service training and consultation.*    Most agencies make a heavy investment in providing in-service training and consultation for their staff. These can also be geared to educate staff members to the intricacies of the ethical aspects of decision making, to sensitize them to the ethical implications of practice, and, in general, to strengthen the ethical level of practice.

*Agency appeals procedures.*    Many agencies have appeals procedures, but often clients are not aware of them. "Forgetting" to inform clients about them may simplify the life of practitioners and administrators, but this does not help raise the level of ethical practice. Appeals procedures do more than correct mistakes made by social workers. One of their most valuable functions is to sensitize social workers to the ethical aspects of practice. An ombudsman or another type of appeals procedure should be readily available to clients and should function without stigma. Ethical social workers will welcome such strategies. Administrative review procedures also have a place in the support system, but they do not take the place of appeals procedures freely available to clients.

*Client's Bill of Rights.*    Many hospitals and other service organizations distribute a Bill of Rights to new clients and patients. These brief statements inform people of the type of information they are entitled to know about their situation. They are also told that they can expect to be treated with dignity and respect, that they will participate in decision making about their situation, that they will be informed about available options, and that they have a right to speak to an ombudsman or other person if they are dissatisfied with their treatment.

Social workers should consider the use of a clear and informative statement to inform new clients about what they can expect from the professional personnel they will encounter, the mechanisms for raising questions or seeking clarification where needed, and the procedures for registering grievances.

*Committee on the Ethics of Social Work Practice.*    Each agency should establish a Committee on the Ethics of Social Work Practice, analogous to Committees on the Rights of Human Subjects that exist in every academic research organization. Practitioners who have an ethical question may consult with the committee about a problem. Such a committee can serve as a forum where social workers can think through thorny ethical questions occurring in everyday practice. Most important, this committee can be the locus for the routine monitoring of ethical practice within the agency.

*Professional associations.*    NASW and other professional associations of social workers must continue to encourage the strengthening of ethical decision making within the profession. The following are some of the ways to do so:

1. Continue to revise and refine the *Code of Ethics*.
2. Encourage the formation of groups to study and review critical ethical decisions arising out of actual practice experiences.
3. Develop a data bank of precedents with ethical implications.
4. Schedule activities that focus on the ethical aspects of practice, both at professional conferences and as part of continuing education programs.
5. Publish an "Ethics Reporter" or a regular ethics column in *Social Work* or in the *NASW News* in order to make social workers more familiar with their *Code of Ethics*.
6. Develop an ethics hotline so that practitioners can obtain advice on ethical issues that arise in their practice. Modern communication technologies, such as fax and electronic mail, can provide instant communication over long distances. At the same time these technologies give the consultant sufficient time to reflect on the question or to consult with others.

With respect to the data bank, it is desirable that social workers begin to collect data on ethical decision making. Such a data bank should not be limited to "success stories" but should also include errors, unanswerable questions, and embarrassing situations. Collection of this type of data will be helpful to practitioners as well as to students. This information will explicate the ethical quandaries experienced by social workers, the preferred solutions, and the results achieved. Such a data base will also be helpful in the creation of case materials, which are so necessary for the systematic development of new social work knowledge. Just as lawyers can draw on case law for guidance in making difficult decisions, so social workers should be able to receive guidance from the suggested data bank.

*Professional complaint procedures.*    NASW's complaint procedures are cumbersome and take too much time. The current procedure provides for three levels of adjudication. A complaint is first presented to the Chapter Committee on Inquiry (COI). Once COI has ascertained that the complaint has met the stipulated criteria (especially that the social worker against whom the complaint has been filed was an NASW member at the time of the alleged violation), the complaint is accepted and a formal hearing is scheduled. After the COI has arrived at a decision about the complaint, it reports its findings to the parties involved and to the chapter executive committee. Either party may appeal the decision, first to the National Committee on Inquiry and finally to the executive committee of the NASW Board of Directors. New adjudication procedures were approved in July 1991. These are designed to assure greater fairness to both parties. They also provide more comprehensive guidelines for the COI and other groups involved in the adjudication. But it is still important to find ways to simplify the procedure and slash the time necessary to adjudicate complaints.

In addition to a complex process, problems also arise because of the existence of relatively few knowledgeable colleagues from whom those charged can seek advice as well as from the fact that even those few knowledgeable individuals are available in relatively few places.

In this final chapter we have presented ideas that may help social workers in their search for more effective ethical practice. The values of the social work profession form the background for ethical decision making. Ethical decision making is the cornerstone for ethical practice.

Ethical decision making begins with the clarification of one's own values. Knowledge of what one really believes is an inescapable basic step for social workers seeking to strengthen their ethical practice. Beyond this, it becomes important for social workers to clarify the values of society and of the various groups with which they work. Clarification of these values permits social workers to become more sensitive to and more aware of the values of others and of possible conflicts between different value systems.

Individual practitioners sometimes feel that they are alone when facing ethical dilemmas, but there are others who can share these ethical problems. Formal peer review, agency consultations, and the professional association must share the burden of thinking through these dilemmas. Some persons have suggested that ethics do not exist outside of community. To base ethical decisions strictly on one's individual conscience can lead a person into very difficult situations and into playing God. All ethics are integral to community. There are many reasons for a professional social worker to "connect" with the professional community. Fellow professionals can provide opportunities to think through ethical questions and dilemmas, to discuss one's ethical concerns with other social work professionals, and to gain colleague support.

## EXERCISES

1.  Identify your strengths and limitations in regard to ethical decision making when you are engaged in social work practice. How can you better prepare yourself for being an ethical social worker?

2. Identify in your field instruction placement, your agency of employment, or other social agency what you consider to be the limitations of the ethical decision-making patterns utilized. If you were going to attempt to improve *one* thing about ethical decision making in the organization, what would you choose to alter and how would you go about trying to improve the situation?

## SUGGESTIONS FOR ADDITIONAL READINGS

Conrad (1989) reviews the development of ethics review committees in the health care field and considers the implications of this development for social work practice.

# Appendix A:
# Additional Exemplars

The exemplars in this appendix have been chosen to illustrate ethical practice problems occurring in the real world of social workers.

➤ **A.1 The Board Member and Mrs. Lang**

Mrs. Lang's husband died a few months ago. It is now evident that she can no longer cope alone. Her family physician urged her to enter a home for the aged, but Mrs. Lang told her social worker that she was not yet ready to leave her own home. The social worker accepted Mrs. Lang's decision since she did not feel that it is ethical to apply pressure on clients. The social worker was also aware that the family doctor had "succeeded" in receiving assent only after he applied heavy pressures on Mrs. Lang.

In reviewing this case with her supervisor, the social worker learned that the family doctor was a board member of the agency. The supervisor thought that cooperating with this board member would be far better than fighting him for the sake of protecting the "right" of one client, especially when it was clear that Mrs. Lang could no longer live alone.

Should the fact that the physician is a board member make any difference in resolving this ethical dilemma?

➤ **A.2 Discriminatory Practices and an Agency Employee**

Several social agencies in your city, including the one for which you work, engage in discriminatory practices against minority group children. There is now a court case about this matter. Lawyers for the plaintiff have asked you to testify about specific instances of such discriminatory practices. You oppose these practices and repeatedly have spoken against them at staff meetings, but you hesitate to testify in court because (1) you are afraid that you may be fired if you testify against your agency, (2) you are not sure whether the confidential relationship you have with your clients permits you to reveal this information, and (3) you are not certain whether it is ethical for you to use agency records for this purpose.

➤ ### A.3 A Multiproblem Family

Pearl Konesky, social worker at the Downriver Consultation Center, wonders what her new clients, the Spinos, are like. According to the short application form filled out by Mildred Spino at the reception desk, she is thirty-three years old, married, a mother of three, and employed as a clerk. She wants help in arranging an abortion. Pearl is hoping that there will not be too many other serious problems because agency policy permits only time-limited services—no more than eight counseling sessions over four weeks.

Before the first session is over, Pearl realizes that the Spinos are a multiproblem family, if there ever was one. The household consists of Walter Spino, age thirty-one, an alcoholic with no steady employment; Irma Spino, age fifteen, a school dropout and six months pregnant (according to her mother, Irma neither wanted an abortion nor was she ready to release her child for adoption); Irma's boyfriend, Mark Rehm, age eighteen, unemployed; Charlene Spino, age fourteen, severely retarded; and Sally Spino, age thirteen, expelled from elementary school because of repeated drug abuse.

By ignoring all problems other than Mildred Spino's request for an abortion, Pearl can adhere to her agency's time-limited service policy. But can a social worker overlook the many other problems which this family presents? Is this ethical?

➤ ### A.4 The Padded Expense Account

Kenneth Boros is a salesman for a large manufacturing company. Lately he has been suffering from crippling migraine headaches. His supervisor suggested that he talk to the company's social worker since the doctors could find no physical cause for these headaches.

While talking with the social worker, Boros mentioned that he felt guilty about padding his expense account. He noted that this was a common practice among the company's sales personnel, but that he still did not feel comfortable about it.

What should be the social worker's response? What is her responsibility to the company? Should she try to reduce Mr. Boros's guilt feelings? Should she try to change his behavior? What are the ethical implications for each option?

➤ **A.5 Birth Control for Teenagers**

Pam Welsh, a fourteen-year-old teen, is not getting along with her parents. After Pam ran away from home twice, her parents took her for therapy to a social worker. During therapy, Pam told her social worker that she is sexually active. She asked the worker for help in avoiding pregnancy. She is afraid of becoming pregnant, but she is even more afraid that her puritanical parents may learn of her sexual activities.

Should the social worker help Pam obtain birth control pills, even though she knows that Pam's parents have taken a strong public stand against supplying them to teens? Is it ethical for the social worker to ignore the parents' values? Can she ignore her clients request? To whom is she accountable?

➤ **A.6 A Three-Generational Family**

The Petros household contains three generations. Scott and Mary Petros are both in their early forties. They have two children, aged eight and ten. Mrs. Petros's seventy-year-old mother has been living with them for the past eight years, ever since she became a widow.

Mary and Scott Petros came to the social worker to seek help for their failing marriage. After working with the couple for a number of sessions, the social worker concluded that one of the major problems was the relationship between Mary Petros and her mother. She feels that the best thing would be for the mother to leave the family and live somewhere else. An old age home is the only place to which she can go, but the town's only old-age home is far less desirable than the Petros home.

Is saving this marriage the only objective? Does the social worker have an obligation for the welfare of Mrs. Petros's mother? Should she be concerned only with the welfare of Mary and Scott? Or does the social worker also have other ethical obligations?

➤ **A.7 Taking on a Private Client**

Christine Ross is the only MSW social worker in a remote mountain community where she staffs the county welfare office. Her friend, Kay Jordan, the principal of the county high school, has told her about a very disturbed student in her school. This student has lately engaged in some very bizarre behavior and Kay has no doubt that he needs professional help. Since the nearest mental health clinic is 130 miles away, Kay asked Christine to provide therapy for this student.

The student is not eligible for service from the county welfare department (which in any case does not provide therapy). Therefore, Kay asked Christine to take him on as a private client. Christine has never before provided therapy for this kind of very disturbed person, but she is willing to try. Is it ethical for her to do so when there is no possibility of obtaining supervision?

### ➤ A.8  Paul and His Illegal Immigrant Parents

Paul Aquizap, a third grader, has shown signs of depression and apathy. He is frequently absent from school. His teacher has referred him to the school social worker since her attempts to contact Paul's parents have not been successful.

On a home visit the social worker discovered that Paul's parents are illegal immigrants, that they speak almost no English, and that they are hardly ever at home since they work very long hours. Paul is left alone at home almost all the time. He finds it difficult to manage.

Should the social worker ignore the illegal status of Paul's parents and focus his attention on helping Paul? Is this legal? Is it ethical?

### ➤ A.9  A Computerized Data Bank

The Forbes Manufacturing Company is designing a computerized data bank that will contain a complete database on all of its employees. This will include employment application data, credit rating, police reports, security check, health data, supervisor's annual report, etc. They also want you to provide information about employees who have contacted you, the company's industrial social worker. They want to know their names, their problems, and what you did for them. What are the ethical considerations that you must consider about this request? What are your obligations to your clients? To your employer?

### ➤ A.10  The Incestuous Father

Sheryl Gulls is a twelve-year-old who has been living with a foster family since her mother died some months ago. She has told her social worker "in confidence" that during the past three years her father made many sexual approaches. A court hearing has been scheduled next month to make a permanent disposition of Sheryl's future.

Sheryl has told her social worker that she wants to live with her father rather than continue living in a foster home. The social worker knows that if she informs the court of what Sheryl has told her about her father's abuse, the judge will reject Sheryl's request—but if she keeps quiet and respects Sheryl's confidence, there is a good chance that the judge will approve Sheryl's request and let her go back to her father.

### ➤ A.11  The Ethics of Team Practice

Timothy Land is a social worker in a day treatment program for deinstitutionalized persons. Professionally Mr. Land is respected by other members of the team and is viewed as a social worker of great promise who will move ahead quickly in his career.

Clients in the program are assigned to treatment groups on the basis of the decision of the psychiatrist and the social worker. There is no written contract as to what is expected of either patients or of staff. Clients are never involved in decisions about group assignment or tasks. If a client does not fulfill the assigned tasks, he or she is typically labeled "disruptive" or "decompensating." These comments are written on the clients' charts.

Land questions the ethical aspects of these procedures. He feels strongly that social work ethics require client participation in all phases of the decision-making process. But Land is not certain to whom he owes primary loyalty and responsibility. Is it to the team? To the clients? Or to his career?

➤ **A.12  An Autistic Young Adult**

Since Gary's family has placed him in a hostel for autistic young adults, they have just about cut all contact with him. Recently they sent him a postcard, telling him that they would no longer be able to visit him regularly since they had moved to another state.

The hostel social worker is aware that Gary misses his family greatly. He also knows that the family has not moved out of the city, but merely to another neighborhood within the city. Should he tell Gary the truth? What is the ethical thing to do?

➤ **A.13  Threats from Your Client**

You have been treating Jason Conger, a severely disturbed person, for several months. In recent weeks he has become increasingly aggressive toward you, claiming (wrongly) that you are planning to harm him. Today he told you that if you do not stop persecuting him, he will get even with you by harming your child.

You are very concerned since you know that Jason has been involved in the past in physically abusing children. Should you report this threat to the police? Should you arrange for a commitment to a mental hospital? Should you withdraw from this case? Or what should you do? What are the ethical dilemmas you must resolve before you can make a decision?

➤ **A.14  Planning Kevin's Suicide**

Kevin Gallagher, a sixteen-year-old high school student, has a spinal condition as a result of a sports injury suffered several years ago. He has been receiving constant and painful treatments since the day he was injured.

Recently Kevin confided to his social worker that he has decided to commit suicide. The reason he wants to put an end to his life is that his widowed father wants to remarry and Kevin feels that he is in the way. His father also has business problems and finds it increasingly difficult to pay for Kevin's very expensive treatments. Kevin feels that he will die sooner or later anyhow. "Why drag it out?" he asks.

Kevin does not want anyone, not even his father, to know about his decision. He asked the social worker for help in finding a foolproof way to end his life. What ethical issues are posed by Kevin's requests? What principles can guide the social worker in this situation?

### ➤ A.15 An Interracial Marriage

Chris, age twenty-eight, has many problems. Until now he has coped with them, but now he has a problem that is too big for him to handle alone. Chris has fallen in love with Amy and wants to marry her. The problem is that both of their families are vehemently opposed to this interracial marriage—Chris is a white Anglo, while Amy is a Vietnamese-American.

The social worker to whom he has turned for help sees nothing wrong with an interracial marriage. She herself is white and has a Native American daughter-in-law. Should the worker share this information with Chris and help him deal with the prejudices of his and Amy's family? Is it ethical for the worker to talk about her own values?

What if this worker felt that interracial marriages made for many difficulties in our society and in this community in particular? Should she share with Chris the problems that her son and daughter-in-law have encountered? Is this ethical?

### ➤ A.16 Mr. Biao's Depression

Harry Biao is a seventy-five-year-old Chinese-American who arrived in this country fifty-three years ago. Until recently he owned a hardware store in Chinatown. His wife died ten years ago and he now lives by himself. The social service homemaker, Mrs. Hua, reports that Mr. Biao appears depressed and almost never leaves his apartment. He is not communicative, regardless of whether she speaks with him in English or Cantonese.

When Mr. Biao's case was presented at a staff meeting, his social worker argued for a strategy that focuses on involving him in the Chinese Community Center's program for the aged. Other social workers suggest that it is best to provide psychotherapy so that Mr. Biao can gain insight into his problem. This has been the agency's customary way of handling problems of this kind. Should Mr. Biao's social worker follow the agency routine and offer psychotherapy even though she feels that this is not the best way of working with this client?

### ➤ A.17 Getting Help for Clyde Lukke

Clyde Lukke voluntarily entered Sunnyside Psychiatric Hospital on Wednesday afternoon. He complained of severe depression and was afraid that he might commit suicide. The admitting psychiatrist diagnosed his case as *depression, recurrent.* The usual treatment at Sunnyside for this diagnostic category is three to five weeks hospitalization, followed by long-term intensive individual therapy.

Five days after admission, Angela Mennikke, the floor social worker, was notified by the business office to prepare the patient for discharge. Ms. Mennikke was surprised since discharge orders are usually discussed by the floor staff before they are entered. Rarely is discharge an administrative decision. Upon inquiry she learned that Mr. Lukke's HMO benefits are limited to one week of psychiatric hospitalization. She also learned that this HMO, like many similar organizations, reimburses only for time-limited group therapy, not for individual therapy.

Should the social worker prepare a routine discharge and let the HMO staff worry about how to help Lukke? Or should she take an advocate stance to ensure that Lukke will get the treatment he needs? What is expected in this situation from a professional social worker who wants to engage in ethical practice?

### ➤ A.18 How Far for Friendship and Loyalty?

You are a social worker in private practice who regularly consults with Dr. Erica Zeitner, a highly experienced social worker and a leader in the mental health community. She chairs or participates in various local task forces, mayor's committees, interdisciplinary work groups, etc. Recently you have begun to suspect that Dr. Zeitner is either using drugs or is having serious psychological problems. A new and unexpected scatter and disorder seem to have entered her life. In her sessions with you she does not seem to be able to focus and follow the discussion. You are very concerned about her apparent difficulties; you also know that she depends on the income from her private practice to support her family. What should you do?

### ➤ A.19 Jennifer, the Agency, and Her Foster Parents

Jennifer has been in foster care for most of her seventeen years. Several months ago she discovered that she was pregnant. She began to see her social worker, Ms. Rosetti, more frequently. Her foster parents are aware of her condition. Because of some of Jennifer's health problems and because of her family history, her physician recommended that she undergo an amniocentesis. The test results revealed that Jennifer's fetus would probably be severely damaged and would have only a marginal chance of surviving more than six months.

When this became known, the agency's assistant director spoke with Ms. Rosetti and asked her if she had discussed an abortion with Jennifer. Unless Jennifer aborted, the agency would have to pay large sums of money for this baby which, at best, would live less than a year.

Ms. Rosetti knows that Jennifer is ambivalent about carrying the fetus to term and is not at all sure whether she wants to be a mother. But Ms. Rosetti also knows that the foster parents with whom Jennifer has an excellent relationship oppose abortion on religious grounds.

➤ **A.20 Who's to Know?**

A local psychologist has just completed a battery of intelligence tests for a teenager with mental retardation served by your agency. You have learned that this boy's test results are just above the score required to continue services for him and his family. Your supervisor, concerned about what will happen if services are cut off, asked you to suggest to the psychologist that she report a slightly lower score, thus ensuring that the agency could continue to provide services to this client.

➤ **A.21 Divorce and the Need to Lie**

June and Warren Eades have come to you for marital counseling. They have been married for three years, have no children, and are now convinced that they are not compatible. After meeting with you for ten weeks, they have come to the joint decision to seek a divorce. From a clinical point of view, you see no reason why this mature decision should not be implemented so that these two adults can be free to pursue other relationships. But you also know that your state does not provide for divorce by mutual consent. Adultery and extreme cruelty are the only causes accepted for divorce.

What are the ethical implications if you refer them to a lawyer who you know will help them fabricate the evidence necessary to obtain a divorce?

➤ **A.22 A New Friend and Peer Consultation**

Last night social worker Mark Sussna met Valery Aylon at a party at a friend's apartment. In the course of the evening they discovered that they shared many interests. It was almost a case of "love at first sight." Mark made a date to meet Valery the following evening.

Today one of Mark's colleagues discussed a complicated case with him. Mark soon realized that the client being discussed was his new friend, Valery Aylon. What should he do? Should he tell his colleague to consult with someone else? Or should he keep silent so that he can find out more about Valery, information which will help him determine whether they are really suitable? Or should he terminate his friendship with Valery? (Note: Peer consultation is the accepted practice in this agency so that *confidentiality* is not an issue.)

➤ **A.23 A Mother's Threats**

Nan Lowell is your client. She has threatened to kill her three-year-old daughter unless the welfare department gives her a larger apartment. You take this threat seriously since you are familiar with the past history of this client. Should you notify the police? Her husband? Or do nothing?

➤ **A.24 One Job or Two?**

Joseph Leggio is a twenty-five-year-old man with mental retardation. He has no living relatives and is able to live in protected environments in the community. Alice Patella, a social worker, recently placed him at a board and care home run by Mrs. Collins, a person with whom Alice has had a long relationship. Mrs. Collins has been supportive of the clients placed in her home, something which is found infrequently. Alice just discovered that Mrs. Collins—who needs the money—has not been supervising the clients placed in her home. Instead, she has hired a discharged psychiatric patient to monitor the residents while she works part-time in a local store. Alice knows that Mrs. Collins needs the income and her assistant, the discharged patient, needs both the extra money and the sense of accomplishment from performing the job. What would you suggest Alice do?

➤ **A.25 Health and Safety, or Housing for the Poor**

Amelia Pena is a social worker employed by an agency whose mission is to develop housing which is desperately needed for poor persons. Ms. Pena is a member of a special committee of staff and board members set up to review the situation which results from the discovery that some of the homes being renovated have lead paint problems. If the agency undertakes to remove the lead paint in order to ensure the safety of future residents, the agency will not be able to offer this new housing to the poor since the purchase price will be prohibitive. But if the lead is not removed, the agency will be morally and legally liable for any resulting damage. The agency does not have sufficient resources to do both—remove the lead and build the housing.

➤ **A.26 Where Should Erica Go?**

Erica Lieber, five years old, was hospitalized for lead poisoning. When discharged, she will return to the same lead-contaminated apartment. As her social worker, you have found no legal method to force the landlord to correct the situation. The family is unable to move. There is a long waiting list for the lead-abatement services that the agency's very limited budget provides. In the normal course of events, the Liebers' turn would come only in five years. In addition, the family's health insurance will not pay for any more of Erica's hospitalization. What should the social worker do in this case?

➤ **A.27 Who Makes Social Work Decisions?**

In the Whitehurst Children's Agency, the social work staff is supervised by Gloria Tabaka, a licensed social worker who is an excellent teacher and supervisor. When Ms. Tabaka has to be away from the agency, whether for a few hours or a day, the only person she trusts sufficiently to act for her is the office manager, Monica Monteleone, who is not a professional social worker nor is she trained in any human service. When Ms. Tabaka is not present and cannot be reached, the staff must go to Ms. Monteleone for decisions about the clients. Admittedly, Ms. Monteleone does know a great deal about many things, but the social work staff is not sure whether social work decisions should be made by a person who has not been certified. Today while Ms. Tabaka is away, you have to make a decision about an emergency child welfare situation that needs your supervisor's approval. Ms. Monteleone disagrees with your recommendation and instead suggests an option which you feel is not professionally defensible. What should you do?

### ➤ A.28  Self-Determination and Eating Habits

Etienne Cormier is mentally ill. Egon Marek serves as his social worker in the Heartland Community Mental Health Center. Mr. Cormier eats out of dumpsters. He is very efficient and has identified a series of dumpsters and stakes them out when he knows food will be available. When Mr. Marek asks him about his eating from the dumpsters, he says he likes to do so and does not want to change his way of life. When Mr. Marek gives him extra food packs, he gives them away and prefers food from the dumpsters. Should Mr. Marek try to find other ways of stopping him from eating from the dumpsters or not? Or should Mr. Marek ignore his eating patterns?

### ➤ A.29  Comparison Shopping the Competition

Marianne Ginot, a clerical staff member in a for-profit family counseling center, needs some help in managing her adolescent daughter. She discusses her problem with Desirée Butler, the social work supervisor of the center. Desirée Butler realized that this was the opportunity that the center staff had been waiting for. The agency could at one and the same time provide some help for Marianne Ginot and obtain information about its competitors. Desirée Butler presented her plan to the administrative staff. It was agreed to send Marianne Ginot to three competing agencies and pay for up to three sessions at each of the agencies, provided Marianne Ginot will report back on the intake procedure, what happened during the first session, the quality of their facilities, and an impression of the experience. Desirée became uncomfortable after the decision was made. With hindsight she realized that she had ignored several ethical issues. What are these?

### ➤ A.30  Obey the Law or Help?

Daphne Ranesco, a social work student, will graduate next week. Today one of her clients, Harry Plimkin, called distraught saying he has become violent with his wife and that he wants help. He tells her he has much respect for her since she has been very helpful to him, especially in controlling his temper. He wants to see her privately for a few sessions because he does not trust anyone else at the agency to help him in this emergency. State regulations do not allow social workers to practice privately until they have had two years of postgraduation profession experience under supervision. Does an emergency such as this one justify breaking the law? Is the prevention of violence more important than abiding by the law? What are Daphne's options? What ethical considerations must be considered for each option?

➤ **A.31  No Other Way to Gather Resources**

You are employed by a rural County Department of Education which has no funds available to help Tom Bishop, your homebound young client or his family to purchase a cheap computer and modem which would enable him to communicate with many learning facilities and with other teenagers. Tom is desperate for activity but cannot travel out of his house because of his physical disabilities, which resulted from a diving accident. You have already asked your colleagues if they know how you might gather these resources, but no one had any helpful suggestions. Tom and his parents have now given you permission to advertise his needs on the electronic network. In your e-mail message you identified your client by gender, age, and a general description of his physical problems, but you did not use his name nor indicate the specific nature of his disabilities. Is this a responsible and ethical use of information? Can your client be recognized in a relatively small and sparsely populated area? What are the ethical issues involved when you use an electronic network to gain needed resources for your client?

➤ **A.32  A Reporter after Death**

A year ago when you were employed by St. Paul's Family Center, you served as social worker of Nicholas Karros, who had been experiencing problems on his job which affected him and his family. About eight months ago Nicholas was killed in an altercation at a local bar. You heard later that he had been the innocent victim. Roberta Frei, a reporter for the local newspaper, approached you yesterday to ask for information about Nicholas because she heard he had been abusive to his wife and children. Ms. Frei wanted this information as part of her preparation for an article on local domestic violence. What should you do? Does the *Code of Ethics* protect dead persons? What ethical issues are involved here?

➤ **A.33  After All, the Polonias Need the Help**

You are a social worker in a counseling agency whose budget is only barely making ends meet. The entire Polonia family has come to you for help with a family problem which is disturbing them all. They are highly motivated. The problem is that there is no provision for family therapy in their insurance plan. Since they cannot afford to pay you, they suggest that the only way to gain third-party reimbursement is to provide a diagnosis for one individual in the family and report that person as the patient. Should you agree and report an individual patient to the insurance plan, even though you treat the entire family?

➤ **A.34 Managed Care Says No, the Agency Says No, What Now?**
Brittany Taylor is a social worker in a group practice. She has been working successfully with Alice Pachler, a middle-aged single parent of limited means. The insurance company has stated that the problem requires only limited service and will only reimburse for two more sessions, but Ms. Taylor believes more time is required. Ms. Taylor's supervisor, when consulted, says the agency cannot afford to carry the case. How should Ms. Taylor handle this?

➤ **A.35 A Peaceful House in a New Land**
Your client is a recent immigrant and has many traditional cultural values. Referred by her physician, she has been having headaches and difficulty with her husband, who is very critical of her housework and of her care for their children. She believes that the woman is responsible for a peaceful house and should put up with her husband's criticisms. In fact, she is proud that he only criticizes her and does not slap or hit her when she does things incorrectly. Your goals as the social worker differ. You think she should protect herself, gain some independence, and be more self-assertive. Should you continue to work with this person? If not, why not? If yes, why?

➤ **A.36 Ethical Research and the Ulanov Family Secret**
You are a social worker employed part-time on a research project exploring family relationships in families with at least one adolescent child. As part of the research protocol you interview each family member separately; all are assured confidentiality. You also interview the family as a unit. While interviewing DeDe Prochoa, a nine-year-old, she tells you that her fifteen-year-old sister, Vicky, has sex with her step-father, Grigori Ulanov. What would you do?

➤ **A.37 Family Service Sets Up an Employee Assistance Program**
Family Service is a multiservice agency operating on a very tight budget. It is one of several similar agencies in town. Recently it was asked by

the Guaranty Insurance Company to establish an employee assistance program. The staff planning committee is meeting to consider several ideas. Your supervisor thinks that the agency should provide this service free as a "loss leader" because if your agency sets up and runs the EAP most of the referrals from the EAP will be sent to Family Service. Providing such a service will mean that the agency has to reduce some other activities because the agency budget has no "play." Is it ethical for the agency to establish the EAP program? What should your agency do?

➤ **A.38  How to Be Fair?**

Your community is in the midst of an annual enrollment period for qualified aging persons to obtain tax-supported inexpensive transportation. Not every applicant will be accepted because only limited funds are available. As you help older persons fill out applications, you know some persons are needy but not providing all the income information in order to qualify. Should you confront them? Should you inform the authorities?

➤ **A.39  Insider Trading**

Recently Mr. Wellington, a friend and neighbor, approached you in the supermarket. You were pleased to see him. Some years ago he helped your parents several times when they were late on mortgage payments by loaning them money free of charge. He tells you that his nine-year-old child has been "acting up" and driving his wife crazy. They went for an initial interview at the local mental health clinic where you serve as the executive director and learned that it would be approximately one month before their son could be seen on a regular basis. Could you do anything to move up the appointment? What should you do?

➤ **A.40  Ellie Rivas Knew What She Wanted Done**

For the past ten years Ellie Rivas has slowly become more and more debilitated. She had heart trouble, diabetes, cancer which was successfully treated, water retention difficulties, and other ailments. Now she is in the hospital intensive care unit. Her physician has just informed the family members that she has perhaps a few weeks to live, her pain will be managed, and she could possibly be moved to a nursing home but would have to be fed directly through a stomach tube. The family, which has a relationship with you, the hospital social worker, want to review the options with you. A daughter has a signed durable power of attorney for health care and Ms. Rivas's instructions, which allow her to make health decisions for Ms. Rivas. Her physician and the hospital also have copies of these documents. Some members of the family believe she should not be fed through the stomach, which will only prolong her life with suffering. Others say she should be fed through a stomach tube because life is sacred, and that it should be valued and sustained under all circumstances. They ask your advice. What would you the social worker do?

➤ **A.41  A House in a New Development**

You are employed in a social agency and have developed a very positive relationship with a client, Chip, a very successful real estate agent who is appreciative of the help you have been able to provide for him. You and your wife are interested in buying a house in a new development where construction has been unable to keep up with the demand for new homes. However, you have less of a down payment than is needed, and you also are not high on the waiting list to get into this desirable area.

When you asked Chip about these two problems, he responded by telling you that he would be glad to move you up on the waiting list and would arrange for a loan for the difference in the down payment. Is there a difference between being moved up on the list and accepting the loan which you will repay? What are your choices?

# Appendix B:
# Codes of Ethics

## National Association
## of Social Workers

### PREAMBLE

This code is intended to serve as a guide to the everyday conduct of members of the social work profession and as a basis for the adjudication of issues in ethics when the conduct of social workers is alleged to deviate from the standards expressed or implied in this code. It represents standards of ethical behavior for social workers in professional relationships with those served, with colleagues, with employers, with other individuals and professions, and with the community and society as a whole. It also embodies standards of ethical behavior governing individual conduct to the extent that such conduct is associated with an individual's status and identity as a social worker.

This code is based on the fundamental values of the social work profession that include the worth, dignity, and uniqueness of all persons as well as their rights and opportunities. It is also based on the nature of social work, which fosters conditions that promote these values.

Reprinted with permission from NASW *Code of Ethics.* Copyright 1993, National Association of Social Workers, Inc.

In subscribing to and abiding by this code, the social worker is expected to view ethical responsibility in as inclusive a context as each situation demands and within which ethical judgment is required. The social worker is expected to take into consideration all the principles in this code that have a bearing upon any situation in which ethical judgment is to be exercised and professional intervention or conduct is planned. The course of action that the social worker chooses is expected to be consistent with the spirit as well as the letter of this code.

In itself, this code does not represent a set of rules that will prescribe all the behaviors of social workers in all the complexities of professional life. Rather, it offers general principles to guide conduct, and the judicious appraisal of conduct, in situations that have ethical implications. It provides the basis for making judgments about ethical actions before and after they occur. Frequently, the particular situation determines the ethical principles that apply and the manner of their application. In such cases, not only the particular ethical principles are taken into immediate consideration, but also the entire code and its spirit. Specific applications of ethical principles must be judged within the context in which they are being considered. Ethical behavior in a given situation must satisfy not only the judgment of the individual social worker, but also the judgment of an unbiased jury of professional peers.

This code should not be used as an instrument to deprive any social worker of the opportunity or freedom to practice with complete professional integrity; nor should any disciplinary action be taken on the basis of this code without maximum provision for safeguarding the rights of the social worker affected.

The ethical behavior of social workers results not from edict, but from a personal commitment of the individual. This code is offered to affirm the will and zeal of all social workers to be ethical and to act ethically in all that they do as social workers.

The following codified ethical principles should guide social workers in the various roles and relationships and at the various levels of responsibility in which they function professionally. These principles also serve as a basis for the adjudication by the National Association of Social Workers of issues in ethics.

In subscribing to this code, social workers are required to cooperate in its implementation and abide by any disciplinary rulings based on it. They should also take adequate measures to discourage, prevent, expose, and correct the unethical conduct of colleagues. Finally, social workers should be equally ready to defend and assist colleagues unjustly charged with unethical conduct.

## I. THE SOCIAL WORKER'S CONDUCT AND COMPORTMENT AS A SOCIAL WORKER

A. *Propriety*—The social worker should maintain high standards of personal conduct in the capacity or identity as social worker.

1. The private conduct of the social worker is a personal matter to the same degree as is any other person's, except when such conduct compromises the fulfillment of professional responsibilities.
2. The social worker should not participate in, condone, or be associated with dishonesty, fraud, deceit, or misrepresentation.
3. The social worker should distinguish clearly between statements and actions made as a private individual and as a representative of the social work profession or an organization or group.

B. *Competence and Professional Development*—The social worker should strive to become and remain proficient in professional practice and the performance of professional functions.

1. The social worker should accept responsibility or employment only on the basis of existing competence or the intention to acquire the necessary competence.
2. The social worker should not misrepresent professional qualifications, education, experience, or affiliations.
3. The social worker should not allow his or her own personal problems, psychosocial distress, substance abuse, or mental health difficulties to interfere with professional judgment and performance or jeopardize the best interests of those for whom the social worker has a professional responsibility.
4. The social worker whose personal problems, psychosocial distress, substance abuse, or mental health difficulties interfere with professional judgment and performance should immediately seek consultation and take appropriate remedial action by seeking professional help, making adjustments in workload, terminating practice, or taking any other steps necessary to protect clients and others.

C. *Service*—The social worker should regard as primary the service obligation of the social work profession.

1. The social worker should retain ultimate responsibility for the quality and extent of the service that individual assumes, assigns, or performs.
2. The social worker should act to prevent practices that are inhumane or discriminatory against any person or group of persons.

D. *Integrity*—The social worker should act in accordance with the highest standards of professional integrity and impartiality.

1. The social worker should be alert to and resist the influences and pressures that interfere with the exercise of professional discretion and impartial judgment required for the performance of professional functions.
2. The social worker should not exploit professional relationships for personal gain.

E. *Scholarship and Research*—The social worker engaged in study and research should be guided by the conventions of scholarly inquiry.

1. The social worker engaged in research should consider carefully its possible consequences for human beings.
2. The social worker engaged in research should ascertain that the consent of participants in the research is voluntary and informed, without any implied deprivation or penalty for refusal to participate, and with due regard for participants' privacy and dignity.
3. The social worker engaged in research should protect participants from unwarranted physical or mental discomfort, distress, harm, danger, or deprivation.
4. The social worker who engages in the evaluation of services or cases should discuss them only for the professional purposes and only with persons directly and professionally concerned with them.
5. Information obtained about participants in research should be treated as confidential.
6. The social worker should take credit only for work actually done in connection with scholarly and research endeavors and credit contributions made by others.

## II. THE SOCIAL WORKER'S ETHICAL RESPONSIBILITY TO CLIENTS

F. *Primacy of Clients' Interests*—The social worker's primary responsibility is to clients.

1. The social worker should serve clients with devotion, loyalty, determination, and the maximum application of professional skill and competence.
2. The social worker should not exploit relationships with clients for personal advantage.

3. The social worker should not practice, condone, facilitate or collaborate with any form of discrimination on the basis of race, color, sex, sexual orientation, age, religion, national origin, marital status, political belief, mental or physical handicap, or any other preference or personal characteristic, condition or status.
4. The social worker should not condone or engage in any dual or multiple relationships with clients or former clients in which there is a risk of exploitation of or potential harm to the client. The social worker is responsible for setting clear, appropriate, and culturally sensitive boundaries.
5. The social worker should under no circumstances engage in sexual activities with clients.
6. The social worker should provide clients with accurate and complete information regarding the extent and nature of the services available to them.
7. The social worker should apprise clients of their risks, rights, opportunities, and obligations associated with social service to them.
8. The social worker should seek advice and counsel of colleagues and supervisors whenever such consultation is in the best interest of clients.
9. The social worker should terminate service to clients, and professional relationships with them, when such service and relationships are no longer required or no longer serve the clients' needs or interests.
10. The social worker should withdraw services precipitously only under unusual circumstances, giving careful consideration to all factors in the situation and taking care to minimize possible adverse effects.
11. The social worker who anticipates the termination or interruption of service to clients should notify clients promptly and seek the transfer, referral, or continuation of service in relation to the clients' needs and preferences.

G. *Rights and Prerogatives of Clients*—The social worker should make every effort to foster maximum self-determination on the part of clients.

1. When the social worker must act on behalf of a client who has been adjudged legally incompetent, the social worker should safeguard the interests and rights of that client.
2. When another individual has been legally authorized to act in behalf of a client, the social worker should deal with that person always with the client's best interest in mind.

3. The social worker should not engage in any action that violates or diminishes the civil or legal rights of clients.

H. *Confidentiality and Privacy*—The social worker should respect the privacy of clients and hold in confidence all information obtained in the course of professional service.

1. The social worker should share with others confidences revealed by clients, without their consent, only for compelling professional reasons.
2. The social worker should inform clients fully about the limits of confidentiality in a given situation, the purposes for which information is obtained, and how it may be used.
3. The social worker should afford clients reasonable access to any official social work records concerning them.
4. When providing clients with access to records, the social worker should take due care to protect the confidences of others contained in those records.
5. The social worker should obtain informed consent of clients before taping, recording, or permitting third party observation of their activities.

I. *Fees*—When setting fees, the social worker should ensure that they are fair, reasonable, considerate, and commensurate with the service performed and with due regard for the clients' ability to pay.

1. The social worker should not accept anything of value for making a referral.

## III. THE SOCIAL WORKER'S ETHICAL RESPONSIBILITY TO COLLEAGUES

J. *Respect, Fairness, and Courtesy*—The social worker should treat colleagues with respect, courtesy, fairness, and good faith.

1. The social worker should cooperate with colleagues to promote professional interests and concerns.
2. The social worker should respect confidences shared by colleagues in the course of their professional relationships and transactions.
3. The social worker should create and maintain conditions of practice that facilitate ethical and competent professional performance by colleagues.
4. The social worker should treat with respect, and represent accurately and fairly, the qualifications, views, and findings of

colleagues and use appropriate channels to express judgments on these matters.

5. The social worker who replaces or is replaced by a colleague in professional practice should act with consideration for the interest, character, and reputation of that colleague.
6. The social worker should not exploit a dispute between a colleague and employers to obtain a position or otherwise advance the social worker's interest.
7. The social worker should seek arbitration or mediation when conflicts with colleagues require resolution for compelling professional reasons.
8. The social worker should extend to colleagues of other professions the same respect and cooperation that is extended to social work colleagues.
9. The social worker who serves as an employer, supervisor, or mentor to colleagues should make orderly and explicit arrangements regarding the conditions of their continuing professional relationship.
10. The social worker who has the responsibility for employing and evaluating the performance of other staff members, should fulfill such responsibility in a fair, considerate, and equitable manner, on the basis of clearly enunciated criteria.
11. The social worker who has the responsibility for evaluating the performance of employees, supervisees, or students should share evaluations with them.
12. The social worker should not use a professional position vested with power, such as that of employer, supervisor, teacher, or consultant, to his or her advantage or to exploit others.
13. The social worker who has direct knowledge of a social work colleague's impairment due to personal problems, psychosocial distress, substance abuse, or mental health difficulties should consult with that colleague and assist the colleague in taking remedial action.

K. *Dealing with Colleagues' Clients*—The social worker has the responsibility to relate to the clients of colleagues with full professional consideration.

1. The social worker should not assume professional responsibility for the clients of another agency or a colleague without appropriate communication with that agency or colleague.
2. The social worker who serves the clients of colleagues, during a temporary absence or emergency, should serve those clients with the same consideration as that afforded any client.

## IV. THE SOCIAL WORKER'S ETHICAL RESPONSIBILITY TO EMPLOYERS AND EMPLOYING ORGANIZATIONS

L. *Commitments to Employing Organization*—The social worker should adhere to commitments made to the employing organization.

1. The social worker should work to improve the employing agency's policies and procedures, and the efficiency and effectiveness of its services.
2. The social worker should not accept employment or arrange student field placements in an organization which is currently under public sanction by NASW for violating personnel standards, or imposing limitations on or penalties for professional actions on behalf of clients.
3. The social worker should act to prevent and eliminate discrimination in the employing organization's work assignments and in its employment policies and practices.
4. The social worker should use with scrupulous regard, and only for the purpose for which they are intended, the resources of the employing organization.

## V. THE SOCIAL WORKER'S ETHICAL RESPONSIBILITY TO THE SOCIAL WORK PROFESSION

M. *Maintaining the Integrity of the Profession*—The social worker should uphold and advance the values, ethics, knowledge, and mission of the profession.

1. The social worker should protect and enhance the dignity and integrity of the profession and should be responsible and vigorous in discussion and criticism of the profession.
2. The social worker should take action through appropriate channels against unethical conduct by any other member of the profession.
3. The social worker should act to prevent the unauthorized and unqualified practice of social work.
4. The social worker should make no misrepresentation in advertising as to qualifications, competence, service, or results to be achieved.

N. *Community Service*—The social worker should assist the profession in making social services available to the general public.

1. The social worker should contribute time and professional expertise to activities that promote respect for the utility, the integrity, and the competence of the social work profession.

2. The social worker should support the formulation, development, enactment and implementation of social policies of concern to the profession.

O. *Development of Knowledge*—The social worker should take responsibility for identifying, developing, and fully utilizing knowledge for professional practice.

1. The social worker should base practice upon recognized knowledge relevant to social work.
2. The social worker should critically examine, and keep current with emerging knowledge relevant to social work.
3. The social worker should contribute to the knowledge base of social work and share research knowledge and practice wisdom with colleagues.

## VI. THE SOCIAL WORKER'S ETHICAL RESPONSIBILITY TO SOCIETY

P. *Promoting the General Welfare*—The social worker should promote the general welfare of society.

1. The social worker should act to prevent and eliminate discrimination against any person or group on the basis of race, color, sex, sexual orientation, age, religion, national origin, marital status, political belief, mental or physical handicap, or any other preference or personal characteristic, condition, or status.
2. The social worker should act to ensure that all persons have access to the resources, services, and opportunities which they require.
3. The social worker should act to expand choice and opportunity for all persons, with special regard for disadvantaged or oppressed groups and persons.
4. The social worker should promote conditions that encourage respect for the diversity of cultures which constitute American society.
5. The social worker should provide appropriate professional services in public emergencies.
6. The social worker should advocate changes in policy and legislation to improve social conditions and to promote social justice.
7. The social worker should encourage informed participation by the public in shaping social policies and institutions.

## SUMMARY OF MAJOR PRINCIPLES

I. **The Social Worker's Conduct and Comportment as a Social Worker**
   A. *Propriety.* The social worker should maintain high standards of personal conduct in the capacity or identity as social worker.
   B. *Competence and Professional Development.* The social worker should strive to become and remain proficient in professional practice and the performance of professional functions.
   C. *Service.* The social worker should regard as primary the service obligation of the social work profession.
   D. *Integrity.* The social worker should act in accordance with the highest standards of professional integrity.
   E. *Scholarship and Research.* The social worker engaged in study and research should be guided by the conventions of scholarly inquiry.

II. **The Social Worker's Ethical Responsibility to Clients**
   F. *Primacy of Clients' Interests.* The social worker's primary responsibility is to clients.
   G. *Rights and Prerogatives of Clients.* The social worker should make every effort to foster maximum self-determination on the part of clients.
   H. *Confidentiality and Privacy.* The social worker should respect the privacy of clients and hold in confidence all information obtained in the course of professional service.
   I. *Fees.* When setting fees, the social worker should ensure that they are fair, reasonable, considerate, and commensurate with the service performed and with due regard for the clients' ability to pay.

III. **The Social Worker's Ethical Responsibility to Colleagues**
   J. *Respect, Fairness, and Courtesy.* The social worker should treat colleagues with respect, courtesy, fairness, and good faith.
   K. *Dealing with Colleagues' Clients.* The social worker has the responsibility to relate to the clients of colleagues with full professional consideration.

IV. **The Social Worker's Ethical Responsibility to Employers and Employing Organizations**
   L. *Commitments to Employing Organizations.* The social worker should adhere to commitments made to the employing organizations.

V. **The Social Worker's Ethical Responsibility to the Social Work Profession**
   M. *Maintaining the Integrity of the Profession.* The social worker should uphold and advance the values, ethics, knowledge, and mission of the profession.
   N. *Community Service.* The social worker should assist the profession in making social services available to the general public.
   O. *Development of Knowledge.* The social worker should take responsibility for identifying, developing, and fully utilizing knowledge for professional practice.

VI. **The Social Worker's Ethical Responsibility to Society**
   P. *Promoting the General Welfare.* The social worker should promote the general welfare of society.

# National Association
# of Black Social Workers

In America today, no Black person, except the selfish or irrational, can claim neutrality in the quest for Black liberation nor fail to consider the implications of events taking place in our society. Given the necessity for committing ourselves to the struggle for freedom, we as Black Americans practicing in the field of social welfare set forth this statement of ideals and guiding principles.

If a sense of community awareness is a precondition to humanitarian acts, then we as Black social workers must use our knowledge of the Black community, our commitments to its self-determination and our helping skills for the benefit of Black people as we marshal our expertise to improve the quality of life of Black people. Our activities will be guided by our Black consciousness, our determination to protect the security of the Black community and to serve as advocates to relieve suffering of Black people by any means necessary.

Therefore, as Black social workers we commit ourselves, collectively, to the interests of our Black brethren and as individuals subscribe to the following statements:

> I regard as my primary obligation the welfare of the Black individual, Black family and Black community and will engage in action for improving social conditions.
>
> I give preference to this mission over my personal interests.
>
> I adopt the concept of a Black extended family and embrace all Black people as my brothers and sisters, making no distinction between their destiny and my own.
>
> I hold myself responsible for the quality and extent of service performed by the agency or organization in which I am employed, as it relates to the Black community.
>
> I accept the responsibility to protect the Black community against unethical and hypocritical practice by any individuals or organizations engaged in social welfare activities.
>
> I stand ready to supplement my paid or professional advocacy with voluntary service in the Black public interest.
>
> I will consciously use my skills, and my whole being, as an instrument for social change, with particular attention directed to the establishment of Black social institutions.

This *Code of Ethics* is reprinted with the permission of the National Association of Black Social Workers, Inc.

# National Federation of Societies
# for Clinical Social Work

## PREAMBLE

Ethical principles affecting the practice of clinical social work are rooted in the basic values of society and the social work profession. The principal objective of the profession of clinical social work is to enhance the dignity and well-being of each individual who seeks its services. It does so through use of clinical social work theory and treatment methods, including psychotherapy.

The following represents codified ethical principles which serve as a standard for clinical social workers as psychotherapists and in their various other professional roles, relationships, and responsibilities. The clinical social worker is expected to take into consideration all the principles in this code that have a bearing upon any situation in which ethical judgment is to be exercised, and to select a course of action consistent with the spirit as well as the letter of the code.

Members of State Societies for Clinical Social Work adhere to these principles. When clinical social workers' conduct is alleged to deviate from these standards, they agree to abide by the recommendations arrived at by State Society disciplinary panels.

It is recognized that the practice of clinical social work is complex and varied and does not lend itself to limitation by a set of rules which will particularize all of its functions. The primary goal of this code is not to restrict the practice of clinical social workers, but to offer general principles to guide their conduct and to inspire their will to act according to ethical principles in all of their professional functions.

## I. GENERAL RESPONSIBILITIES OF CLINICAL SOCIAL WORKERS

Clinical social workers maintain high standards of the profession in all of their professional roles. Clinical social workers value professional competence, objectivity and integrity. They consistently examine, use, and attempt to expand the knowledge upon which practice is based, working to ensure that their services are used appropriately and accepting responsibility for the consequences of their work.

This *Code of Ethics* was revised in May 1988, and is presented here with the permission of the National Federation of Societies for Clinical Social Work, Inc.

a) As psychotherapy practitioners, clinical social workers bear a heavy responsibility because their recommendations and professional actions may alter the lives of others. The social worker's primary responsibility is to the client. However, when the interest of the individual patient or client conflicts with the welfare of his family or of the community at large, the clinical social worker weighs the consequences of any action and arrives at a judgment based on all considerations.

b) As employees of institutions or agencies, clinical social workers are responsible for remaining alert to and attempting to moderate institutional pressures and/or policies that conflict with the standards of their profession. If such conflict arises, clinical social workers' primary responsibility is to uphold the ethical standards of their profession.

c) As teachers, clinical social workers are responsible for careful preparation so that their instruction maintains high standards of scholarship and objectivity.

d) Clinical social workers practice only within their sphere of competence. They accurately represent their abilities, education, training, and experience. They avail themselves of opportunities for continuing professional education to maintain and enhance their competence. When indicated, they seek consultation from colleagues or other appropriate professionals.

e) Clinical social workers do not exploit their professional relationships sexually, financially, or for any other personal advantage. They maintain this standard of conduct toward all who may be professionally associated with them, such as clients, colleagues, supervisees, employees, students, and research participants.

f) Clinical social workers refrain from undertaking any professional activity in which their personal problems or conflicts might lead to the inadequate provision of service. If involved in such a situation, they seek appropriate professional assistance to help them determine whether they should suspend, terminate, or limit the scope of their professional involvement.

## II. RESPONSIBILITY TO CLIENTS

The clinical social worker's primary responsibility is to the client. Clinical social workers respect the integrity, protect the welfare, and maximize the self-determination of the clients with whom they work.

a) Clinical social workers inform clients of the extent and nature of services available to them as well as the limits, rights, opportunities, and obligations associated with service which might affect the client's decision to enter into or continue the relationship.

b) Clinical social workers enter and/or continue professional relationships based on their ability to meet the needs of clients appropriately. The clinical social worker terminates service to clients, and professional relationships with them, when such service and relationships are no longer required or no longer serve the client's best interests. The clinical social worker who anticipates the interruption or termination of service to clients gives reasonable notification and provides for transfer, referral or continuation of service in relation to the client's needs and preferences. Clinical social workers do not withdraw services precipitously except under extraordinary circumstances, giving careful consideration to all factors in the situation and taking care to minimize possible adverse effects.

c) Clinical social workers use care to prevent the intrusion of their own personal needs into relationships with clients. They recognize that the private and personal nature of the therapeutic relationship may unrealistically intensify clients' feelings toward them, thus increasing their obligation to maintain professional objectivity. Therefore, specifically:

1. Clinical social workers avoid entering treatment relationships in which their professional judgment will be compromised by prior association with or knowledge of a client. Examples might include treatment of one's family members, close friends, associates, employees, or others whose welfare could be jeopardized by such a dual relationship.

2. Clinical social workers do not engage in or condone sexual activities with clients.

3. Clinical social workers do not initiate, and should avoid when possible, personal relationships or dual roles with current clients, or with any former clients whose feelings toward them may still be derived from or influenced by the former professional relationship.

d) The clinical social worker takes care to ensure an appropriate setting for practice to protect both the client and the social worker from actual or imputed mental and/or physical harm. If the clinical social worker judges that there is a threat to safety, reasonable steps are taken to prevent the client from causing harm to self or others.

e) When the clinical social worker must act on behalf of a client, the action should always safeguard the interests and concerns of that client. When another person has been authorized to act on behalf of a client, the clinical social worker should deal with that person with the client's best interests in mind.

## III. RELATIONSHIPS WITH COLLEAGUES

Clinical social workers act with integrity in their relationships with colleagues and members of other professions. They know and take into account the traditions, practices, and areas of competence of other professionals and cooperate with them fully for the welfare of clients.

a) The clinical social worker represents accurately the views, qualifications, and findings of colleagues and, when expressing judgment on these matters, does so in a manner that does not compromise the best interests of clients.
b) Clinical social workers know that a client's health and safety may depend on receiving appropriate service from members of other professional disciplines. They are responsible for maintaining knowledge of, and appropriately utilizing, the expertise of such professionals on the client's behalf.
c) In referring clients to allied professionals, clinical social workers ensure that those to whom they refer clients are recognized members of their own disciplines and are competent to carry out the professional services required.
d) If a clinical social worker's services are sought by an individual who is already receiving similar services from another professional, consideration for the client's welfare shall be paramount. It requires the clinical social worker to proceed with great caution, carefully considering both the existing professional relationship and the therapeutic issues involved.
e) As supervisors or employers, clinical social workers accept their responsibility to provide competent professional guidance to colleagues, employees, and students. They foster working conditions that ensure fairness, privacy, and protection from physical or mental harm. They evaluate fairly and with consideration the performance of those under their supervision, and share evaluations with supervisees. They do not abuse the power inherent in their position.
f) Clinical social workers take appropriate measures to discourage, prevent, expose, and correct unethical or incompetent behavior by colleagues, but take equally appropriate steps to assist and defend colleagues unjustly charged with such conduct. They do

not encourage the unsupervised practice of social work by those who fail to meet accepted standards of training and experience.[1]

## IV. REMUNERATION

Fees set by clinical social workers are in accord with professional standards that protect the client and the profession.

  a) In establishing rates for professional services, clinical social workers take into account both the ability of the client to pay and the value of the services rendered.
  b) Clinical social workers do not participate in illegal fee-splitting arrangements, nor do they give or accept kickbacks for referrals. However, it is not unethical for clinical social workers to utilize referral services for which a fee is charged, nor to participate in contractual arrangements under which they agree to discount fees.
  c) Clinical social workers employed by an agency or clinic and also engaged in private practice conform to agency regulations regarding their dual roles.

## V. CONFIDENTIALITY

The safeguarding of the client's right to privacy is a basic responsibility of the clinical social worker. Clinical social workers have a primary obligation to maintain the confidentiality of material that has been transmitted to them in any of their professional roles, including the identity of the client.

  a) Clinical social workers reveal confidential information to others only with the informed consent of the client, except in those circumstances in which not to do so would violate the law or would result in clear and imminent danger to the client or to others. Unless specifically contraindicated by such situations, clients should be informed in advance of any limitations of confidentiality, and informed and written consent should be obtained from

---

[1] i.e., a master's degree in social work from a school of social work accredited by the Council on Social Work Education, or a doctoral degree in social work, that included a sequence of clinically oriented course work and supervised clinical field placement, plus at least 2 years or its part-time equivalent of post-master's or doctoral full-time supervision in direct-service clinical experience in a clinical setting. (Standards for Health Care Providers in Clinical Social Work, National Federation of Societies for Clinical Social Work, 1974.)

the client before confidential information is revealed. Such consent includes telling the client about the purposes for which information is obtained and how it may be used.

b) When confidential information is used for the purposes of professional education, research, consultation, etc., every effort will be made to conceal the true identity of the client. Such presentations will be limited to material necessary for the professional purpose, and this material will be shared only with other responsible individuals.

c) Special care needs to be taken regarding confidentiality when the client is a vulnerable adult or minor child. In disclosing information to parents, guardians, the court, or others, the clinical social worker acts to protect the best interest of the primary client. Clinical social workers uphold their obligation to observe applicable law, including state mandates to report actual or potential abuse.

d) In keeping client records, clinical social workers remain aware of the limits of confidentiality and of the conditions under which they may be required to reveal recorded information. Accordingly, they maintain records adequate to ensure proper diagnosis and treatment, but take precautions to minimize the exposure of the client to any harm that might result from improper disclosure. Clients are permitted to examine their records if they request access. Clinical social workers make provisions for maintaining confidentiality in the storage and disposal of these records, whether written or on audio or visual tape.

## VI. SOCIETAL AND LEGAL STANDARDS

Clinical social workers show sensible regard for the social codes and ethical expectations in their communities, recognizing that violations of accepted societal, ethical, and legal standards on their part may compromise the fulfillment of their professional responsibilities or reduce public trust in the profession.

a) Clinical social workers do not, in any of their capacities, practice, condone, facilitate, or collaborate with any form of discrimination on the basis of race, sex, sexual orientation, age, religion, socioeconomic status, or national origin.

b) Clinical social workers practice their profession in compliance with legal standards. They do not participate in arrangements undermining the law. However, when they believe laws affecting clients or their practice are in conflict with the principles and standards of the profession, clinical social workers make known the conflict and work toward change that will benefit the public interest.

c) Clinical social workers recognize a responsibility to participate in activities contributing toward improved social conditions within their community.

## VII. PURSUIT OF RESEARCH AND SCHOLARLY ACTIVITIES

In planning, conducting and reporting a study, the investigator has the responsibility to make a careful evaluation of its ethical acceptability, taking into account the following additional principles for research with human subjects. To the extent that this appraisal, weighing scientific and humane values, suggests a compromise of any principle, the investigator incurs an increasingly serious obligation to seek advice and to observe stringent safeguards to protect the rights of the research participants.

a) In conducting research in institutions or organizations, clinical social workers obtain appropriate authority to carry out such research. Host organizations are given proper credit for their contributions.

b) Ethically acceptable research begins with the establishment of a clear and fair agreement between the investigator and the research participant that clarifies the responsibilities of each. The investigator has the obligation to honor all promises and commitments included in that agreement.

c) Responsibility for the establishment and maintenance of acceptable ethical practice in research always remains with the investigator. The investigator is also responsible for the ethical treatment of research participants by collaborators, assistants, students, and employees, all of whom, however, incur parallel obligations.

d) Ethical practice requires the investigator to inform the participant of all features of the research that might reasonably be expected to influence willingness to participate, and to explain all other aspects of the research about which the participant inquires. Failure to make full disclosure imposes additional force to the investigator's abiding responsibility to protect the welfare and dignity of the research participant. After the data are collected, the investigator provides the participant with information about the nature of the study in order to remove any misconceptions that may have arisen.

e) The ethical investigator protects participants from physical and mental discomfort, harm, and danger. If a risk of such consequences exists, the investigator is required to inform the participant of that fact, secure consent before proceeding, and take all possible measures to minimize distress. A research procedure must not be used if it is likely to cause serious or lasting harm to a participant.

f) The methodological requirements of the study may necessitate concealment, deception, or minimal risk. In such cases the investigator is required to justify the use of these techniques and to ensure, as soon as possible, the participant's understanding of the reasons and sufficient justification for the procedure in question.

g) Ethical practice requires the investigator to respect the individual's freedom to decline to participate in or withdraw from research, and to so inform prospective participants. The obligation to protect this freedom requires special vigilance when the investigator is in a position of power over the participant, as, for example, when the participant is a student, client, employee, or otherwise is in a dual relationship with the investigator. It is unethical to penalize a participant in any way for withdrawing from or refusing to participate in a research project.

h) Information obtained about the individual research participants during the course of an investigation is confidential unless otherwise agreed in advance. When the possibility that others may obtain access to such information exists, to protect confidentiality, the participants will be informed that it is part of the procedure to obtain informed consent.

i) Investigations of human participants using drugs are conducted only in conjunction with licensed physicians.

j) Research findings must be presented accurately and completely, with full discussion of both their usefulness and their limitations. Clinical social workers are responsible for attempting to prevent any distortion or misuse of their findings.

k) Clinical social workers take credit only for work actually done in scholarly and research endeavors and give appropriate credit to the contributions of others.

## VIII. PUBLIC STATEMENTS

Public statements, announcements of services, and promotional activities of clinical social workers serve the purpose of providing sufficient information to aid consumers in making informed judgments and choices. Clinical social workers state accurately, objectively, and without misrepresentation their professional qualifications, affiliations, and functions as well as those of the institutions or organizations with which they or their statements may be associated. They should correct the misrepresentations of others with respect to these matters.

a) In announcing availability for professional services, a clinical social worker may use any information so long as it describes his or her credentials and the services provided accurately and without misrepresentation. Information usually found helpful by the client includes his or her name; highest relevant academic degree from an accredited institution; specialized post-graduate training; date, type, and level of certification or licensure; address and telephone number; office hours; type of services provided; appropriate fee information; foreign language spoken; and policy with regard to third-party payments.

b) Brochures or catalogs bearing a clinical social worker's name announcing any services offered shall describe the services accurately but shall not falsely or deceptively claim or imply superior personal or professional competence.

c) The clinical social worker is responsible for assuring that the content of all advertising communicated to the public on his or her behalf, whether by audio-visual or any other means, is in conformance with the ethical standards of the profession.

d) Clinical social workers provide diagnostic and therapeutic services only in the context of a professional relationship. Such services are not given by means of public lectures or demonstrations, newspaper or magazine articles, radio or television programs, or anything of a similar nature. Professional use of the media or other public forum is appropriate when the purpose is to educate the public about professional matters regarding which the clinical social worker has special knowledge or expertise.

e) Clinical social workers do not offer to perform any services beyond the scope permitted by law or beyond the scope of their competence. They do not engage in any form of advertising which is false, fraudulent, deceptive or misleading. The clinical social worker vigilantly guards against exploiting the therapeutic relationship with a client for commercial gain.

f) Clinical social workers respect the rights and reputation of any professional organization with which they are affiliated. They shall not falsely imply sponsorship or certification by such an organization. When making public statements, the clinical social worker will make clear which are personal opinions and which are authorized statements on behalf of the organization.

# Canadian Association of Social Workers

## PREAMBLE

### Philosophy

The profession of social work is founded on humanitarian and egalitarian ideals. Social workers believe in the intrinsic worth and dignity of every human being and are committed to the values of acceptance, self-determination and respect of individuality. They believe in the obligation of all people, individually and collectively, to provide resources, services and opportunities for the overall benefit of humanity. The culture of individuals, families, groups, communities and nations has to be respected without prejudice.

Social workers are dedicated to the welfare and self-realization of human beings; to the development and disciplined use of scientific knowledge regarding human and societal behaviors; to the development of resources to meet individual, group, national and international needs and aspirations; and to the achievement of social justice for all.

### Professional Practice Conflicts

If a conflict arises in professional practice, the standards declared in this Code take precedence. Conflicts of interest may occur because of demands from the general public, workplace, organizations or clients. In all cases, if the ethical duties and obligations or ethical responsibilities of this Code would be compromised, the social worker must act in a manner consistent with this Code.

### Nature of this Code

The first seven statements in this code establish ethical duties and obligations. These statements provide the basis of a social worker's relationship with a client and are based on the values of social work. A breach of any of these statements forms the basis of a disciplinary action. The remaining three statements are characterized as ethical responsibilities and are to be seen as being different from the ethical duties and obligations. These ethical responsibilities are not likely to form the basis of any disciplinary action if breached. However these sections may form the basis of inquiry. These ethical responsibilities may be used in conjunction with breaches of other sections of this code and may form the basis of necessary background information in any action for discipline. Of equal importance, these ethical responsibilities are desirable goals to be achieved by the social work profession which by its nature is driven by an adherence to the values that form the basis of these desirable ethical behaviours.

## Ethical Duties and Obligations

1. A social worker shall maintain the best interest of the client as the primary professional obligation.
2. A social worker shall carry out her or his professional duties and obligations with integrity and objectivity.
3. A social worker shall have and maintain competence in the provision of a social work service to a client.
4. A social worker shall not exploit the relationship with a client for personal benefit, gain or gratification.
5. A social worker shall protect the confidentiality of all information acquired from the client or others regarding the client and the client's family during the professional relationship unless

    (a) the client authorizes in writing the release of specified information,
    (b) the information is released under the authority of a statute or an order of a court of competent jurisdiction, or
    (c) otherwise authorized by this Code.

6. A social worker who engages in another profession, occupation, affiliation or calling shall not allow these outside interests to affect the social work relationship with the client.
7. A social worker in private practice shall not conduct the business of provision of social work services for a fee in a manner that discredits the profession or diminishes the public's trust in the profession.

## Ethical Responsibilities

8. A social worker shall advocate for workplace conditions and policies that are consistent with the Code.

9. A social worker shall promote excellence in the social work profession.
10. A social worker shall advocate change
    (a) in the best interest of the client, and
    (b) for the overall benefit of society, the environment and the global community.

## 1. PRIMARY PROFESSIONAL OBLIGATION

1.   A social worker shall maintain the best interest of the client as the primary professional obligation.

1.1   The social worker is to be guided primarily by this obligation. Any action which is substantially inconsistent with this obligation is an unethical action.

1.2   A social worker in the practice of social work shall not discriminate against any person on the basis of race, ethnic background, language, religion, marital status, sex, sexual orientation, age, abilities, socio-economic status, political affiliation or national ancestry.

1.3   A social worker shall inform a client of the client's right to consult another professional at any time during the provision of social work services.

1.4   A social worker shall immediately inform the client of any factor, condition or pressure that affects the social worker's ability to perform an acceptable level of service.

1.5   A social worker shall not become involved in a client's personal affairs that are not relevant to the service being provided.

1.6   A social worker shall not state an opinion, judgment or use a clinical diagnosis unless there is a documented assessment, observation or diagnosis to support the opinion, judgment or diagnosis.

1.7   Where possible, a social worker shall provide or secure social work services in the language chosen by the client.

## 2. INTEGRITY AND OBJECTIVITY

2.   A social worker shall carry out his or her professional duties and obligations with integrity and objectivity.

2.1   The social worker shall identify and describe education, training, experience, professional affiliations, competence, and nature of service in an honest and accurate manner.

2.2   The social worker shall explain to the client her or his education, experience, training, competence, nature of service and action at the request of the client.

2.3   A social worker shall cite an educational degree only after it has been received from the institution.

2.4   A social worker shall not claim formal social work education in an area of expertise or training solely by attending a lecture, demonstration, conference, panel discussion, workshop, seminar or other similar teaching presentation.

2.5   The social worker shall not make a false, misleading or exaggerated claim of efficacy regarding past or anticipated achievement with respect to clients.

2.6   The social worker shall distinguish between actions and statements made as a private citizen and actions and statements made as a social worker.

## 3. COMPETENCE IN THE PROVISION OF SOCIAL WORK SERVICES

3.   A social worker shall have and maintain competence in the provision of a social work service to a client.

3.1   The social worker shall not undertake a social work service unless the social worker has the competence to provide the service or the social worker can reasonably acquire the necessary competence without undue delay, risk or expense to the client.

3.2   Where a social worker cannot reasonably acquire the necessary competence in the provision of a service to a client, the social worker shall decline to provide the service to the client, advising the client of the reason and ensuring that the client is referred to another professional person if the client agrees to the referral.

3.3.   The social worker, with the agreement of the client, may obtain advice from other professionals in the provision of service to a client.

3.4   A social worker shall maintain an acceptable level of health and well-being in order to provide a competent level of service to a client.

3.5   Where a social worker has a physical or mental health problem, disability or illness that affects the ability of the social worker to provide competent service or that would threaten the health or well-being of the client, the social worker shall discontinue the provision of social work service to a client

  (a) advising the client of the reason and,

(b) ensuring that the client is referred to another professional person if the client agrees to the referral.

3.6   The social worker shall have, maintain and endeavor periodically to update an acceptable level of knowledge and skills to meet the standards of practice of the profession.

## 4. LIMIT ON PROFESSIONAL RELATIONSHIP

4.   A social worker shall not exploit the relationship with a client for personal benefit, gain or gratification.

4.1   The social worker shall respect the client and act so that the dignity, individuality and rights of the person are protected.

4.2   The social worker shall assess and consider a client's motivation and physical and mental capacity in arranging for the provision of an appropriate service.

4.3   The social worker shall not have a sexual relationship with a client.

4.4   The social worker shall not have a business relationship with a client, borrow money from a client, or loan money to a client.

4.5   The social worker shall not have a sexual relationship with a social work student assigned to the social worker.

4.6   The social worker shall not sexually harass any person.

## 5. CONFIDENTIAL INFORMATION

5.   A social worker shall protect the confidentiality of all information acquired from the client or others regarding the client and the client's family during the professional relationship unless
   (a) the client authorizes in writing the release of specified information,
   (b) the information is released under the authority of a statute or an order of a court of relevant jurisdiction, or
   (c) otherwise authorized under this Code.

5.1   The requirement of confidentiality also applies to social workers who work as
   (a) supervisors,
   (b) managers,
   (c) educators, or
   (d) administrators.

5.2   A social worker who works as a supervisor, manager or administrator shall establish policies and practices that protect the confidentiality of client information.

5.3    The social worker may disclose confidential information to other persons in the workplace who, by virtue of their responsibilities, have an identified need to know as determined by the social worker.

5.4    Clients shall be the initial or primary source of information about themselves and their problems unless the client is incapable or unwilling to give information or when corroborative reporting is required.

5.5    The social worker has the obligation to ensure that the client understands what is being asked, why and to what purpose the information will be used, and to understand the confidentiality policies and practices of the workplace setting.

5.6    Where information is required by law, the social worker shall explain to the client the consequences of refusing to provide the requested information.

5.7    Where information is required from other sources, the social worker

(a) shall explain the requirement to the client, and

(b) shall attempt to involve the client in selecting the sources to be used.

5.8    The social worker shall take reasonable care to safeguard the client's personal papers or property if the social worker agrees to keep the property at the request of the client.

## Recording Information

5.9    The social worker shall maintain only one master file on each client.

5.10    The social worker shall record all relevant information, and keep all relevant documents in the file.

5.11    The social worker shall not record in a client's file any characterization that is not based on clinical assessment or fact.

## Accessibility of Records

5.12    The social worker who contracts for the delivery of social work services with a client is responsible to the client for maintaining the client record.

5.13    The social worker who is employed by a social agency that delivers social work services to clients is responsible

(a) to the client for the maintaining of a client record, and

(b) to the agency to maintain the records to facilitate the objectives of the agency.

5.14   A social worker is obligated to follow the provision of a statute that allows access to records by clients.

5.15   The social worker shall respect the client's right of access to a client record subject to the social worker's right to refuse access for just and reasonable cause.

5.16   Where a social worker refuses a client the right to access a file or part of a file, the social worker shall advise the client of the right to request a review of the decision in accordance with the relevant statute, workplace policy or other relevant procedure.

## Disclosure

5.17   The social worker shall not disclose the identity of persons who have sought a social work service or disclose sources of information about clients unless compelled legally to do so.

5.18   The obligation to maintain confidentiality continues indefinitely after the social worker has ceased contact with the client.

5.19   The social worker shall avoid unnecessary conversation regarding clients.

5.20   The social worker may divulge confidential information with consent of the client, preferably expressed in writing, where this is essential to a plan of care or treatment.

5.21   The social worker shall transfer information to another agency or individual, only with the informed consent of the client or guardian of the client and then only with the reasonable assurance that the receiving agency provides the same guarantee of confidentiality and respect for the right of privileged communication as provided by the sending agency.

5.22   The social worker shall explain to the client the disclosure of information requirements of the law or of the agency before the commencement of the provision of social work services.

5.23   The social worker in practice with groups and communities shall notify the participants of the likelihood that aspects of their private lives may be revealed in the course of their work together, and therefore require a commitment from each member to respect the privileged and confidential nature of the communication between and among members of the client group.

5.24   Subject to section 5.26, the social worker shall not disclose information acquired from one client to a member of the client's family without the informed consent of the client who provided the information.

5.25  A social worker shall disclose information acquired from one client to a member of the client's family where

(a) the information involves a threat of harm to self or others,

(b) the information was acquired from a child of tender years and the social worker determines that its disclosure is in the best interests of the child.

5.26  A social worker shall disclose information acquired from a client to a person or a police officer where the information involves a threat of harm to that person.

5.27  A social worker may release confidential information as part of a discipline hearing of a social worker as directed by the tribunal or disciplinary body.

5.28  When disclosure is required by order of a court, the social worker shall not divulge more information than is reasonably required and shall where possible notify the client of this requirement.

5.29  The social worker shall not use confidential information for the purpose of teaching, public education or research except with the informed consent of the client.

5.30  The social worker may use non-identifying information for the purpose of teaching, public education or research.

## Retention and Disposition of Information

5.31  Where the social worker's documentation is stored in a place or computer maintained and operated by an employer, the social worker shall advocate for the responsible retention and disposition of information contained in the file.

## 6. OUTSIDE INTEREST

6.  A social worker who engages in another profession, occupation, affiliation or calling shall not allow these outside interests to affect the social work relationship with the client.

6.1  A social worker shall declare to the client any outside interests that would affect the social work relationship with the client.

6.2  A social worker shall not allow an outside interest:

(a) to affect the social worker's ability to practise social work;

(b) to present to the client or to the community that the social worker's ability to practise social work is affected; or

(c) to bring the profession of social work into disrepute.

## 7. LIMIT ON PRIVATE PRACTICE

7.   A social worker in private practice shall not conduct the business of provision of social work services for a fee in a manner that discredits the profession or diminishes the public's trust in the profession.

7.1   A social worker shall not use the social work relationship within an agency to obtain clients for his or her private practice.

7.2   Subject to section 7.3 a social worker who enters into a contract for service with a client
   (a) shall disclose at the outset of the relationship, the fee schedule for the social work services,
   (b) shall not charge a fee that is greater than that agreed to and disclosed to the client, and
   (c) shall not charge for hours of service other than the reasonable hours of client services, research, consultation and administrative work directly connected to the case.

7.3   A social worker in private practice may charge differential fees for services except where an increased fee is charged based on race, ethnic background, language, religion, marital status, sex, sexual orientation, age, abilities, socio-economic status, political affiliation or national ancestry.

7.4   A social worker in private practice shall maintain adequate malpractice, defamation and liability insurance.

7.5   A social worker in private practice may charge a rate of interest on delinquent accounts as is allowed by law.

7.6   Notwithstanding section 5.17 a social worker in private practice may pursue civil remedies to ensure payment for services to a client where the social worker has advised the client of this possibility at the outset of the social work service.

## 8. ETHICAL RESPONSIBILITIES TO THE WORKPLACE

8.   A social worker shall advocate for workplace conditions and policies that are consistent with the Code.

8.1   Where the responsibilities to an employer are in conflict with the social worker's obligations to the client, the social worker shall document the issue in writing and shall bring the situation to the attention of the employer.

8.2   Where a serious ethical conflict continues to exist after the issue has been brought to the attention of the employer, the social worker shall bring the issue to the attention of the Association or regulatory body.

8.3    A social worker shall follow the principles in the Code when dealing with
  (a) a social worker under the supervision of the social worker,
  (b) an employee under the supervision of the social worker, and
  (c) a social work student under the supervision of the social worker.

## 9. ETHICAL RESPONSIBILITIES TO THE PROFESSION

9.    A social worker shall promote excellence in the social work profession.

9.1    A social worker shall report to the appropriate association or regulatory body any breach of this Code by another social worker which adversely affects or harms a client or prevents the effective delivery of a social service.

9.2    A social worker shall report to the association or regulatory body any unqualified or unlicensed person who is practising social work.

9.3    A social worker shall not intervene in the professional relationship of a social worker and client unless requested to do so by the client and unless convinced that the best interests and well-being of the client require such intervention.

9.4    Where a conflict arises between a social worker and other professionals, the social worker shall attempt to resolve the professional differences in ways that uphold the principles of this Code and the honour of the social work profession.

9.5    A social worker engaged in research shall ensure that the involvement of clients in the research is a result of informed consent.

## 10. ETHICAL RESPONSIBILITIES FOR SOCIAL CHANGE

10.    A social worker shall advocate change
  (a) in the best interest of the client, and
  (b) for the overall benefit of society, the environment and the global community.

10.1    A social worker shall identify, document and advocate for the elimination of discrimination.

10.2    A social worker shall advocate for the equal distribution of resources to all persons.

10.3    A social worker shall advocate for the equal access of all persons to resources, services and opportunities.

10.4    A social worker shall advocate for a clean and healthy environment and shall advocate the development of environmental strategies consistent with social work principles.

10.5   A social worker shall provide reasonable professional services in a state of emergency.

10.6   A social worker shall promote social justice.

# Feminist Therapy Code of Ethics:
# Ethical Guidelines for Feminist Therapists

## I. CULTURAL DIVERSITIES AND OPPRESSION

A. A feminist therapist increases her accessibility to and for a wide range of clients from her own and other identified groups through flexible delivery of services. When appropriate, the feminist therapist assists clients in accessing other services.

B. A feminist therapist is aware of the meaning and impact of her own ethnic and cultural background, gender, class, and sexual orientation, and actively attempts to become knowledgeable about alternatives from sources other than her clients. The therapist's goal is to uncover and respect cultural and experiential differences.

C. A feminist therapist evaluates her ongoing interactions with her clientele for any evidence of the therapist's biases or discriminatory attitudes and practice. The feminist therapist accepts responsibility for taking action to confront and change any interfering or oppressing biases she has.

## II. POWER DIFFERENTIALS

A. A feminist therapist acknowledges the inherent power differentials between client and therapist, and models effective use of personal power. In using the power differential to the benefit of the client, she does not take control or power which rightfully belongs to her client.

B. A feminist therapist discloses information to the client which facilitates the therapeutic process. The therapist is responsible for using self-disclosure with purpose and discretion in the interests of the client.

C. A feminist therapist negotiates and renegotiates formal and/or informal contacts with clients in an on-going mutual process.

D. A feminist therapist educates her clients regarding their rights as consumers of therapy, including procedures for resolving differences and filing grievances.

## III. OVERLAPPING RELATIONSHIPS

A. A feminist therapist recognizes the complexity and conflicting priorities inherent in multiple or overlapping relationships. The therapist

This *Code of Ethics* is printed with the permission of the Feminist Therapy Institute, Inc., 50 South Steele, #850, Denver, CO 80209.

accepts responsibility for monitoring such relationships to prevent potential abuse of or harm to the client.

B. A feminist therapist is actively involved in her community. As a result, she is especially sensitive about confidentiality. Recognizing that her clients' concerns and general well-being are primary, she self-monitors both public and private statements and comments.

C. A feminist therapist does not engage in sexual intimacies nor any overtly or covertly sexualized behaviors with a client or former client.

## IV. THERAPIST ACCOUNTABILITY

A. A feminist therapist works only with those issues and clients within the realm of her competencies.

B. A feminist therapist recognizes her personal and professional needs, and utilizes ongoing self-evaluation, peer support, consultation, supervision, continuing education, and/or personal therapy to evaluate, maintain, and improve her work with clients, her competencies, and her emotional well-being.

C. A feminist therapist continually re-evaluates her training, theoretical background, and research to include developments in feminist knowledge. She integrates feminism into psychological theory, receives ongoing therapy training, and acknowledges the limits of her competencies.

D. A feminist therapist engages in self-care activities in an ongoing manner. She acknowledges her own vulnerabilities and seeks to care for herself outside of the therapy setting. She models for the ability and willingness to self-nurture in appropriate and self-empowering ways.

## V. SOCIAL CHANGE

A. A feminist therapist actively questions other therapeutic practices in her community that appear abusive to clients or therapists, and when possible, intervenes as early as appropriate or feasible, or assists clients in intervening when it is facilitative to their growth.

B. A feminist therapist seeks multiple avenues for impacting change, including public education and advocacy within professional organizations, lobbying for legislative actions, and other appropriate activities.

# Bibliography

This bibliography lists the books and articles cited in this book, as well as additional literature on ethical problems in professional practice that may be of interest to the reader.

Abramson, M. (1985). The autonomy-paternalism dilemma in social work practice. *Social Casework, 66*, 387–93.

Abramson, M. (1989). Autonomy vs. paternalistic beneficence: Practice strategies. *Social Casework, 70*, 101–105.

Abramson, M. (1990). Keeping secrets: Social workers and AIDS. *Social Work, 35*, 169–73.

Acock, A. C., & Fuller, T. (1984). The attitude-behavior relationship and parental influence: Circular mobility in Thailand. *Social Forces, 62*, 973–94.

Adler, S. S. (1989). Truth telling to the terminal ill. *Social Work, 34*, 158–60.

Albert, R. (1986). *Law and social work practice.* New York: Springer Publishing.

Algana, F. J., et al. (1979). Evaluating reaction to interpersonal touch in a counseling interview. *Journal of Counseling Psychology, 26*, 465–72.

American Association of State Social Work Boards (1995). *Social work laws and board regulations: A state comparison study.* Author.

American Medical Association (1988). Council report. Council on Ethics and Judicial Affairs. *Journal of the American Medical Association, 259*, 1360–61.

American Psychiatric Association (1994). *Diagnostic and statistical manual of mental disorders* (4th ed.). Washington, D.C.: Author.

Anderson, S., & Mandell, D. (1989). The use of self-disclosure by professional social workers. *Social Casework, 70,* 259–67.

Andrews, Arlene B., & Patterson, Elizabeth G. (1995). Searching for solutions to alcohol and other drug abuse during pregnancy: Ethics, values, and constitutional principles. *Social Work, 40* (1), 55–64.

Arras, John D. (1993). The emerging epidemic of TB in patients with AIDS: Tension between civil liberties and public health. Presentation at Shock Trauma, University of Maryland Medical System, April 16, 1993.

Ashford, J. B., Macht, M. W., & Mylym, M. (1987). Advocacy by social workers in the public defender's office. *Social Work, 32,* 199–204.

Barker, R. L. (1982). *The business of psychotherapy.* New York: Columbia University Press.

Barker, R. L. (1988a). "Client dumping": Some ethical considerations. *Journal of Independent Social Work, 2* (1), 1–5.

Barker, R. L. (1988b). Just whose code of ethics should the independent practitioner follow? *Journal of Independent Social Work, 2* (4), 1–5.

Barksdale, C. (1989). Child abuse reporting: A clinical dilemma. *Smith College Studies in Social Work, 59* (2), 170–82.

Bates, C. M., & Brodsky, A. M. (1988). *Sex in the therapy hour.* New York: Guilford Press.

Bayles, M. D. (1981). *Professional ethics.* Belmont, Calif.: Wadsworth Publishing.

Bayles, Michael D. (1987). Moral theory and application. In John Howie (Ed.), *Ethical principles and practice* (pp. 1–23). Carbondale, Ill.: Southern Illinois University Press.

Beit-Hallahmi, B. (1975). Encountering orthodox religions in psychotherapy. *Psychotherapy, 12,* 357–59.

Bem, D. J. (1970). *Beliefs, attitudes and human affairs.* Pacific Grove, Calif.: Brooks/Cole Publishing.

Berliner, A. K. (1989). Misconduct in social work practice. *Social Work, 34,* 69–72.

Bernstein, S. (1960). Self-determination: "King or citizen in the realm of values." *Social Work, 5* (1), 3–8.

Bernstein, Saul B. (1993). What happened to self-determination? *Social Work with Groups, 16* (1/2), 3–14.

Bernstein, S. R. (1990). Contracted services: Issues for the nonprofit agency manager. In *Towards the 21st century: Challenges for the voluntary sector.* Proceedings of the 1990 Conference of the Association of Voluntary Action Scholars. London, England.

Besharov, Douglas J. (1990). Gaining control over child abuse reports. *Public Welfare, 48* (2) (Spring), 34–40.

Besharov, D. J., & Besharov, S. H. (1987). Teaching about liability. *Social Work, 32,* 517–22.

Black, D. (1972). The boundaries of legal sociology. *Yale Law Journal, 81,* 1086–1101.

Bloom, M. (1975). *The paradox of helping: Introduction to the philosophy of scientific helping.* New York: John Wiley & Sons.

Bogodanoff, M., & Elbaum, P. L. (1978). Touching: A legacy from the encounter movement to social work practice. *Social Work in Health Care, 4,* 209–19.

Borenzweig, H. (1983). Touching in clinical social work. *Social Casework, 64,* 238–42.

Borys, D. S., & Pope, K. S. (1989). Dual relationships between therapist and client: A national study of psychologists, psychiatrists, and social workers. *Professional Psychology: Research and Practice, 20,* 283–93.

Bouthoutsos, J. (1985). Therapist-client sexual involvement. *American Journal of Orthopsychiatry, 55,* 177–82.

Brager, G. A. (1968). Advocacy and political behavior. *Social Work, 13* (2), 5–15.

Brennan, J. G. (1983). The Stockdale course. In M. J. Collins (Ed.), *Teaching values and ethics in college* (pp. 69–80). San Francisco: Jossey-Bass.

Brieland, D., & Korr, W. S. (1987). Social work education: The foundation for professional ethics. *Arete, 12* (2), 33–39.

Brown, B. S. (1968). Social change: A professional challenge. Unpublished paper.

Brown, H. J. (1970). Social work values in a developing country. *Social Work, 15* (1), 107–12.

Butz, R. A. (1985). Reporting child abuse and confidentiality in counseling. *Social Casework, 66,* 83–90.

Cain, L. P. (1979). Social worker's role in teen-age abortion. *Social Work, 24,* 52–56.

Callahan, D. (1987, October/November). Terminating treatment: Age as a standard. *Hastings Center Reporter,* 21–25.

Callahan, J. (1994). The ethics of assisted suicide. *Health and Social Work, 19* (4), 237–44.

Canadian Association of Social Workers. (1994). *Code of ethics.* Ottawa, Ont.: Author.

Canda, E. R. (1988). Spirituality, religious diversity, and social work practice. *Social Casework, 69,* 238–47.

Caputo, Richard K. (1991). Managing information systems: An ethical framework and information needs matrix. *Administration in Social Work, 15* (4), 53–64.

Carlton, W. (1978). *In our professional opinion: The primacy of clinical judgment over moral choice.* Notre Dame, Ind.: University of Notre Dame Press.

Christensen, K. E. (1986). Ethics of information technology. In G. R. Geiss & N. Viswanathan (Eds.), *The human edge* (pp. 72–91). Binghamton, N.Y.: Haworth Press.

Cnaan, Ram A. (1989). "Social work education and direct practice in the computer age." *Journal of Social Work Education, 25* (3) (Fall), 235–43.

Cohen, R. (1980a). The (revised) NASW Code of Ethics. *NASW News, 25* (April), 19.

Cohen, R. (1980b). Ethics: Responsibility to more than profession's clients. *NASW News, 25* (June), 10.

Coleman, E., & Schaefer, S. (1986). Boundaries of sex and intimacy between client and counselor. *Journal of Counseling and Development, 64,* 341–44.

Congress, Elaine P. (1992). Ethical decision making of social work supervisors. *Clinical Supervisor, 10* (1), 157–69.

Conrad, A. P. (1988). Ethical considerations in the psychosocial process. *Social Casework, 69,* 603–10.

Conrad, A. P. (1989). Developing an ethics review process in a social service agency. *Social Thought, 15* (3/4), 102–15.

Conte, H. R., Plutchik, R., Picard, S., & Karasu, T. B. (1989). Ethics in the practice of psychotherapy. *American Journal of Psychotherapy, 43,* 32–42.

Coughlin, B. J. (1966). Interrelationship of governmental and voluntary welfare services. *The Social Welfare Forum 1966.* New York: Columbia University Press.

Council on Social Work Education (1992). *Curriculum Policy Statement.* Alexandria, Va.: Author.

Curtis, P. A., & Lutkus, A. M. (1985). Client confidentiality in police social work settings. *Social Work, 30,* 355–60.

Cwikel, J. G., & Cnaan, R. A. (1991). Ethical dilemmas in applying second-wave information technology to social work practice. *Social Work, 36* (2), 114–20.

Cyrns, A. G. (1977). Social work education and student ideology: A multivariate study of professional socialization. *Journal of Education for Social Work, 13* (1), 44–51.

Daro, Deborah (1988). *Confronting child abuse: Research for effective program design* (p. 20). New York: Free Press.

Davis, L. V. (1985). Female and male voices in social work. *Social Work, 30,* 106–13.

Dean, Ruth G., & Rhodes, Margaret L. (1992). Ethical-clinical tensions in clinical practice. *Social Work, 37* (2), 128–32.

Denton, W. H. (1989). DSM-III-R and the family therapist: Ethical considerations. *Journal of Marriage and Family Therapy, 15,* 367–77.

Denton, W. (1990). A family systems analysis of DSM-III-R. *Journal of Marital and Family Therapy, 16* (2) (April), 113–25.

DeYoung, M. (1988). The good touch/bad touch dilemma. *Child Welfare, 67,* 60–68.

Diener, E., & Crandall, R. (1978). *Ethics in social and behavioral research.* Chicago: University of Chicago Press.

Diggs, B. J. (1970). Rules and utilitarianism. In K. Pahel & M. Schiller (Eds.), *Readings in contemporary ethical theory* (pp. 260–82). Englewood Cliffs, N.J.: Prentice-Hall.

Dobrin, A. (1989). Ethical judgments of male and female social workers. *Social Work, 34,* 451–55.

Dolgoff, Ralph, & Skolnik, Louise. (1992). Ethical decision making: The NASW Code of ethics and group work practice: Beginning explorations. *Social Work with Groups 15* (4), 99–112.

Dunkel, J., & Hatfield, S. (1986). Countertransference issues in working with persons with AIDS. *Social Work, 31,* 114–17.

Dworkin, G. (1985). Behavioral control and design. *Social Research, 52,* 543–54.

Egley, Lance C. (1992). Defining the *Tarasoff* Duty. *Journal of Psychiatry and Law,* 19 (1/2) (Spring/Summer), 93–133.

Ellis, A. (1974). *Humanistic psychotherapy: The rational-emotive approach.* New York: McGraw-Hill.

Eth, S. (1988). The sexually active, HIV infected patient: Confidentiality versus the duty to protect. *Psychiatric Annals, 18,* 571–76.

Feldman, K. A., & Newcomb, T. M. (1970). *The impact of college on students.* San Francisco: Jossey-Bass.

Feminist Therapy Institute (1987). *Feminist code of ethics.* Denver, Colo. Author.

Festinger, L. (1957). *A theory of cognitive dissonance.* New York: Harper & Row.

Finkelhor, David (1990). Is child abuse overreported? *Public Welfare, 48* (1), 22–29.

Finn, Jerry (1990). Security, privacy, and confidentiality in agency microcomputer use. *Families in Society: The Journal of Contemporary Human Services,* (May), 283–90.

Fisher, D. (1987). Problems for social work in a strike situation: Professional, ethical, and value considerations. *Social Work, 32,* 252–54.

Fishkin, J. S. (1982). *The limits of obligation.* New Haven, Conn.: Yale University Press.

Fleck-Henderson, Ann (1991). Moral reasoning in social work practice. *Social Service Review* (June), 185–202.

Fletcher, J. F. (1966). *Situation ethics, the new morality.* Philadelphia: Westminster Press.

Flexner, A. (1915). Is social work a profession? *Proceedings of National Conference of Charities and Corrections* (pp. 576–90). Chicago: Hindman.

Foster, Larry W., Sharp, J., Scesny, Alice, McLellan, L., & Cotman, K. (1993). Bioethics: Social work's response and training needs. *Social Work in Health Care, 19* (1), 15–38.

Frank, J. (1974). *Persuasion and healing* (Rev. ed.). New York: Schocken Books.

Frankena, W. K. (1973). *Ethics* (2d ed.). Englewood Cliffs, N.J.: Prentice-Hall.

Frankena, W. K. (1980). *Thinking about morality.* Ann Arbor, Mich.: University of Michigan Press.

Frankl, V. (1968). *The doctor and the soul.* New York: Alfred A. Knopf.

Freedberg, S. (1989). Self-determination: Historical perspectives and effects on current practice. *Social Work, 34,* 33–38.

Gerhart, U. C., & Brooks, A. D. (1985). Social workers and malpractice: Law, attitudes, and knowledge. *Social Casework, 66,* 411–16.

Gewirth, A. (1978). *Reason and morality.* Chicago: University of Chicago Press.

Gibelman, Margaret, & Schervish, P. H. (1993). *Who we are: The social work labor force as reflected in the NASW membership.* Washington, D.C.: NASW.

Gilbert, N., & Specht, H. (1976). Advocacy and professional ethics. *Social Work, 21,* 288–93.

Gilligan, C. (1982). *In a different voice: Psychological theory and women's development.* Cambridge, Mass.: Harvard University Press.

Gillis, J. S. (1974). Social influence therapy: The therapist as manipulator. *Psychology Today, 8* (7), 90–95.

Girardi, J. A., Keese, R. M., Traver, L. B., & Cooksey, D. R. (1988). Psychotherapist responsibility for notifying individuals at risk for exposure to HIV (AIDS). *Journal of Sex Research, 25,* 1–27.

Givelber, D., Bowers, W., & Blitch, C. (1984). *Tarasoff*: Myth and reliability. *Wisconsin Law Review, 2,* 443–97.

Glaser, R. D., & Thorpe, J. S. (1986). Unethical intimacy: A survey of sexual contact and advances between psychology educators and female graduate students. *American Psychologist, 41,* 42–51.

Glasser, P. H. (1984). Being honest with ourselves: What happens when our values conflict with our clients? *Practice Digest, 6* (4), 6–10.

Glassman, Carol (1992). Feminist dilemmas in practice. *Affilia, 7* (2), 160–66.

Gochros, H. L. (1988). Risks of abstinence: Sexual decision making in the AIDS era. *Social Work, 33,* 254–56.

Goffman, E. (1959). *The presentation of self in everyday life*. Garden City, N.Y.: Doubleday Anchor Books.

Goldstein, H. (1973). *Social work: A unitary approach*. Columbia, S.C.: University of South Carolina Press.

Goldstein, H. (1987). The neglected moral link in social work practice. *Social Work, 32*, 181–86.

Golton, M. (1971). Private practice in social work. In R. Morris (Ed.), *The encyclopedia of social work*. New York: National Association of Social Workers.

Gordon, W. E. (1965a). Knowledge and value: Their distinction and relationship in clarifying social work practice. *Social Work, 10* (3), 32–39.

Gordon, W. E. (1965b). Toward a social work frame of reference. *Journal of Education in Social Work, 1*, 19–26.

Gothard, S. (1989). Power in the court: The social worker as an expert witness. *Social Work, 34*, 65–67.

Gould, Carol C. (1992). New paradigms in professional ethics: Feminism, communitarianism, and democratic theory. *Professional Ethics, 1* (1/2), (Spring/Summer), 143–54.

Gould, K. H. (1988). Old wine in new bottles: A feminist perspective on Gilligan's theory. *Social Work, 33*, 411–15.

Gray, L. A., & Harding, A. K. (1988). Confidentiality limits with clients who have the AIDS virus. *Journal of Counseling and Development, 66*, 219–23.

Green, S. L., & Hansen J. C. (1989). Ethical dilemmas faced by family therapists. *Journal of Marriage and Family Therapy, 15*, 149–58.

Greenwood, E. (1957). Attributes of a profession. *Social Work, 2* (3), 45–55.

Group for the Advancement of Psychiatry (1994). *Forced into treatment: The role of coercion in clinical practice*. Report No. 137. Washington, D.C.: American Psychiatric Press.

Haley, J. (1976). *Problem-solving therapy*. New York: Harper & Row.

Halleck, S. L. (1963). The impact of professional dishonesty on behavior of disturbed adolescents. *Social Work, 8* (2), 48–56.

Halleck, S. L. (1981). Covert values in the treatment of psychosis. *American Journal of Psychotherapy, 35*, 173–86.

Halmos, P. (1965). *Faith of the counselor*. London: Constable.

Handler, J. F., & Hollingsworth, E. J. (1971). *The deserving poor*. Chicago: Markham.

Haney, C., Banks, C., & Zimbardo, P. G. (1973). Interpersonal dynamics in a simulated prison. *International Journal of Criminology and Penology, 1*, 69–97.

Hasenfeld, Y. (1987). Power in social work practice. *Social Service Review, 61*, 469–83.

Hayes, D. D., & Varley, B. K. (1965). The impact of social work education on students' values. *Social Work, 10* (4), 40–46.

Himes, K. (1989). The relationship of religion and morality. *Social Thought, 15* (3/4), 33–41.

Hiratsuka, Jon (1994). When it's a helper who needs help. *NASW News* (June), 1994, 3.

Hogan, Patricia Turner, & Siu, Sau-Fong (1988). Minority children and the child welfare system: An historical perspective. *Social Work, 33* (6) (November/December), 493–98.

Hokenstad, M. C. (1987). Preparation for practice: The ethical dimension. *Social Work Education Reporter, 25*, 1–4.

Holroyd, J., & Brodsky, A. (1977). Psychologists' attitudes and practices regarding erotic and nonerotic physical contact with patients. *American Psychologist, 32*, 843–49.

Hoshino, G. (1978). Social services: The problem of accountability. In S. Slavin (Ed.), *Social Administration* (pp. 299–309). Binghamton, N.Y.: Haworth Press.

Howe, E. (1980). Public professions and the private model of professionalism. *Social Work, 25*, 179–91.

Howell, Mary C. (1988). Ethical dilemmas encountered in the care of those who are disabled and also old. *Educational Gerontology, 14* (5), 439–49.

Hughes, E. C. (1965). Professions. In K. S. Lynn (Ed.), *The professions in America*. Boston: Beacon Press.

Hughes, Ronald C. (1993a). Child welfare services for the catastrophically ill newborn: Part I—A confusion of responsibility. *Child Welfare, 72* (4) (July/August), 323–40.

Hughes, Ronald C. (1993b). Child welfare services for the catastrophically ill newborn: Part II—A guiding ethical paradigm. *Child Welfare, 72* (5) (September/October), 423–37.

Imre, R. E. (1982). *Knowing and caring*. Lanham, Md.: University Press of America.

Imre, R. E. (1989). Moral theory for social work. *Social Thought, 15* (1), 18–27.

Iserson, Kenneth V. (1986). An approach to ethical problems in emergency medicine. In Kenneth V. Iserson et al. (Eds.), *Ethics in emergency medicine* (pp. 35–41). Baltimore: Williams & Wilkins.

Ivanoff, A., Blythe, B. J., & Tripodi, T. (1994). *Involuntary clients in social work practice: A research-based approach*. New York: Aldine De Gruyter.

Jones, J. A., & Alcabes, A. (1989). Clients don't sue: The invulnerable social worker. *Social Casework, 70*, 414–20.

Jones, W. T., Sontag, F., Beckner, M. O., & Fogelin, R. J. (1977). *Approaches to ethics*. New York: McGraw-Hill.

Jordan, S. M. (1985). *Decision-making for incompetent persons*. Springfield, Ill.: Charles C. Thomas, Publisher.

Joseph, M. V. (1983). The ethics of organization. *Administration in Social Work, 7* (Fall), 48–57.

Joseph, M. V. (1985). A model for ethical decision-making in clinical practice. In C. B. Germain (Ed.), *Advances in clinical social work practice* (pp. 207–17). Silver Spring, Md.: NASW.

Judah, E. H. (1979). Values: The uncertain component of social work. *Journal of Education for Social Work, 15* (2), 79–86.

Kagle, Jill Doner, & Gielbelhausen, Pam N. (1994). Dual relationships and professional boundaries. *Social Work, 39* (2) (March), 213–20.

Kapp, M. B. (1988). Forcing services on at-risk older adults: When doing good is not so good. *Social Work in Health Care, 13* (4), 1–13.

Keith-Lucas, A. (1977). Ethics in social work. *Encyclopedia of Social Work* (pp. 350–55). Washington, D.C.: National Association of Social Workers.

Kelley, P., Alexander, P., & Cullinane, M. A. (1987). Ethical issues in private practice. *Journal of Independent Social Work, 1* (2), 5–83.

Kirk, S. A., & Kutchins, H. (1988). Deliberate misdiagnosis in mental health practice. *Social Service Review, 62*, 225–37.

Kitchner, K. S. (1984). Intuition, critical evaluation and ethical principles: The foundation of ethical decisions in counseling psychology. *Counseling Psychology, 12*, 43–55.

Kluckhohn, C. (1951). Values and value-orientations in the theory of action: An exploration in definition and clarification. In T. Parsons & E. A. Shils (Eds.), *Toward a general theory of action* (pp. 388–433). Cambridge, Mass.: Harvard University Press.

Knapp, S., & VandeCreek, L. (1990). Application of the duty to protect to HIV-positive patients. *Professional Psychology, 21*, 161–66.

Kohlberg, L. (1976). Moral stages and moralization: The cognitive-developmental approach. In T. Lickona (Ed.), *Moral development and behavior: Theory, research and social issues* (pp. 31–53). New York: Holt, Rinehart & Winston.

Kopels, S., & Kagle, Jill Doner (1993). Do social workers have a duty to warn? *Social Service Review, 67* (1), 101–26.

Kugelman, Wendy (1992). Social work ethics in the practice arena: A qualitiative study. *Social Work in Health Care, 17* (4), 59–80.

Kuhse, H., & Singer, P. (1985). Ethics and the handicapped newborn infant. *Social Research, 52*, 505–42.

Kupferman, K., & Smaldino, C. (1987). The vitalizing and the revitalizing experience of reliability: The place of touch in psychotherapy. *Clinical Social Work Journal, 15*, 223–35.

Kurzweil, Z. (1980). Why heteronomous ethics? In M. Kranzberg (Ed.), *Ethics in an age of pervasive technology* (pp. 68–71). Boulder, Colo.: Westview Press.

Kutchins, H., & Kirk, S. A. (1987). DSM-III and social work malpractice. *Social Work, 32,* 205–11.

Kutchins, H., & Kirk, S. A. (1988). The business of diagnosis: DSM-III and clinical social work. *Social Work, 33,* 215–20.

Kutchins, H., & Kirk, S. A. (1989). DSM-III-R: The conflict over new psychiatric diagnoses. *Health and Social Work, 14,* 91–101.

Kutchins, Herbert, & Kirk, Stuart A. (1995). Review of *Diagnostic and statistical manual of mental disorders* (4th ed.). *Social Work, 40* (2), 286–87.

Laing, R. D. (1967). *Politics of experience.* New York: Pantheon Books.

Lamb, D. H., Clark, C., Drumheller, P., Frizzell, K., & Surrey, L. (1989). Applying *Tarasoff* to AIDS-related psychotherapy issues. *Professional Psychology: Research and Practice, 20,* 37–43.

Land, H. (1988). The impact of licensing on social work: Values, ethics and choices. *Journal of Independent Social Work, 2,* 87–99.

Leukefeld, C. G., & Fimbres, M. (Eds.). (1987). *Responding to AIDS: Psychosocial initiatives.* Silver Spring, Md.: NASW.

Levy, C. (1976a). Personal versus professional values: The practitioner's dilemma. *Clinical Social Work Journal, 4,* 110–20.

Levy, C. (1976b). The value base of social work. *Journal for Education in Social Work, 9,* 34–42.

Levy, C. (1982). *Guide to ethical decisions and actions for social service administrators.* Binghamton, N.Y.: Haworth Press.

Levy, C. (1988). What's ethics, what's practice, what's both? *Social Work, 33,* 477–78.

Lewis, H. (1984). Ethical assessment. *Social Casework, 65,* 203–11.

Lewis, H. (1987). Teaching ethics through ethical teaching. *Journal of Teaching in Social Work, 1* (1), 3–14.

Lewis, H. (1989). Ethics and the private non-profit human service organization. *Administration in Social Work, 13* (2), 1–14.

Lewis, K. N., & Walsh, W. B. (1980). Effects of value-communication style and similarity of values on counselor evaluation. *Journal of Counseling Psychology, 27,* 305–14.

Lindenthal, J. J., Jordan, T. J., Lentz, J. D., & Thomas, C. S. (1988). Social workers' management of confidentiality. *Social Work, 33,* 157–58.

Lindley, R. (1987). Family therapy and respect for people. In R. Walrond-Skinner & D. Watson (Eds.), *Ethical issues in family therapy* (pp. 104–17). London: Routledge & Kegan Paul.

Loewenberg, F. M. (1978). Professional values and professional ethics in social work education. In B. L. Baer & R. Federico (Eds.), *Educating the baccalaureate social worker* (pp. 115–29). Cambridge, Mass.: Ballinger Publishing.

Loewenberg, F. M. (1983). *Fundamentals of social intervention* (2d ed.). New York: Columbia University Press.

Loewenberg, F. M. (1987). Another look at unethical professional conduct. *Journal of Applied Social Sciences, 11,* 220–29.

Loewenberg, F. M. (1988). *Religion and social work practice in contemporary American society.* New York: Columbia University Press.

Loewenberg, Frank (1992). Notes on ethical dilemmas in wartime: Experiences of Israeli social workers during Operation Desert Shield. *International social work, 35* (4) 429–39.

Lytle-Vieira, J. E. (1987). Kramer vs. Kramer revisited: The social work role in child custody cases. *Social Work, 32,* 5–10.

McCann, C. W. (1977). The codes of ethics of the NASW: An inquiry into its problems and perspectives. In B. E. Olvett (Ed.), *Values in Social Work Education* (pp. 10–19). Salt Lake City: University of Utah Graduate School of Social Work.

MacIver, R. (1922). The social significance of professional ethics. *Annals, 101,* 5–11.

MacMurray, J. (1961). *Persons in relation.* Atlantic Highlands, N.J.: Humanities Press.

Maesen, W. A. (1991). Fraud in mental health practice: A risk management perspective. *Administration and Policy in Mental Health, 18* (6), 431–32.

Marcuse, P. (1976). Professional ethics and beyond: Values in planning. *Journal of the American Institute of Planners, 42,* 264–74.

Maritain, J. (1934). *Introduction to philosophy.* London: Sheed & Ward.

Marson, Steve. Social work discussion list (SOCWORK@UMAB.BITNET). October 18, 1993.

Maslow, A. H. (1962). *The farther reaches of human nature.* New York: Penguin Books.

Maslow, A. H. (1969). Toward a humanistic biology. *American Psychologist, 24,* 724–35.

Melton, G. B. (1988). Ethical and legal issues in AIDS-related practice. *American Psychologist, 43,* 941–47.

Meyer, C. H. (1985). Different voices: Comparable worth. *Social Work, 30,* 99.

Miller, D. J., & Thelen, M. H. (1986). Knowledge and beliefs about confidentiality in psychotherapy. *Professional Psychology: Research and Practice, 17,* 15–19.

Miller, H. (1968). Value dilemmas in social casework. *Social Casework, 13,* 27–33.

Miller, L. (1990). Voluntary organizations in turbulent times. In *Towards the 21st century: Challenges for the voluntary sector.* Proceedings of the 1990 Conference of the Association of Voluntary Action Scholars. London, England.

Moran, J. R. (1989). Social work education and students' humanistic attitudes. *Journal of Education for Social Work, 25* (1), 13–19.

Morrison, C. F. (1989). AIDS: Ethical implications for psychological intervention. *Professional Psychology: Research and Practice, 20,* 166–71.

Moser, C. (1980). Letter. *NASW News, 25* (9), 6.

Muehleman, T., Pickens, B. K., & Robinson, F. (1985). Informing clients about the limits to confidentiality, risk and their rights: Is self-disclosure inhibited? *Professional Psychology: Research and Practice, 16,* 385–97.

Murray, E. J. (1956). A content-analysis method for studying psychotherapy. *Psychological Monographs, 70* (13).

National Association of Black Social Workers (n.d.). *Code of ethics.*

National Association of Social Workers (1993). *Code of ethics.* Washington, D.C.: Author.

National Association of Social Workers (1990). People in the news. *NASW News, 35* (5) (May), 17.

National Association of Social Workers (1993). Warning issued on long reach of liability, *38* (7) (July), 9.

National Association of Social Workers (1993). NASW and FTC enter into consent agreement. *NASW News, 38* (5) (May), 4.

National Association of Social Workers (1994). Client self-determination in end-of-life decisions. *Social Work Speaks,* Washington, D.C.: Author, 58–61.

National Association of Social Workers (1993). A study of trends in adjudication of complaints concerning violations of NASW's code of ethics—Overview of results.

National Association of Social Workers (1995). A study cites most reported ethics breaches. *NASW News, 40* (4) (April), 4.

National Association of Social Workers (1995). Lawsuits: No more immunity. *NASW News, 40* (1) (January), 7.

NASW (1985). *Compilation of public social policy statements.* Silver Spring, Md.

NASW Ad Hoc Committee on Advocacy. (1969). The social worker advocate: Champion of social victims. *Social Work, 14* (2), 16–23.

National Federation of Societies of Clinical Social Work (1988). *Code of ethics.* Arlington, Va.

Navarro, Mireya (1993). Confinement for TB: Weighing rights vs. health. *New York Times,* November 21, pp. 1, 45.

Netting, F. E. (1987). Ethical issues in volunteer management and accountability. *Social Work, 32,* 250–52.

Netting, F. E., Kettner, P. M., & McMurty, S. L. (1993). *Social work macro practice.* White Plains, N.Y.: Longman Publishing Group.

Newhill, Christina E. (1992). Assessing danger to others in clinical social work practice. *Social Service Review, 66* (1) (March), 64–84.

Novak, D. H., et al. (1979). Changes in physicians' attitudes toward telling the cancer patient. *Journal of the American Medical Association, 241,* 537–42.

Organization for Economic Cooperation and Development (1994). *OECD in figures: Statistics on the member countries.* No. 188 (June/July), 44–45.

Parloff, M. B., et al. (1978). Research on therapist variables. In S. L. Garfield & A. E. Bergin (Eds.), *Handbook of psychotherapy and behavior change* (2d ed.) (pp. 233–87). New York: John Wiley & Sons.

Pemberton, J. D. (1965). Is there a moral right to violate the law? *The Social Welfare Forum, 1965* (pp. 183–96). New York: Columbia University Press.

Perlman, G. L. (1988). Mastering the law of privileged communications: A guide for social workers. *Social Work, 33,* 425–29.

Perlman, H. H. (1965). Self-determination: Reality or illusion? *Social Service Review, 39,* 410–22.

Perlman, H. H. (1976). Believing and doing: Values in social work education. *Social Casework, 57,* 381–90.

Pilseker, C. (1978). Values: A problem for everyone. *Social Work, 23,* 54–57.

Pincus, A., & Minahan, A. (1973). *Social work practice.* Itasca, Ill.: F. E. Peacock Publishers.

Pope, K. S. (1988). How clients are harmed by sexual contact with mental health professionals: The syndrome and its prevalence. *Journal of Counseling and Development, 67,* 222–26.

Pope, K. S., & Bouthoutsos, J. C. (1986). *Sexual intimacy between therapist and patient.* New York: Praeger Publishers.

Pope, K. S., Tabachnick, B. G., & Keith-Spiegel, P. (1987). Ethics of practice: The beliefs and behaviors of psychologists and therapists. *American Psychologist, 42,* 993–1006.

Pope, Kenneth S., & Vasquez, Melba T. (1991). *Ethics in psychotherapy and counseling.* San Francisco: Jossey-Bass.

Price, D. (1990). Between Scylla and Charybdis: Charting a course to reconcile the duty of confidentiality and the duty to warn in the AIDS context. *Dickinson Law Review, 94,* 435–87.

Proctor, E. K., Morrow-Howell, Nancy, & Lott, Cynthia L. (1993). Classification and correlates of ethical dilemmas in hospital social work. *Social Work, 38* (2), 166–77.

Pumphrey, M. W. (1959). *The teaching of values and ethics in social work education.* New York: CSWE.

Rabkin, J. G., & Struening, E. L. (1976). *Ethnicity, social class and mental illness.* New York: Institute on Pluralism & Group Identity.

Rachels, R. (1986). *The elements of moral philosophy*. New York: Random House.

Rawlings, Steve W. (1993). *Household and family characteristics: March 1992*, U.S. Bureau of the Census. Current population reports, P-20-467. Washington, D.C.: U.S. Government Printing Office.

Rawls, J. (1971). *A theory of justice*. Cambridge, Mass.: Harvard University Press.

Rawls, J. (1988). The obligation to obey the law. In R. M. Baird & S. E. Rosenbaum (Eds.), *Morality and the law* (pp. 125–40). Buffalo, N.Y.: Prometheus Books.

Reamer, F. G. (1982). Conflicts of professional duty in social work. *Social Casework, 63*, 579–85.

Reamer, F. G. (1983). Ethical dilemmas in social work practice. *Social Work, 28*, 31–35.

Reamer, F. G. (1987). Ethics committees in social work. *Social Work, 32*, 188–92.

Reamer, F. G. (1988). AIDS and ethics: The agenda for social workers. *Social Work, 33*, 460–64.

Reamer, F. G. (1989). Toward ethical practice: The relevance of ethical theory. *Social Thought, 15* (3/4), 67–78.

Reamer, F. G. (1990). *Ethical dilemmas in social service* (2d ed.). New York: Columbia University Press.

Reamer, Frederic E. (1993). *The philosophical foundations of social work*. New York: Columbia University Press.

Reid, W. J., & Hanrahan, P. (1982). Recent evaluations of social work: Ground for optimism. *Social Work, 27*, 328–40.

Reiser, S. J., Burstajn, H. J., Applebaum, P. S., & Gutheil, T. G. (1987). *Divided staffs, divided selves: A case approach to mental health ethics*. Cambridge, England: Cambridge University Press.

Rhodes, M. L. (1985). Gilligan's theory of moral development as applied to social work. *Social Work, 30*, 101–105.

Rhodes, M. L. (1986). *Ethical dilemmas in social work practice*. London: Routledge & Kegan Paul.

Rhodes, Margaret L. (1990). Ethical judgments and gender: Responses to Dobrin. *Social Work, 35* (2), 179–83.

Richmond, M. E. (1917). *Social diagnosis*. New York: Russell Sage Foundation.

Roback, Howard B., Purdon, Scot E., Ochoa, Elizabeth, & Bloch, Frank (1992). Confidentiality dilemmas in group psychotherapy: Management strategies and utility of guidelines. *Small Group Research, 23* (2) (May), 169–84.

Roberts, C. S. (1989). Conflicting professional values in social work and medicine. *Health and Social Work, 14*, 211–18.

Robertson, J. A. (1985). The geography of competency. *Social Research*, *52*, 555–79.

Rogers, C. R. (1951). *Client-centered therapy*. Boston: Houghton Mifflin.

Rogers, C. R. (1977). *Carl Rogers on personal power*. New York Delacorte.

Rooney, Ronald H. (1992). *Strategies for work with involuntary clients*. New York: Columbia University Press.

Ross, J. W. (1989). AIDS, rationing of care, and ethics. *Family & Community Health*, *12* (2), 24–33.

Ross, Judith W. (1992). Editorial: Are social work ethics compromised? *Health and Social Work*, *17* (3) (August), 163–64.

Rothman, J. (1989). Client self-determination: Untangling the knot. *Social Service Review*, *63*, 598–612.

Rubin, A. (1985). Practice effectiveness: More grounds for optimism. *Social Work*, *30*, 469–76.

Ryan, C. C., & Rowe, M. J. (1988). AIDS: Legal and ethical issues. *Social Casework*, *69*, 324–33.

Salomon, E. L. (1967). Humanistic values and social casework. *Social Casework*, *48*, 26–32.

Sammons, C. C. (1978). Ethical issues in genetic intervention. *Social Work*, *23*, 237–42.

Schild, S., & Black, R. B. (1984). *Social work and genetic counseling: A guide to practice*. Binghamton, N.Y.: Haworth Press.

Schultz, L. G. (1975). Ethical issues in treating sexual dysfunction. *Social Work*, *20*, 126–28.

Schutz, W. C. (1967). *Joy*. New York: Grove Press.

Schwartz, G. (1989). Confidentiality revisited. *Social Work*, *34*, 223–36.

Seeling, M. (1987). Legal and ethical issues for independent social work. *Journal of Independent Social Work*, *2* (2), 81–86.

Selznick, P. (1961). Sociology and natural law. *Natural Law Forum*, *6*, 84–108.

Sharwell, G. R. (1974). Can values be taught? *Journal of Education for Social Work*, *10* (Spring), 99–105.

Shaw, G. B. (1932). *The doctor's dilemma*. London: Constable.

Shirk, E. (1965). *The ethical dimension*. New York: Appleton-Century-Crofts.

Siegel, M. (1979). Privacy, ethics, and confidentiality. *Professional Psychology*, *10*, 249–58.

Singer, Peter (1993). *Practical ethics* (2d ed.). Cambridge, England: Cambridge University Press.

Siporin, M. (1975). *Introduction to social work practice*. New York: Macmillan.

Siporin, M. (1982). Moral philosophy in social work today. *Social Service Review*, *56*, 516–38.

Siporin, M. (1983). Morality and immorality in working with clients. *Social Thought, 9* (Fall), 10–28.

Siporin, M. (1985a). Deviance, morality and social work therapy. *Social Thought, 11* (4), 11–24.

Siporin, M. (1985b). Current social work perspectives for clinical practice. *Clinical Social Work Journal, 13,* 198–217.

Siporin, M., & Glasser, P. (1986). Family functioning, morality and therapy. In P. Glasser & D. Watkins (Eds.), *Religion and social work.* Newbury Park, Calif.: Sage Publications.

Smyer, Michael A. (1993). Aging and decision-making capacity. In M. A. Smyer (Ed.), *Mental health and aging: progress and prospects.* New York: Springer Publishing.

*Social Work* (March 1991), *36* (2), 106–44. This issue contains a series of articles on the theme "Ethics and Professional Relationships."

Sonne, J., Meyer, C. B., & Marshall, V. (1985). Clients' reactions to sexual intimacy in therapy. *American Journal of Orthopsychiatry, 55,* 183–89.

Spero, M. H. (1990). Identification between the religious patient and therapist in social work and psychoanalytic psychotherapy. *Journal of Social Work and Policy in Israel, 3,* 83–98.

Star, B. (1980). Patterns of family violence. *Social Casework, 61,* 339–46.

Strom, Kimberly. (1992). Reimbursement demands and treatment decisions: A growing dilemma for social workers. *Social Work, 37* (5), 398–403.

Swoboda, J., et al. (1978). Knowledge of and compliance with privileged communications and child-abuse reporting laws. *Professional Psychologist, 9,* 448–57.

Szasz, T. (1986). The case against suicide prevention. *American Psychologist, 41,* 806–12.

Taylor, L., & Adelman, H. S. (1989). Reframing the confidentiality dilemma to work in children's best interest. *Professional Psychology: Research and Practice, 20,* 79–83.

Taylor-Brown, Susan, & Garcia, Alejandro (1995). Social workers and HIV-affected families: Is the profession prepared? *Social Work, 40* (1), 14–15.

Thomas, R. Murray, & Diver-Stamnes, Ann. (1993). *What wrongdoers deserve: The moral reasoning behind responses to misconduct.* Westport, Conn.: Greenwood Press.

Thomlison, R. J. (1984). Something works: Evidence from practice effectiveness studies. *Social Work, 29,* 51–56.

Timms, N. (1983). *Social work values: An enquiry.* London: Routledge & Kegan Paul.

Torczyner, Jim (1991). Discretion, judgment, and informed consent:

Ethical and practice issues in social action. *Social Work, 36* (2), 122–28.

Totten G., Lamb, D. H., & Reeder, G. D. (1990). *Tarasoff* and confidentiality in AIDS-related psychotherapy. *Professional Psychology, 21,* 155–60.

Towle, C. (1965). *Common human needs.* New York: National Association of Social Workers.

Tropman, John E., Erlich, John L., & Rothman, Jack (1995). *Tactics and techniques of community intervention* (3d ed.). Itasca, Ill.: F. E. Peacock Publishers.

Truax, C. B. (1966). Reinforcement and nonreinforcement in Rogerian psychotherapy. *Journal of Abnormal Psychology, 71,* 1–9.

VandeCreek, L., Knapp, S., & Herzog, C. (1988). Privileged communications for social workers. *Social Casework, 69,* 28–34.

Van Hoose, W. H., & Kottler, J. A. (1985). *Ethical and legal issues in counseling and psychotherapy* (2d ed.). San Francisco: Jossey-Bass.

Varley, B. K. (1963). Socialization in social work education. *Social Work, 8* (4), 102–9.

Varley, B. K. (1968, Fall). Social work values: Changes in value commitment of students from admission to MSW graduation. *Journal of Education for Social Work, 4,* 67–76.

Vigilante, J. L. (1974). Between values and science: "Education for the profession during a moral crisis or is proof truth?" *Journal of Education for Social Work, 10* (Fall), 107–15.

Vigilante, J. L. (1983). Professional values. In A. Rosenblatt & D. Waldfogel (Eds.), *Handbook of clinical social work* (pp. 58–69). San Francisco: Jossey-Bass.

Walden, T., Wolock, I., & Demone, H. W., Jr. (1990). Ethical decision making in human services: A comparative study. *Families in Society, 71,* 67–75.

Walrond-Skinner, S., & Watson, D. (1987). *Ethical issues in family therapy.* London: Routledge & Kegan Paul.

Watkins, S. A. (1989). Confidentiality and privileged communications: Legal dilemma for family therapists. *Social Work, 34,* 133–36.

Weick, A., & Pope. L. (1988). Knowing what's best: A new look at self-determination. *Social Casework, 69,* 10–16.

Weil, M., & Sanchez, E. (1983). Impact of *Tarasoff* decision on clinical social work practice. *Social Service Review, 57,* 112–24.

Wheeler, David L. (1993). Physician-anthropologist examines what ails America's medical system: Instead of treating patients, Melvin Konner probes health care in general. *Chronicle of Higher Education,* June 2, 1993, A6–A7.

Wicclair, Mark R. (1993). *Ethics & the Elderly.* New York: Oxford University Press.

Wigmore, J. (1961). *Evidence in trials at common law* (rev. ed.). Boston: Little, Brown.

Willbach, D. (1989). Ethics and family therapy: The case management of family violence. *Journal of Marriage and Family Therapy, 15*, 43–52.

Williams, R. M., Jr. (1967). Individual and group values. *Annals, 371*, 20–37.

Willis, C. (1987). Legal and ethical issues of touch in dance/movement therapy. *American Journal of Dance Therapy, 10*, 41–53.

Wodarski, John S., Pippin, James A., & Daniels, Maurice (1988). The effects of graduate social work education on personality, values and interpersonal skills. *Journal of Social Work Education, 24*, (3), 266–77.

Yu, Muriel, & O'Neal, Brenda (1992). Issues of confidentiality when working with persons with AIDS. *Clinical Social Work Journal, 20* (4) (Winter), 421–30.

Yurkow, J. (1991). "Abuse and neglect of the frail elderly." *Pride Institute Journal of Long Term Home Health Care, 10* (1) (Winter), 36–39.

Zygmond, M. J., & Boorhem, H. (1989). Ethical decision-making in family therapy. *Family Process, 28*, 269–80.

# Index

ETHICAL DECISIONS FOR SOCIAL WORK PRACTICE
Fifth edition
Edited by Robert Cunningham
Production supervision by Kim Vander Steen
Cover design by Lesiak/Crampton Design, Park Ridge, Illinois
Composition by Point West, Inc., Carol Stream, Illinois
Paper, Finch Opaque
Printed and bound by Quebecor Printing